SIGNAL PROCESSING IN C

SIGNAL PROCESSING IN C

Christopher E. Reid
Thomas B. Passin

John Wiley & Sons, Inc.

New York · Chichester · Brisbane · Toronto · Singapore

This publication is designed to provide accurate and authoritative information in regard to the subject matter covered. It is sold with the understanding that the publisher is not engaged in rendering legal, accounting, or other professional service. If legal advice or other expert assistance is required, the services of a competent professional person should be sought. FROM A DECLARATION OF PRINCIPLES JOINTLY ADOPTED BY A COMMITTEE OF THE AMERICAN BAR ASSOCIATION AND A COMMITTEE OF PUBLISHERS.

Library of Congress Cataloging-in-Publication Data

Reid, Christopher, 1956–
    Signal processing in C / Christopher Reid, Thomas Passin.
      p.   cm.
    Includes bibliographical references.
    ISBN 0-471-52713-0
    ISBN 0-471-56954-2 (Disk)
    ISBN 0-471-56955-0 (Book-Disk Set)
    1. Signal processing—Digital techniques—Data processing. 2. C (Computer program language) I. Passin, Thomas. II. Title.
TK5102.5.R3765   1992
621.382'2—dc20   91-24772

Printed and bound by R.R. Donnelley & Sons, Inc.
10 9 8 7 6 5 4 3 2

Acknowledgments

This book was an outgrowth of a much longer process than we originally anticipated. The original idea came from a friend of mine, Peter Siy. He wanted a book that would provide for him all those signal processing routines he had to keep coding for himself, but he could not find one that suited his needs. Out of that need, the idea for this book was born. He shared his idea with me, and together we came up with the original outline and proposal package.

Unfortunately, once the contract was obtained, he became very busy with other projects and was not able to spend sufficient time on this book. Feeling the need for substantial help, I therefore invited another friend of mine, Thomas Passin, to help as a consulting technical editor. He has had influence beyond what that official title may suggest. Although he did not directly write any of the text, he has had a large impact on the organization and readability of this book. His own unique point of view and experience shines through in many places. His contribution has improved the technical quality and organization of this book substantially.

Finally, I would like to thank my wife, Jane, and our children, Tobias, Alexander, Hannah, and Obadiah, for their considerable patience with me. Writing this book has taken time away from our traditional family activities.

Contents

List of Figures

Introduction

There is more to signal processing than a collection of loosely associated facts and theorems. The successful practice of digital signal processing requires a fundamental understanding of the subject *and* a programming technique that will serve well for a wide variety of applications. The goal of this book is to help you achieve both of these ends.

PROJECT ORIENTATION

What is the best way to learn the fundamentals of digital signal processing? What is the best way to learn a modern C programming style? In both cases, at least for most people, the answer is practice. Reading theoretical books and articles is also important, but without practice these ideas cannot be internalized.

This book is therefore arranged around two projects, which together require an understanding of all the fundamentals of digital signal processing. The first project builds a musical synthesizer, which requires the fundamentals of digital signal processing as well as a structured programming approach. The second project builds on the first by analyzing the digitized waveform of a glockenspiel and a piano, finding a digital filter that best approximates each instrument. The results of the second project can be combined with the first to yield a more convincing musical synthesizer. Finally, the reader is challenged to carry the process further by doing the same for a trumpet and French horn.

The content of this book is driven by these projects. This approach organizes the presentation around a central goal, similar to the process experienced by every researcher working on a new problem. At every step of the way it is clear why the current topic is important to the project at hand. Contrast this with the typical textbook approach, where the material is organized according to some concept in the mind of the author, exercises are devised to support the subjects, and the reader is left wondering how it all connects.

The project-oriented approach also facilitates the natural and necessary marriage between computer programming and digital signal processing. Nothing can be done with digital signal processing unless someone writes a program. Yet, in most books, either the theory is expostulated with no attention to programming or programs are presented with little attention to the theory.

However, the more typical academic development, found in such books as Oppenheim and Schafer's[7], covers more topics in digital signal processing, and books like Parks'[8] covers digital filtering in more depth, than is possible in this book. This book does not attempt to replace such books. While we believe that everyone learns best when pursuing a project of personal interest, this book cannot replace the scope of comprehensive academic books or the specialization of single-topic books.

THE THREE PARTS

The first project, in part I of the book, simulates a bell choir using the simplest of all possible oscillating systems, a damped simple harmonic oscillator. The end product of this part is a program that reads a musical score from a disk file and creates a file containing the digital waveform. This waveform is suitable for playing through a typical 12-bit D/A converter. It is instructive and fun to experiment with the various constants describing the simple harmonic oscillators, listening to the different sounds produced.

The second part of the book contains several chapters that are needed as support for the other two parts. These chapters are more academic in their approach. The inclusion of these chapters makes the book reasonably self-contained so that the novice reader will not have to keep referring to other textbooks. However, this book is not meant to replace the standard texts.

The third part of the book contains the second project. The waveforms of a glockenspiel and a piano are analyzed in order to design a digital filter that approximates their sounds. This project requires an understanding of IIR and FIR filters as well as C programming techniques that are used to implement the filters. The resulting simulated glockenspiel and piano can be used to replace the simple harmonic oscillators used in Chapter 5 to build the bell choir.

Finally, the reader is challenged to extend the music synthesizer by adding the glockenspiel and piano voices to the music synthesizer. Waveforms from these instruments as well as from a trumpet and French horn are included on the companion disks for your own experimentation. Achieving a satisfactory result for all of these instruments is a challenging project that will deepen your understanding of signal processing and entertain you at the same time.

ENHANCED READABILITY

Digital signal processing is a complex subject, and every reader brings to this book a different mix of knowledge and ignorance. It is impossible to write a book that will address everyone's needs equally well. However, I have endeavored to aid both novice and more experienced readers by clearly labeling the many chapters, sections, and subsections with descriptive titles. These titles will help novice readers by advising them of the contents of each part of the book and will make it easier to refer back to a difficult point. More advanced readers may be able to skim or skip entirely a section that contains material they already understand.

As another aid to readability, I have repeated key formulas in several places in the book, rather than always referring the reader back to the place that particular formula was first stated. This should reduce "page flipping," which is always necessary when reading a technical book but can get in the way of understanding difficult material.

Finally, each chapter contains a brief description of its contents, the reason for its existence, and which chapters depend on its contents. This should enable readers to choose their own thread through the book, without skipping material that is essential for future chapters.

SCOPE

This book is not a replacement for any existing text on digital signal processing. No attempt is made to be encyclopedic. Rather, the topics covered are those necessary to achieve the projects contained in the book. These topics include all the basics of digital signal processing.

Some topics are unique to this book or are treated in a different way than is usual. In particular, the development of discrete-time simple harmonic oscillators from their continuous-time counterparts is unique to this book. The group-theoretic approach to a deeper understanding of Fourier transforms in general, and the fast Fourier transform in particular, is also unique. This is also the only book that integrates basic DSP theory with C program development. The C programming style that developed in this text will carry you through most any assignment or project of your own.

A MENU-DRIVEN DSP ENVIRONMENT AND COMPANION LIBRARY

Everything in this book was tested and/or proven afresh while I was writing. All the code actually runs (except perhaps for errors introduced when putting it into the text) and all the techniques discussed are illustrated with graphics newly generated especially for this book.

This involved much more work than I anticipated at first. I planned from the beginning to develop a new, cohesive library of signal processing routines for both your use and mine. However, as the work proceeded, I found myself writing more and more special-purpose routines to test this concept or that or to generate a particular graphic for the text. I realized that what I really needed was a general, menu-driven, digital signal processing environment that could perform all the functions and produce all the graphs I might need. I wrote such a program and used it intensively throughout the whole book.

You may buy the Companion Library and Companion DSP Environment by completing the business reply form bound into the end of this book. The Companion Library contains all the source code for all DSP routines used for any purpose in this book, and many others besides. The Companion DSP Environment provides a menu-driven environment for your IBM-PC style computer that uses the Companion Library routines. It is a spiffed-up version of the utility I wrote for myself.

If the order form is missing you may write to me at the following address:

Reid Associates
Companion Software
P.O. Box 495
Chelmsford, MA 01824

SIGNAL PROCESSING IN C

PART 1

Bells and Bell Choirs

*T*he first project of this book culminates with the synthetic bell choir programs in Chapter 5. Each bell of the bell choir is simulated using the simplest possible oscillating system, a damped simple harmonic oscillator. In spite of the simplicity of this system compared to a real bell, the effect is convincing. The programs developed in Chapter 5 and contained in the music directory on the companion disk read a musical score from a disk file and produce a file containing a digital waveform suitable for playing through a standard D/A converter.

Chapter 1 examines the most basic concepts of digital signal processing: What is a discrete-time frequency? How are discrete-time frequencies related to continuous-time frequencies? Chapter 2 develops the continuous-time solutions to the differential equation for a damped simple harmonic oscillator. An understanding of the continuous-time system is necessary for the discrete-time solutions developed in Chapter 3. Chapter 4 uses the discrete-time solutions developed in Chapter 3 to simulate a bell and an organ pipe. Although the sound of the bell is quite convincing, the organ pipe sounds more like a cheap tin whistle. Chapter 5 shows how these simple harmonic oscillators can be used to write a music synthesizer program. This includes an introduction to the modern style of programming used in this book.

CHAPTER 1

The Fundamentals of Digital Signal Processing

This chapter addresses the most fundamental question of digital signal processing: What is a *discrete-time frequency* and how is it related to continuous-time frequencies? If you think you know the answers, read this chapter anyway. It is short, and it presents a viewpoint somewhat different from that found in other expositions. A thorough understanding of these basic issues goes a long way toward clearing up all kinds of muddled thinking about digital signal processing.

As is often the case in a complicated subject, the fundamentals of digital signal processing are actually quite simple once they are grasped. These underlying foundation stones are easily lost in the complicated superstructure built on top of them. These basic issues can be understood through everyday experience, such as watching wagon wheels in old Western movies turning backwards when you know that that cannot really be happening (see Section 1.3).

1.1 DISCRETE-TIME FREQUENCIES AND WAVEFORMS

What is a continuous-time frequency? You may think you know the answer, and you may just write down a single number or letter, ω or f, to represent a "frequency"—but think again. The answer is really a bit more complicated.

The most elementary notion of a frequency is a real number, ω, that in turn specifies a waveform, $\cos(\omega t + \phi)$, for some initial phase angle, ϕ. In signal processing, it is convenient to generalize this notion to a complex frequency, $s = -d + j\omega$, where the real number, d, is the damping term, which governs the exponential decay of the waveform, and $j = \sqrt{-1}$. The waveform specified by this frequency is a pair of damped sinusoids, one real, the other imaginary:

$$e^{st} = e^{(-d+j\omega)t}$$

$$= e^{-dt}(\cos(\omega t) + j \sin(\omega t)) \tag{1.1}$$

3

Thus, even in the continuous-time world, the specification of a frequency is not as simple as you may have thought. It requires a specification, $s = -d + j\omega$, *and* an implied method of generating a waveform from it, Equation 1.1.

What is a discrete-time frequency? By analogy with the continuous-time case, a discrete-time frequency must consist of a complex number and an implied method of generating a waveform. A discrete-time frequency is any complex number, z. The "waveform" generated by this frequency is a geometric sequence of the form

$$1, z, z^2, z^3, z^4, \ldots, z^k, \ldots \tag{1.2}$$

Where is the oscillation associated with such a frequency? Consider first the special case

$$z = e^{j\omega\Delta t} = \cos(\omega\Delta t) + j\sin(\omega\Delta t)$$

where Δt is the time between sample points. When graphed on the complex plane, this complex number is on the unit circle, and so is every power of it:

$$z^k = e^{jk\omega\Delta t} = \cos(k\omega\Delta t) + j\sin(k\omega\Delta t)$$

The oscillation that is normally associated with a frequency is contained in the real and imaginary parts of this discrete waveform.

What is the relationship between a continuous-time frequency and a discrete-time frequency? A continuous-time frequency of the form $s = -d + j\omega$ generates a waveform specified by Equation 1.1, which oscillates with frequency ω. The corresponding discrete-time frequency is

$$z = e^{s\Delta t} = e^{(-d+j\omega)\Delta t} \tag{1.3}$$

where Δt is the sample interval. With this definition, the two waveforms will agree at any point in time $t = n\Delta t$, because

$$z^n = e^{sn\Delta t} = e^{st}$$

which is the value of the continuous-time waveform at time t.

Many different continuous-time frequencies result in the same discrete-time frequency. Any two continuous-time frequencies s and s' that differ by $s - s' = j2\pi k/\Delta t$ (that is, by $k/\Delta t$ Hz, where k is an integer) correspond to the same discrete-time frequency:

$$z = e^{s\Delta t}$$

$$= e^{[s'+(s-s')]\Delta t}$$

$$= e^{s'\Delta t + j2\pi k}$$

$$= e^{s'\Delta t}$$

$$= z'$$

If the discrete-time frequency, z, is not on the unit circle, the associated waveform will be spiraling either in or out (away from the origin) depending on whether $|z| < 1$ or $|z| > 1$, respectively, as illustrated in Figure 1.1.

There are two special cases worth considering. If z is a positive real number, it still qualifies as a discrete frequency. The waveform it generates does not oscillate. It either grows geometrically, shrinks, or stays constant, depending on the magnitude of z. When z is a negative real number, the waveform bounces back and forth between positive and negative real numbers, growing or

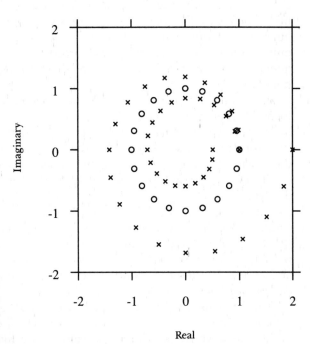

Figure 1.1   A discrete-time frequency is any complex number, z. The waveform it generates is the geometric sequence, $1, z, z^2, \dots$. In this figure, three different values of z are chosen. All three lie on the same line through the origin, but one is inside, one is on, and the other is outside the unit circle. The waveform generated by the value of z on the unit circle does not grow or decay. The one outside grows geometrically, and the one inside decays geometrically.

shrinking according to the magnitude of z. This is the highest frequency that can be represented in discrete time: one cycle for every two data points.

1.2   THE NYQUIST FREQUENCY: THE HIGHEST DISCRETE-TIME FREQUENCY

Is there such a thing as a highest frequency? Yes, there is, in the discrete-time world. A discrete-time frequency z has two components that can be treated independently:

$$z = re^{j\omega\Delta t}$$

The *magnitude* of z, $|z| = r$, determines whether the waveform it generates will grow, shrink, or remain constant in magnitude. The *phase*, $\exp(j\omega\Delta t)$, determines how fast the waveform progresses around the circle. The *highest* frequency is the one that travels around the circle the fastest. For this discussion, only frequencies on the unit circle need to be considered. Certainly the frequency, $z = -1$, travels around the circle quickly, taking only two data points per cycle.

Now imagine yourself watching a movie of a complex discrete-time waveform of frequency z. The kth frame of the movie shows a black circle with a bright red dot on it at the location of z^k on the complex plane. The movie starts on frame 0, so the dot is at the complex number 1 in the first frame of the movie, no matter what frequency is being used.

If the frequency, z, is in the upper half of the complex plane, the red dot will appear to move from 1 upward and around the circle counterclockwise until it arrives at z. In the next frame, the dot will again appear to move counterclockwise, *less than halfway around the circle*, until it reaches z^2.

If the frequency, z, is in the lower half of the complex plane, the red dot will appear to move from 1 downward and around the circle clockwise until it arrives at z. In the next frame, the dot will again appear to move clockwise, *less than halfway around the circle*, until it reaches z^2.

This means that the frequencies z in the upper half of the complex plane are the positive frequencies and those in the lower half of the complex plane are the negative frequencies. It is really only a matter of convention which are negative and which are positive frequencies, but they will appear to be rotating in opposite directions, and that is what is important.

That leaves the frequency $z = -1$ sitting right in the middle. In fact, if you watch a movie generated by this frequency, you will not get a feeling of motion *around* the circle, because the circle will never be defined by its path. It will simply appear to be bouncing back and forth along the real axis. This is the highest distinguishable discrete-time frequency, often called the *Nyquist* frequency. It is one cycle per two data points, or π radians per data point.

ALIASING AND BANDPASS SAMPLING

This brings us to the other fundamental fact of discrete-time signals. How do these discrete-time frequencies relate to frequencies in continuous time? You have probably seen the answer for yourself while watching wagon wheels in the cowboy-and-Indian movies. As the wagon gains speed, the wheel seems to start out okay, moving in concert with the wagon, but after a while it starts moving backward, then forward again, but too slowly to keep up with the wagon, and so forth.

In this case, the frame rate of the original movie determines how the data points are spaced in time, each frame representing a new data sample. The spokes of the wagon wheel complicate the picture some, so let's simplify it by putting a bright red light on the wheel so we can watch it, ignoring the spokes. If the wagon wheel makes less than half a turn between frames of the movie, the red light will appear to be moving in concert with the wagon. As soon as the wheel makes more than half a turn per movie frame, it will appear to be moving backward, against the motion of the wagon. When the wagon wheel makes exactly one turn per frame of the movie, it will appear to be standing still, even though the wagon is streaking forward. When the wheel speeds up a bit more, the wheel again appears to change direction, moving in the right direction again, but much too slowly to be keeping up with the wagon.

This variation in the apparent speeds of the wagon wheel demonstrates what is called *aliasing*. The term is used because one frequency of the wagon wheel in real life can masquerade as another, slower frequency, or even one of the opposite sense, on the film.

Notice that the terms *positive* and *negative* frequencies were not used in the wagon wheel discussion because the direction of motion of the wagon was not specified. By convention, motion in the counterclockwise direction is a positive frequency, so a wagon moving slowly from right to left on the movie screen will have wheels rotating in the positive direction. A wagon moving in the other direction, left to right, will have wheels moving with a negative frequency. This means that both positive and negative frequencies are needed to discuss the motion even of slowly rotating wheels, on the movie screen or in real life.

Aliasing occurs as soon as the wagon wheel makes more than half a turn per movie frame. Of course, if the wagon is known to be going fast enough so that the wheels are making more than one turn per frame, but not more than two, we can measure the speed of the wagon by measuring the apparent speed of the wheels and remembering to make the appropriate correction. This is often done in discrete-time signal processing. If all the frequencies of interest are between 2π and 4π radians per data point and all other frequencies are absent, then, even though our samples do not tell us the whole story, we know what has really been happening and can make the proper corrections. This process is usually called *bandpass sampling*. It is no more complicated than knowing that the wagon wheels cannot possibly be moving so slowly, or backward, while the wagon is moving rapidly forward.

1.4   DISCRETE-TIME SOLUTIONS ARE EXACT

There is one more similarity between wagon wheels and discrete-time signal processing that is important to understand. If the camera shutter is fast enough so that the wheel does not blur when the picture is taken, the discrete-time version of the events being filmed shows the position of the wheel exactly where it really was when the frame was snapped. Just like the movie of the wagon wheel, the discrete-time solutions of the simple harmonic oscillator developed in Chapter 3 will track the continuous-time solutions *exactly*. However, approximations are sometimes used that blur the situation somewhat.

1.5   BUILDING ON THE FOUNDATION

The two principal cornerstones of discrete-time signal processing, then, are that a discrete-time frequency is a complex number, z, and that wagon wheels in old Westerns represent the whole story about converting continuous-time frequencies to discrete-time frequencies, including aliasing, bandpass sampling, and the Nyquist frequency. The wagon wheels are even good models of complex frequencies. The motion of a complex waveform around the unit circle on the complex plane is precisely analogous to the motion of our imagined red light on the wagon wheel.

With a foundation like that, digital signal processing must be pretty easy, right? Well, no, it isn't. That would be like saying that the special effects of movies such as *Star Wars* must be easy because they are somehow related to illusions that can be obtained from discrete-time motion picture frames. Illusions on the movie screen are based on discrete-time pictures, however, and all of digital signal processing is based on these simple cornerstones. You can understand both disciplines from a fundamental viewpoint if you keep a clear understanding of the foundations in mind.

CHAPTER 2

Continuous-Time Simple Harmonic Oscillators

In our music synthesizer, each bell will be represented by a simple harmonic oscillator. This chapter solves the equations for a continuous-time oscillator, and Chapter 3 does the same for the discrete-time version. Comparing the two cases will tell us nearly everything about the differences between discrete-time and continuous-time signal processing.

But why study a simple harmonic oscillator? Why not start out with something more complicated? As it turns out, even the most complicated linear, time-invariant systems in both the continuous-time and discrete-time worlds can be understood as a collection of interacting simple harmonic oscillators. The simple harmonic oscillator is central to linear system theory.

Why the *linear* and *time-invariant* restrictions? The restriction to linear systems is essential because of the enormous complexity of even simple nonlinear systems. Nonlinear systems are the topic of much current research, popularly known as chaos theory, catastrophe theory, and fractals.

The time-invariant restriction is less critical, but still necessary unless some other restriction is imposed on the time variations. Mixing is an example of a linear (for the proof that it is linear, see Section 2.1), time-dependent process that can be easily modeled in digital signal processing. More complicated time-dependent systems are, in general, difficult to model and are not generally treated as part of digital signal processing.

This chapter is necessary for a full understanding of Chapter 3, which develops the discrete-time solutions to the simple harmonic oscillator equations. However, it is possible to skip these two chapters and go directly to Chapter 4. The necessary equations from these two chapters are repeated in that chapter or referred to directly.

2.1 LINEARITY AND TIME-INVARIANCE

Digital signal processing is the study of discrete-time, linear, time-invariant systems. It is appropriate, therefore, to take some time explaining these terms.

A *linear* system or operator, $\mathscr{L}$, is any operator that satisfies

$$\mathscr{L}(af + bg) = a\mathscr{L}(f) + b\mathscr{L}(g) \tag{2.1}$$

where f and g are two functions in the domain of the operator and a and b are arbitrary constants. If the constants are real, we say the operator is linear over the field of real numbers, or *real-linear*. If they are allowed to be complex, then the operator is linear over the complex field, or *complex-linear*.

It is possible for an operator to be real-linear without being complex-linear. For example, consider an operator R that reflects complex numbers through the real axis by taking complex conjugates. As an operator on the complex-valued functions, R is real-linear. However, it is not complex-linear, as is proved by the following counterexample. Let $f(t) = 1$ and $g(t) = 0$. When these functions are used and $\mathscr{L} = R$ in Equation 2.1, the result is

$$R(af + bg) = aR(f) + bR(g)$$

which reduces to

$$R(a) = a$$

This is true if a is real, but not if a has an imaginary term. For example, if $a = j = \sqrt{-1}$, the equation becomes

$$R(j) = j$$

which is not true. Thus, R is real-linear but not complex-linear.

Mixing is a common operator in signal processing. It will come as a surprise to many people that mixing is a linear operator. Do not confuse this assertion with the methods used to create a mixer in an electrical circuit. The circuit that implements a mixer contains nonlinear elements, but the end effect is actually a linear operation. Of course, inaccuracies in the actual circuit may cause its behavior to depart somewhat from the ideal mixer, but that is usually a small effect, when the circuit is operating properly, and is not usually of interest.

The general mixer, M_g, multiplies a signal x by another waveform, g. The ideal mixer is defined by

$$M_g(x(t)) = g(t)x(t)$$

This is a linear operator, since for any two waveforms x and y and any two constants a and b, we can compute

$$M_g(ax(t) + by(t)) = g(t)(ax(t) + by(t))$$
$$= ag(t)x(t) + bg(t)y(t)$$
$$= aM_g(x(t)) + bM_g(y(t))$$

which proves linearity.

There are only two common signal processing techniques that are time-dependent. Mixing is one; filtering a waveform by applying a Fourier transform on successive overlapping windows is the other (see Section 10.5). Adaptive signal processing techniques are time-dependent by definition (otherwise they cannot adapt) and may well be nonlinear. However, these are more advanced techniques and are not considered in this book; they are not yet in widespread use.

2.2   TWO SIMPLE HARMONIC OSCILLATORS

Tuning forks, mass-and-spring systems, low-amplitude pendulums, and *RLC* circuits are all examples of simple harmonic oscillators, at least to a good approximation. The ideal mass-and-spring system satisfies the equation

$$mx'' + bx' + kx = F \tag{2.2}$$

where x is the displacement of the mass from its equilibrium position, m is the mass of the weight on the end of the spring, b is the coefficient of friction, F is the driving force, and k is the spring constant.

An *RLC* circuit is another example of a simple harmonic oscillator. The equation for this circuit is

$$LQ'' + RQ' + \frac{1}{C}Q = v \tag{2.3}$$

where Q is the charge on the capacitor, Q' is the current in the circuit, C is the capacitance, R is the electrical resistance, L is the inductance, and v is the driving voltage source.

When we compare Equations 2.3 and 2.2, it is evident that the charge Q in the electric circuit is analogous to the displacement x in the spring-and-mass system; the inductance L is equivalent to the mass m on the end of the spring; the electrical resistance is equivalent to the friction in the mass-and-spring system; and the inverted capacitance, $1/C$, is equivalent to the spring constant.

2.3 REDUCTION TO FIRST-ORDER EQUATIONS

There are at least three equivalent ways to solve equations like Equations 2.2 and 2.3. One is to factor the differential equation like a polynomial. Another is to substitute a cleverly constructed function for the function x or Q, respectively. The third is to reduce the second-order equation to a system of first-order differential equations and solve the system of equations using matrix methods.

Both the factoring and the matrix method will be used in this chapter. They are closely related and carry over directly to the discrete-time case.

How can a differential equation be factored? At least superficially, the differential Equation 2.2 is similar to a second-order polynomial. The only difference is that instead of powers of a variable we have derivatives of a function. At this point it is useful to introduce the notation D for the operator that is differentiation with respect to time. In other words, for any function of time f, the differential operator D is defined by

$$D f(t) = f'(t) = \frac{d}{dt} f(t)$$

Why do we need three different symbols to mean the same thing? Each of these three ways to represent the time derivative operator has advantages in certain settings. When one converts a differential equation into a polynomial, the D notation is most convenient.

By using the D notation for differentiation with respect to time, the differential equation

$$mx'' + bx' + kx = F$$

can be rewritten as

$$mD^2x + bDx + kx = F$$

Because the differential operator is linear, this equation can be written as

$$(mD^2 + bD + k)x = F$$

in which case it is evident that the polynomial in D, $mD^2 + bD + k$, can be considered separately as another linear differential operator.

If the coefficients are constant, as they are in this case, then the polynomial differential operator can be factored into first-order terms just like an ordinary polynomial. The above polynomial differential operator can be written as

$$mD^2 + bD + k = m\left(D^2 + \frac{b}{m}D + \frac{k}{m}\right)$$

$$= m\left(D^2 - (z + \bar{z})D + z\bar{z}\right)$$

$$= m(D - z)(D - \bar{z}) \tag{2.4}$$

where, just as for an ordinary polynomial,

$$z = \frac{-b + \sqrt{b^2 - 4km}}{2m} \tag{2.5}$$

$$\bar{z} = \frac{-b - \sqrt{b^2 - 4km}}{2m}$$

If $b^2 - 4km < 0$, then z is complex and $\bar{z}$ is its complex conjugate. Otherwise, $\bar{z}$ is simply the other real root of the polynomial. It will be convenient below to write

$$d = \frac{b}{2m}$$

$$\omega = \frac{\sqrt{4km - b^2}}{2m}$$

so that the two roots are

$$z = -d + j\omega$$

$$\bar{z} = -d - j\omega$$

The frequency of oscillation is ω (if it is real) and d is the damping coefficient.

How is this used to solve the differential equation? By using Equation 2.4 for the differential operator, the original differential equation, Equation 2.2, can be written as

$$(D - z)(D - \bar{z})x = \frac{1}{m}F \tag{2.6}$$

The important thing to realize is that this can be viewed as a pair of first-order differential equations. One of the first-order equations is obtained by solving for the function $g = (D - \bar{z})x$ instead of x. With this definition of g, Equation 2.6 becomes

$$(D - z)g = \frac{1}{m}F$$

a first-order differential equation that is easily solved. The other first-order differential equation that comes from Equation 2.6 is obtained similarly, by defining a function $h = (D - z)x$, which evidently satisfies the differential equation

$$(D - \bar{z})h = \frac{1}{m}F$$

Here we are using the fact that $(D - z)(D - \bar{z}) = (D - \bar{z})(D - z)$, which is true only because the coefficients are independent of time. Once the solutions for g and h are found, the function x satisfying Equation 2.6 can be calculated as

$$x = \frac{g - h}{z - \bar{z}}$$

2.4 THE MATRIX EQUATION VIEWPOINT

The previous section showed one way to reduce the second-order equation to a system of two first-order equations, which can then be solved and used to obtain the original function. While the solution in this case can be obtained without the explicit matrix method developed in this section, the matrix approach is nonetheless implicit in the process. Moreover, it is easy to get lost in the details of solving even the second-order equation, so that the generally useful techniques are hidden by the details of the particular case. For these reasons, I have chosen to make the matrix approach explicit. This section presents the general technique, which will then be used in the particular case of interest.

As I said, it is not necessary to use the matrix method to solve the equation for a simple harmonic oscillator. If you don't want to spend the time learning this general technique, you can simply skip this section and the next, picking up again at Section 2.6, where the three categories of solution are explained. The matrix method is used again in Section 3.2, but that section is not needed for any later material in the book. Skipping this material will not unduly hamper your understanding of the remaining material.

2.4.1 Matrix Formalism for Second-Order Equations

The matrix method begins by transforming the general nth order linear constant-coefficient differential equation into a system of n first-order equations. The quickest road is to transform Equation 2.2 into the system of two first-order equations

$$Dx - x' = 0$$

$$mDx' + bx' + kx = F$$

where x and x' are the two functions to be solved for. This can be cast into a matrix equation:

$$D\begin{pmatrix} x \\ x' \end{pmatrix} - \begin{pmatrix} 0 & 1 \\ -\dfrac{k}{m} & -\dfrac{b}{m} \end{pmatrix} \begin{pmatrix} x \\ x' \end{pmatrix} = \begin{pmatrix} 0 \\ \dfrac{F}{m} \end{pmatrix} \tag{2.7}$$

where the derivative of a vector is taken componentwise.

Have we made any progress? Yes, we have, but before discussing how to solve an equation such as Equation 2.7, let's take a moment to consider the relationship between this equation and the system of equations for g and h in the previous section. The equations for g and h in terms of x and x' can be expressed by the matrix equation

$$\begin{pmatrix} g \\ h \end{pmatrix} = \begin{pmatrix} -\bar{z} & 1 \\ -z & 1 \end{pmatrix} \begin{pmatrix} x \\ x' \end{pmatrix} \tag{2.8}$$

Using this transformation, Equation 2.7 can be transformed into the system of equations for g and h. It will be easier to see how this is done by introducing some shorthand notation, as follows:

$$\mathbf{A} = \begin{pmatrix} 0 & 1 \\ -\dfrac{k}{m} & -\dfrac{b}{m} \end{pmatrix}$$

$$\mathbf{S} = \begin{pmatrix} -\bar{z} & 1 \\ -z & 1 \end{pmatrix}$$

$$f = \frac{F}{m}$$

Then Equation 2.7 becomes

$$D\begin{pmatrix} x \\ x' \end{pmatrix} - \mathbf{A}\begin{pmatrix} x \\ x' \end{pmatrix} = \begin{pmatrix} 0 \\ f \end{pmatrix}$$

and Equation 2.8 becomes

$$\begin{pmatrix} g \\ h \end{pmatrix} = \mathbf{S}\begin{pmatrix} x \\ x' \end{pmatrix}$$

Equation 2.7 can be transformed into an equation for g and h by multiplying from the left by $\mathbf{S}$, which gives

$$\mathbf{S}\left(D\begin{pmatrix} x \\ x' \end{pmatrix}\right) - \mathbf{SA}\begin{pmatrix} x \\ x' \end{pmatrix} = \mathbf{S}\begin{pmatrix} 0 \\ f \end{pmatrix} \tag{2.9}$$

Since **S** is a constant matrix and matrix multiplication is linear, the first term can be rewritten as

$$\mathbf{S}\left(D\begin{pmatrix} x \\ x' \end{pmatrix}\right) = D\mathbf{S}\begin{pmatrix} x \\ x' \end{pmatrix} = D\begin{pmatrix} g \\ h \end{pmatrix}$$

The second term in Equation 2.9 can be written in terms of g and h, as follows:

$$\mathbf{SA}\begin{pmatrix} x \\ x' \end{pmatrix} = \mathbf{SAS}^{-1}\mathbf{S}\begin{pmatrix} x \\ x' \end{pmatrix} = \left(\mathbf{SAS}^{-1}\right)\begin{pmatrix} g \\ h \end{pmatrix}$$

The transformation of **A** into the matrix $\mathbf{SAS}^{-1}$ is called a *similarity* transform of **A**. Using all these facts, the matrix Equation 2.7 has been transformed into

$$D\begin{pmatrix} g \\ h \end{pmatrix} - \mathbf{SAS}^{-1}\begin{pmatrix} g \\ h \end{pmatrix} = \begin{pmatrix} f \\ f \end{pmatrix} \tag{2.10}$$

which looks very much like the system of equations for g and h. Of course, it must be exactly the same set of equations. This is verified by calculating the similarity transform

$$\mathbf{SAS}^{-1} = \begin{pmatrix} \bar{z} & 0 \\ 0 & z \end{pmatrix}$$

which you can calculate for yourself.

2.4.2   The General Pattern for Matrix Equations

Thus, the original differential equation, Equation 2.2 can be reduced to a system of first-order equations, Equation 2.7, in a canonical way. The original differential equation can be factored, as in Equation 2.6, leading to a system of uncoupled first-order equations for g and h. This process is equivalent to finding a similarity transform for the matrix equation, Equation 2.7, that diagonalizes the matrix, obtaining Equation 2.10.

This same procedure works for an arbitrary constant-coefficient linear differential equation

$$D^n x + a_{n-1}D^{n-1}x + \cdots + a_1 Dx + a_0 x = f$$

which can be written canonically as a system of first-order equations:

$$D\begin{pmatrix} x \\ x' \\ \vdots \\ D^{n-1}x \end{pmatrix} - \begin{pmatrix} 0 & 1 & 0 & \cdots & 0 \\ 0 & 0 & 1 & \ddots & \vdots \\ \vdots & \vdots & \ddots & \ddots & 0 \\ 0 & 0 & \cdots & 0 & 1 \\ -a_{n-1} & \cdots & -a_2 & -a_1 & -a_0 \end{pmatrix} \begin{pmatrix} x \\ x' \\ \vdots \\ D^{n-1}x \end{pmatrix} = \begin{pmatrix} 0 \\ 0 \\ \vdots \\ 0 \\ f \end{pmatrix} \qquad (2.11)$$

In shorthand notation this equation can be written formally in the same way as Equation 2.7,

$$D\mathbf{v} - \mathbf{A}\mathbf{v} = \mathbf{w} \qquad (2.12)$$

where $\mathbf{v}$ is the vector of functions, $\mathbf{A}$ is the matrix expressing the coefficients of the original equation, and $\mathbf{w}$ is the driving vector.

2.4.3 Solving the Matrix Equations—General Case

The system of equations, Equation 2.12, can be solved formally without ever looking at the specifics of the coefficients from the original equation. In fact, the method is exactly the same one that is used to solve any first-order linear differential equation. If we ignore, for a moment, the fact that $\mathbf{A}$ is a matrix and $\mathbf{v}$ and $\mathbf{w}$ are vectors, then the standard method for solving Equation 2.12 can be used as follows. Multiply both sides of Equation 2.12 by $\exp(-\mathbf{A}t)$ (which is never zero) to obtain

$$e^{-\mathbf{A}t}D\mathbf{v} - e^{-\mathbf{A}t}\mathbf{A}\mathbf{v} = e^{-\mathbf{A}t}\mathbf{w}$$

and rewrite the left-hand side to obtain

$$D\left(e^{-\mathbf{A}t}\mathbf{v}\right) = e^{-\mathbf{A}t}\mathbf{w}$$

which can be immediately integrated with respect to time, giving

$$e^{-\mathbf{A}t}\mathbf{v}(t) = \mathbf{v}(0) + \int_0^t e^{-\mathbf{A}\tau}\mathbf{w}(\tau)\,d\tau \qquad (2.13)$$

Solving for $\mathbf{v}$ gives the final solution:

$$\mathbf{v}(t) = e^{\mathbf{A}t}\mathbf{v}(0) + e^{\mathbf{A}t}\int_0^t e^{-\mathbf{A}\tau}\mathbf{w}(\tau)\,d\tau \qquad (2.14)$$

It turns out that Equation 2.14 makes perfect sense, even when we wake up and remember that $\mathbf{A}$ is a matrix and $\mathbf{v}$ and $\mathbf{w}$ are vectors. The definition of the exponential of a matrix is exactly the same as the ordinary definition of the exponential. For any square matrix $\mathbf{Z}$, its exponential is defined by the Taylor series

$$e^{\mathbf{Z}} = \mathbf{1} + \mathbf{Z} + \frac{\mathbf{Z}^2}{2!} + \frac{\mathbf{Z}^3}{3!} + \cdots$$

$$= \sum_{k=0}^{\infty} \frac{\mathbf{Z}^k}{k!}$$

where $\mathbf{1} = \mathbf{Z}^0$ should be interpreted as the identity matrix. It turns out that no matter what square matrix we begin with, its exponential is invertible. This is easily proved, but first we need to establish the following formula. Given any two square matrices $\mathbf{X}$ and $\mathbf{Y}$ that commute (that is, $\mathbf{XY} = \mathbf{YX}$), then

$$e^{\mathbf{X}} e^{\mathbf{Y}} = e^{\mathbf{X}+\mathbf{Y}}$$

This can be proved by a straightforward multiplication of the Taylor series defining these exponentials; we will not go through the calculation here. It is obvious that $\mathbf{Z}$ commutes with $-\mathbf{Z}$ for any square matrix $\mathbf{Z}$, so, in particular, this formula shows that

$$e^{\mathbf{Z}} e^{-\mathbf{Z}} = e^{\mathbf{0}} = \mathbf{1}$$

which is the identity matrix.

Thus, in particular, Equation 2.13 can be transformed into matrix Equation 2.14 by multiplying both sides by the inverse of $\exp(-At)$, which is $\exp(At)$. The integration on the right-hand side of Equation 2.14 should be interpreted as the component-by-component integration of each element of the vector that results from the matrix-times-vector multiplication in the integrand.

Now we can come back to the special case we are interested in at the moment: Equation 2.7. We are immediately faced with the problem of calculating the exponential of the matrix

$$e^{\mathbf{A}t} = \mathbf{1} + \mathbf{A}t + \frac{1}{2}\mathbf{A}^2 t^2 + \frac{1}{3!}\mathbf{A}^3 t^3 + \cdots$$

$$\mathbf{A} = \begin{pmatrix} 0 & 1 \\ -\dfrac{b}{m} & -\dfrac{k}{m} \end{pmatrix}$$

The problem, of course, is calculating all these powers $\mathbf{A}^k$ of the matrix and then adding up the power series in some reasonable way. However, there is a way out of this difficulty. We know that there is a similarity transform that converts this matrix into a diagonal matrix. This same similarity transform can be used on the exponential of the matrix, which can be shown as follows:

$$\mathbf{S}e^{\mathbf{Z}}\mathbf{S}^{-1} = \mathbf{S}\left(1 + \mathbf{Z} + \frac{\mathbf{Z}^2}{2} + \cdots\right)\mathbf{S}^{-1}$$

$$= \mathbf{S}\left(\sum_{k=0}^{\infty} \frac{1}{k!}\mathbf{Z}^k\right)\mathbf{S}^{-1}$$

$$= \sum_{k=0}^{\infty} \frac{1}{k!}\mathbf{S}\mathbf{Z}^k\mathbf{S}^{-1}$$

and in a moment we will show that this can be written as

$$= \sum_{k=0}^{\infty} \frac{1}{k!}\left(\mathbf{S}\mathbf{Z}\mathbf{S}^{-1}\right)^k$$

$$= e^{\mathbf{S}\mathbf{Z}\mathbf{S}^{-1}}$$

The one step that needs to be verified is that the similarity transform can be brought inside the kth-power function. It will be sufficient to show how this works for one example:

$$\mathbf{S}\mathbf{Z}^2\mathbf{S}^{-1} = \mathbf{S}\mathbf{Z}\mathbf{Z}\mathbf{S}^{-1}$$

$$= \mathbf{S}\mathbf{Z}\mathbf{S}^{-1}\mathbf{S}\mathbf{Z}\mathbf{S}^{-1}$$

$$= \left(\mathbf{S}\mathbf{Z}\mathbf{S}^{-1}\right)^2$$

This can be proved for the general case using an easy induction proof, which is left for you to construct if you are interested.

Another important fact from linear algebra is that every matrix can be diagonalized with a similarity transform. The exponential of a diagonal matrix is easily calculated as follows. Let the diagonal matrix be

$$\mathbf{D} = \begin{pmatrix} d_0 & 0 & \cdots & 0 \\ 0 & d_1 & \ddots & \vdots \\ \vdots & \ddots & \ddots & 0 \\ 0 & \cdots & 0 & d_{n-1} \end{pmatrix}$$

Since the kth power of this matrix is just the diagonal matrix with entries equal to the kth power of these diagonal values, it is easy to see that the exponential of the matrix is

$$
e^{\mathbf{D}} = \begin{pmatrix} e^{d_0} & 0 & \cdots & 0 \\ 0 & e^{d_1} & \ddots & \vdots \\ \vdots & \ddots & \ddots & 0 \\ 0 & \cdots & 0 & e^{d_{n-1}} \end{pmatrix}
$$

Thus, the exponential of any matrix can be obtained by first transforming it to a diagonal matrix, then taking the exponential, then transforming back. In particular, if

$$\mathbf{D} = \mathbf{SAS}^{-1}$$

then we can calculate as follows:

$$
\begin{aligned}
e^{\mathbf{A}t} &= e^{\mathbf{S}^{-1}\mathbf{D}t\mathbf{S}} \\
&= \mathbf{S}^{-1}e^{\mathbf{D}t}\mathbf{S}
\end{aligned}
$$

The first term in Equation 2.14 is exactly as we want it for most purposes, because it gives the homogeneous part of the solution in terms of the initial conditions on x and all of its derivatives. However, the second term is difficult to calculate as it stands, since it involves the complicated matrix multiplications. It is easier to calculate this term by transforming it into the diagonal form. This is done by substituting

$$\mathbf{A} = \mathbf{S}^{-1}\mathbf{DS}$$

for $\mathbf{A}$ everywhere, and simplifying as follows:

$$
\begin{aligned}
e^{\mathbf{A}t}\int_0^t e^{-\mathbf{A}\tau}\mathbf{w}(\tau)\,d\tau &= e^{\mathbf{S}^{-1}\mathbf{DS}t}\int_0^t e^{-\mathbf{S}^{-1}\mathbf{DS}\tau}\mathbf{w}(\tau)\,d\tau \\
&= \mathbf{S}^{-1}e^{\mathbf{D}t}\mathbf{S}\int_0^t \mathbf{S}^{-1}e^{-\mathbf{D}\tau}\mathbf{S}\mathbf{w}(\tau)\,d\tau \\
&= \mathbf{S}^{-1}e^{\mathbf{D}t}\int_0^t e^{-\mathbf{D}\tau}\mathbf{S}\mathbf{w}(\tau)\,d\tau
\end{aligned}
$$

In other words, the way to use Equation 2.14 most conveniently is in the form

$$\mathbf{v}(t) = e^{\mathbf{A}t}\mathbf{v}(0) + \mathbf{S}^{-1}e^{\mathbf{D}t}\int_0^t e^{-\mathbf{D}\tau}\mathbf{S}\mathbf{w}(\tau)\,d\tau \tag{2.15}$$

where $\mathbf{S}$ is the matrix that transforms A to its diagonal form: $\mathbf{D} = \mathbf{SAS}^{-1}$.

2.5 APPLICATION TO THE MASS-AND-SPRING SYSTEM

Now let's use the method we have just outlined to solve Equation 2.7. The transformation of the matrix $\mathbf{A}$ to its diagonal form is given by Equation 2.8. Thus, in this particular case,

$$e^{\mathbf{A}t} = \mathbf{S}^{-1} \begin{pmatrix} e^{\bar{z}t} & 0 \\ 0 & e^{zt} \end{pmatrix} \mathbf{S}$$

$$= \frac{1}{z - \bar{z}} \begin{pmatrix} 1 & -1 \\ z & -\bar{z} \end{pmatrix} \begin{pmatrix} e^{\bar{z}t} & 0 \\ 0 & e^{zt} \end{pmatrix} \begin{pmatrix} -\bar{z} & 1 \\ -z & 1 \end{pmatrix}$$

$$= \frac{1}{z - \bar{z}} \begin{pmatrix} z e^{zt} - \bar{z} e^{\bar{z}t} & e^{\bar{z}t} - e^{zt} \\ -|z|^2 \left(e^{\bar{z}t} - e^{zt} \right) & z e^{\bar{z}t} - \bar{z} e^{zt} \end{pmatrix}$$

This complicated matrix can be simplified considerably by using the notation

$$z = -d + j\omega$$

in which case the matrix, after collecting terms, is

$$e^{\mathbf{A}t} = e^{-dt} \begin{pmatrix} \cos(\omega t) - \dfrac{d \sin(\omega t)}{\omega} & -\dfrac{\sin(\omega t)}{\omega} \\ (d^2 + \omega^2) \dfrac{\sin(\omega t)}{\omega} & \cos(\omega t) + d \dfrac{\sin(\omega t)}{\omega} \end{pmatrix} \tag{2.16}$$

The matrix $\exp(-\mathbf{A}t)$ can be obtained from this one by simply changing the sign of t everywhere. When this is done and the matrix is substituted into Equation 2.14, the equation becomes

$$\begin{pmatrix} x(t) \\ x'(t) \end{pmatrix} = e^{-dt} \begin{pmatrix} x(0)\cos(\omega t) + (x(0)d + x'(0))\dfrac{\sin(\omega t)}{\omega} \\ * \end{pmatrix}$$

$$+ \mathbf{S}^{-1} e^{\mathbf{D}t} \int_0^t \begin{pmatrix} e^{-\bar{z}\tau} f(\tau) \\ e^{-z\tau} f(\tau) \end{pmatrix} d\tau$$

where the asterisk $*$ is used as a place holder, because we are only interested in the top component.

The second term on the right-hand side needs additional work. Careful calculations show that

$$\mathbf{S}^{-1}e^{\mathbf{D}t}\int_0^t \begin{pmatrix} e^{-\bar{z}\tau}f(\tau) \\ e^{-z\tau}f(\tau) \end{pmatrix} d\tau = \mathbf{S}^{-1}\begin{pmatrix} e^{\bar{z}t} & 0 \\ 0 & e^{zt} \end{pmatrix}\begin{pmatrix} \int_0^t e^{-\bar{z}\tau}f(\tau)\,d\tau \\ \int_0^t e^{-z\tau}f(\tau)\,d\tau \end{pmatrix}$$

$$= \mathbf{S}^{-1}\begin{pmatrix} e^{\bar{z}t}\int_0^t e^{-\bar{z}\tau}f(\tau)\,d\tau \\ e^{zt}\int_0^t e^{-z\tau}f(\tau)\,d\tau \end{pmatrix}$$

$$= \frac{1}{z-\bar{z}}\begin{pmatrix} e^{zt}\int_0^t e^{-z\tau}f(\tau)\,d\tau - e^{\bar{z}t}\int_0^t e^{-\bar{z}\tau}f(\tau)\,d\tau \\ * \end{pmatrix}$$

which, using $z = -d + j\omega$, can be written as

$$= \begin{pmatrix} e^{-dt}\int_0^t e^{d\tau}\dfrac{\sin[\omega(t-\tau)]}{\omega}f(\tau)\,d\tau \\ * \end{pmatrix}$$

Extracting only the top component, which is of primary interest, the solution is

$$x(t) = e^{-dt}\left\{ x(0)\cos(\omega t) + [x(0)d + x'(0)]\frac{\sin(\omega t)}{\omega} \right\}$$

$$+ e^{-dt}\int_0^t e^{d\tau}\frac{\sin[\omega(t-\tau)]}{\omega}f(\tau)\,d\tau \tag{2.17}$$

2.6 THE THREE CATEGORIES OF SOLUTIONS

There are three categories of solutions to the simple harmonic oscillator, corresponding to the values of ω. They are called *overdamped* (ω imaginary), *underdamped* (ω real), and *critically damped* ($\omega = 0$).

The reason for these terms is evident from the *impulse response* of the system in each case. For the mass-and-spring system, the damping term is bx'. For the *RLC* circuit, the damping term is RQ'. In the critically damped case, the system does not oscillate in response to an impulse but returns to zero quickly. If the damping is higher, the system will not oscillate but will not return to its rest position as quickly. If the damping is lower, the system will repeatedly overshoot its resting position, oscillating with a decaying amplitude.

The impulse response of a system can be thought of as what happens when it is hit sharply with a hammer. The hammer, however, must be an ideal one: The blow delivered must be instantaneous. In order to deliver any energy to the system within a zero time span, the blow must also be infinitely strong. The function that does this is the Dirac delta function, $\delta(t)$. More precisely, it is a distribution that is defined by the equation

$$\int_a^b y(\tau)\delta(\tau)\,d\tau = y(0)$$

supposing only that $a \le 0 \le b$. Mathematically, the impulse response of a simple harmonic oscillator is obtained by putting $f(\tau) = \delta(\tau)$ into Equation 2.17, assuming the system was initially at rest, $x(0) = 0$, and not moving, $x'(0) = 0$. The impulse response is therefore,

$$x(t) = e^{-dt}\frac{\sin(\omega t)}{\omega} \tag{2.18}$$

2.6.1 Overdamped

The overdamped case occurs when ω is imaginary. For the mass-and-spring system, according to Equation 2.5, this means that $b^2 > 4km$. For this case, write

$$\gamma = j\omega = \frac{\sqrt{b^2 - 4km}}{2m}$$

Then the equation becomes

$$x(t) = \frac{e^{-dt}\sinh(\gamma t)}{\gamma}$$

In this case, there is no oscillation in the impulse response. Figure 2.1 is a plot of both the overdamped and the critically damped impulse responses. The overdamped response is the one that is slower in reaching its equilibrium position.

2.6.2 Critically Damped

Obtaining the impulse response for the critically damped case requires a little more work, since $\omega = 0$. However, Equation 2.18 can be saved by taking the limit as $\omega \to 0$. The most straightforward way to do this is to expand the sine as a power series, as follows:

$$\lim_{\omega \to 0}\frac{\sin(\omega t)}{\omega} = \lim_{\omega \to 0}\frac{1}{\omega}\left[\omega t - \frac{\omega^3 t^3}{3!} + \frac{\omega^5 t^5}{5!} + \cdots\right]$$

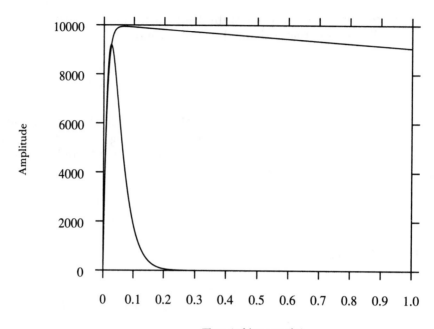

Time (arbitrary units)

Figure 2.1   The overdamped and critically damped motions of the simple harmonic oscillator are plotted together in this figure. The critically damped solution is the one that decays to zero faster. These solutions were obtained for fixed spring constant k and fixed mass m. Only the friction coefficient b was varied.

$$= \lim_{\omega \to 0} \left[t - \frac{\omega^2 t^3}{3!} + \frac{\omega^4 t^5}{5!} + \cdots \right]$$

$$= t.$$

Therefore, the impulse response in the critically damped case is

$$x(t) = te^{-dt}$$

Figure 2.1 plots this curve along with the overdamped impulse response for comparison. The critically damped motion is the one that decays to its equilibrium position most quickly *for a fixed spring constant and mass,* in the spring-and-mass system, or *for a fixed capacitance and inductance,* in the *RLC* circuit.

2.6.3   Underdamped

The underdamped case, ω real and not zero, is given by Equation 2.18. This is the only case that displays any oscillation. This is a damped sinusoid and is

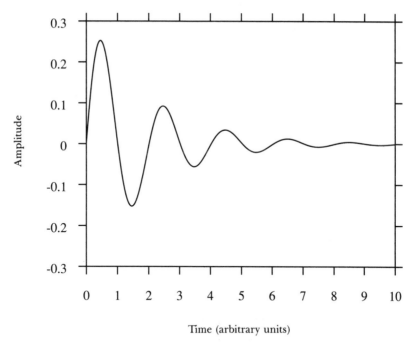

Figure 2.2 The underdamped simple harmonic oscillator "rings like a bell" in response to an impulse.

plotted in Figure 2.2. Notice that the frequency of the oscillation,

$$\omega = \frac{\sqrt{4km - b^2}}{2m}$$

for the mass-and-spring system, or

$$\omega = \frac{\sqrt{4L/C - R^2}}{2L}$$

depends on the damping or resistance, as well as the mass and spring constant, or inductance and capacitance.

It may seem surprising that the frequency of oscillation depends on the friction or resistance in the system. It can be understood intuitively in the mass-and-spring system. Any friction added to the system will slow its motions, thus lengthening the period of oscillation. Similarly, in the *RLC* circuit, the electrical resistance *R* resists the motion of charge in the circuit.

Discrete-Time Simple Harmonic Oscillators

The goal of this chapter is to obtain a discrete-time version of the general solution to the motion of a simple harmonic oscillator, Equation 2.17. The complete solution, while not particularly complicated, does require significant effort to obtain. Section 3.1 therefore develops the first-order case, which is then used to solve the second-order problem in Section 3.3.

This chapter requires careful study for a full understanding. It is an introduction to some of the core subjects of digital signal processing and how those techniques can be used to mimic the real world. However, it is not necessary that you understand everything on the first reading. All the results from this chapter that are needed to proceed with the construction of the bell choir and organ of the next two chapters are repeated concisely at the beginning of Chapter 4.

3.1 FIRST-ORDER DISCRETE-TIME SOLUTIONS

A discrete-time version of Equation 2.17 is the goal of this chapter. This section shows how to solve the simpler first-order equation. Two such solutions are then combined to obtain the solution to the simple harmonic oscillator equation. The general first-order equation is

$$(D - z)y = f \tag{3.1}$$

3.1.1 First-Order, Homogeneous

When $f = 0$, Equation 3.1 is called *homogeneous*, meaning simply that the equation is not forced. In that case, the continuous-time solution is trivially obtained:

$$y(t) = y(0)e^{zt}$$

The discrete-time version should track this equation exactly, so it is clear that, for a time interval of Δt, the discrete-time solution is

$$y_n = y(n\Delta t) = y(0)e^{nz\Delta t} \tag{3.2}$$

In other words, the discrete-time frequency is

$$q = e^{z\Delta t}$$

and the waveform is

$$g_n = g(0)q^n$$

exactly as claimed in Equation 1.2 on page 4.

A recurrence formula is normally used in digital signal processing instead of Equation 3.2. Of course, it is possible to use this equation directly, but in most applications the filter or oscillator is being forced, which requires the complete solutions of the next section, and makes it difficult or impossible to use an equation like 3.2 directly. Even in the homogeneous case considered in this section, the recurrence relation generates the waveform with much less computation than required by Equation 3.2. The recurrence formula equivalent to Equation 3.2 is

$$y_0 = y(0) \tag{3.3}$$

$$y_{n+1} = e^{z\Delta t} y_n \tag{3.4}$$

In an application program, the discrete-time frequency, $q = \exp(z\Delta t)$, is computed once and then used to generate as many data points as required, each new data point requiring only one (possibly complex) multiplication. This is much more efficient than using Equation 3.2 for each data point.

3.1.2   First-Order, Forced

The forcing function, f, introduces some complications, as it did for the continuous-time solutions. The method is the same as used for the matrix case of Equation 2.14, and the solution to Equation 3.1 is easily seen to be

$$y(t) = e^{zt}y(0) + e^{zt}\int_0^t e^{-z\tau}f(\tau)\,d\tau$$

The goal is now to obtain a recurrence formula similar to Equation 3.4 that will make calculations of this formula efficient.

Equation 3.4 suggests calculating the difference,

$$y_{n+1} - e^{z\Delta t}y_n$$

since in the homogeneous case this difference is zero. This is indeed the right way to proceed and results in the computation

$$y_{n+1} - e^{z\Delta t}y_n = e^{(n+1)z\Delta t}y(0) + e^{(n+1)z\Delta t}\int_0^{(n+1)\Delta t} e^{-z\tau}f(\tau)\,d\tau$$

$$- e^{z\Delta t}\left(e^{nz\Delta t}y(0) + e^{nz\Delta t}\int_0^{n\Delta t} e^{-z\tau}f(\tau)\,d\tau\right)$$

$$= e^{(n+1)z\Delta t}\int_{n\Delta t}^{(n+1)\Delta t} e^{-z\tau}f(\tau)\,d\tau$$

The recurrence relation is, therefore,

$$y_{n+1} = e^{z\Delta t}y_n + (T_z f)_{n+1} \tag{3.5}$$

where T_z has been defined to be the integral operator

$$(T_z f)(t) = e^{zt}\int_{t-\Delta t}^t e^{-z\tau}f(\tau)\,d\tau \tag{3.6}$$

and, as always, the subscript notation on a function means that

$$(T_z f)_n = (T_z f)(n\Delta t)$$

3.1.3 First-Order, Approximating the Integral

Now we can see what sort of trouble the forcing function causes. The integral, Equation 3.6, cannot be evaluated without knowing the analytical *form* of the forcing function, while in most signal processing applications, only the *value* of the forcing function is known and only at the sampled times. The only solution to this problem is to take sample points close enough together (small Δt) such that the forcing function does not "change much" between the sample points. In that case, the integral can be adequately approximated by one means or another.

The easiest method is to use the *mean-value theorem*, which says that as long as the forcing function f is continuous on the interval from $n\Delta t$ to $(n + 1)\Delta t$, there is some time, γ, in this interval such that

$$(T_z f)_{n+1} = e^{z(n+1)\Delta t} \int_{n\Delta t}^{(n+1)\Delta t} e^{-z\tau} f(\tau) \, d\tau$$

$$= f(\gamma) e^{z(n+1)\Delta t} \int_{n\Delta t}^{(n+1)\Delta t} e^{-z\tau} \, d\tau$$

which can be integrated to give

$$(T_z f)_{n+1} = f(\gamma) e^{z(n+1)\Delta t} \frac{e^{-zn\Delta t} - e^{-z(n+1)\Delta t}}{z}$$

$$= f(\gamma) \frac{e^{z\Delta t} - 1}{z}$$

The only problem is that we cannot know the values of f on the interval, and even if we did, we would not know which one to choose. Therefore, this formula is used simply by choosing $\gamma = n\Delta t$ or $\gamma = (n + 1)\Delta t$, one of the end points where the function is known.

Using the function value at one end point is equivalent to approximating the integral by the area of a rectangle. Other approximations are better, under the right circumstances. Another method is to draw a straight line from one function value to the next and use the area of the resulting trapezoid. Other approximations are possible. All these approximations result in using some linear combination of the function values at the end points instead of simply the value at one end point. The general form is, therefore,

$$(T_z f)_{n+1} \approx (\alpha f_n + \beta f_{n+1}) \frac{e^{z\Delta t} - 1}{z} \tag{3.7}$$

where we would normally use $\alpha + \beta = 1$, both positive.

As will be shown in Chapter 14, combining adjacent input values this way is equivalent to a zero at the Nyquist frequency. To see what this means, consider the case $\alpha = \beta = 0.5$. In that case, consider what happens to the forcing function if it is at the Nyquist frequency, $f_n = (-1)^n$. The average of successive points is always zero, so no energy gets through to drive the equation; that is why it is called a zero. At the other extreme, if $f_n = 1$ is a constant, then the driving force is unchanged by Equation 3.7, regardless of the values of α and β, except for the scale factor $(e^{z\Delta t} - 1)/z$.

That scale factor is important and can be very different from 1. In fact, if $z\Delta t$ is small enough in magnitude, the exponential can be approximated by the first two terms of its Taylor expansion, $\exp(z\Delta t) \approx 1 + z\Delta t$, which means the factor in Equation 3.7 is, approximately,

$$\frac{e^{z\Delta t} - 1}{z} \approx \frac{1 + z\Delta t - 1}{z} = \Delta t$$

Ignoring this factor can make a very big difference in the magnitude of your answers.

3.1.4 First-Order, Impulse Response

In some special cases, the integral in Equation 3.6 can be calculated exactly, allowing a comparison between the actual value and the approximation in Equation 3.7. Two special cases are considered. The first is when $f(t) = \delta(t)$, the Dirac delta function. This case will be used to produce the bell tones of Section 4. The other case is when $f(t) = \exp(st)$ is a pure tone.

First, if $f(t) = \delta(t)$, the computation is particularly easy:

$$(T_z\delta)_{n+1} = \begin{cases} e^{z\Delta t} & \text{if } n = 0 \\ 0 & \text{otherwise} \end{cases}$$

Therefore, the recurrence formula for a single ideal impulse at time 0 is

$$y_0 = y(0)$$

$$y_1 = e^{z\Delta t}y_0 + e^{z\Delta t}$$

$$y_{n+1} = e^{z\Delta t}y_n \qquad \forall n \geq 1$$

The best approximation to this that can be obtained from Equation 3.7 is to choose $\alpha = 1$, $\beta = 0$, and $f_0 = 1/\Delta t$, so that the forcing function carries unit energy. Then the approximation gives

$$e^{z\Delta t} \int_0^{\Delta t} e^{-z\tau} f(\tau) \, d\tau \approx \frac{e^{z\Delta t} - 1}{z\Delta t}$$

This is not a very good approximation, but since in this case, the error is only a matter of scale, it is easily compensated. We should not expect a very good approximation from Equation 3.7 in this case, since the function is not continuous and changes dramatically during the time interval.

3.1.5 First-Order, Pure Tone

The other case to be considered is $f(t) = \exp(st)$, which is a bit harder than the impulse case. In this case, the integral is evaluated as follows:

$$\left(T_z e^{st}\right)_{n+1} = e^{z(n+1)\Delta t} \int_{n\Delta t}^{(n+1)\Delta t} e^{-z\tau} e^{s\tau} \, d\tau \tag{3.8}$$

$$= e^{z(n+1)\Delta t} \int_{n\Delta t}^{(n+1)\Delta t} e^{(s-z)\tau} \, d\tau$$

$$= e^{z(n+1)\Delta t} \frac{e^{(s-z)(n+1)\Delta t} - e^{(s-z)(n\Delta t)}}{s - z}$$

$$= \frac{e^{(z-s)\Delta t} - 1}{z - s} e^{s(n+1)\Delta t} \tag{3.9}$$

Therefore, if the forcing function is of the form $f(\tau) = \exp(s\tau)$, then the recurrence formula giving the discrete-time solution to the first-order linear differential Equation 3.1 is

$$y_0 = y(0)$$

$$y_{n+1} = e^{z\Delta t} y_n + \frac{e^{(z-s)\Delta t} - 1}{z - s} e^{s(n+1)\Delta t}$$

This complicated-looking formula is actually quite simple to use in practice. The multiplier of y_n is a constant, as is the fraction in the second term on the right. Thus, each iteration of this formula requires only two (possibly complex) multiplications.

Please note that this solution is not the same as presenting the simple harmonic oscillator with a series of impulses. The most important difference is that the scale factor multiplying the driving function is a function of s, the driving frequency, as well as of z.

Now compare the exact solution with the approximation, Equation 3.7, for this case, which works out to be

$$\left(T_z e^{st}\right)_{n+1} \approx \left(\alpha e^{-s\Delta t} + \beta\right) \frac{e^{z\Delta t} - 1}{z} e^{s(n+1)\Delta t}$$

Since there are two constants to be determined, we can force this approximation to be equal to the exact solution for two different values of s. It is usually desirable to have the correct response for small frequencies, particularly $s = 0$, which reduces to the condition

$$(\alpha + \beta) \frac{e^{z\Delta t} - 1}{z} = \frac{e^{z\Delta t} - 1}{z}$$

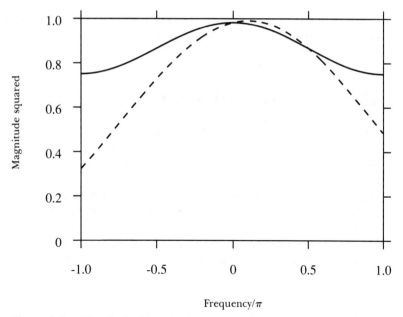

Frequency/π

Figure 3.1. The dashed line is the squared magnitude of the theoretically correct integral, Equation 3.9. The solid line is the squared magnitude of the approximation Equation 3.7 where α and β were chosen by forcing a match at frequency $\pi/2$.

which trivially reduces to the condition

$$\alpha + \beta = 1$$

What other point should be chosen? That decision is not particularly easy. However, once another frequency is chosen, the values of α and β are calculated by solving the equation

$$\left|\alpha e^{-s\Delta t} + \beta\right|^2 \left|\frac{e^{z\Delta t} - 1}{z}\right|^2 = \left|\frac{e^{(z-s)\Delta t} - 1}{z - s}\right|^2$$

which reduces to a quadratic equation for α by using $\beta = 1 - \alpha$.

Figure 3.1 shows the theoretical and approximated integrals for the case $z = -0.01 + j(0.1\pi)$ as a function of $s = j\phi$, assuming $\Delta t = 1$. The dashed line is the squared magnitude of the theoretically correct solution, Equation 3.9. The solid line is the magnitude squared value of the approximation, Equation 3.7, obtained by forcing a match at $s = j\pi/2$.

The discrepancy shown in Figure 3.1 is somewhat disheartening. However, we can do much better later, when we consider the full solution to the simple harmonic oscillator equation. The basic reason for this is that for a single pole, the theoretical value of the integral in Equation 3.9 is not symmetric around

0, while the approximation in Equation 3.7 is always symmetric. When a real-coefficient differential equation is considered, any complex pole is matched by its complex conjugate pole, thus restoring the symmetry around zero.

3.2   THE DISCRETE-TIME MATRIX SOLUTION

This section shows how the discrete-time solution for any n^{th}-order constant-coefficient linear differential equation can be obtained in matrix form. This solution is not used directly for the later development, but I think it does provide insight into the general process. It is not much extra work to obtain this general solution, so I have included it here. You may, however, skip directly to Section 3.3 without loss of continuity and without missing any material needed for later development.

As we saw in Chapter 2, every nth-order, constant-coefficient linear differential equation can be reduced to the $n \times n$ first-order matrix Equation 2.12:

$$\mathbf{Dv} - \mathbf{Av} = \mathbf{w}$$

where $\mathbf{v}$ is a vector function with n components, $\mathbf{A}$ is an $n \times n$ constant matrix, and $\mathbf{w}$ is the vector of forcing functions. The continuous-time solution to this matrix equation can be written as in Equation 2.14:

$$\mathbf{v}(t) = e^{\mathbf{A}t}\mathbf{v}(0) + e^{\mathbf{A}t}\int_0^t e^{-\mathbf{A}\tau}\mathbf{w}(\tau)\,d\tau$$

This equation can be used to obtain a recurrence formula for the discrete-time solution just as we did for the general first-order equation, obtaining the recurrence formula Equation 3.5. The procedure is exactly the same.

The discrete-time vector values we are interested in obtaining are $\mathbf{v}_k = \mathbf{v}(k\Delta t)$ for some fixed sample interval Δt. The generalized discrete-time frequency is evidently

$$e^{\mathbf{A}\Delta t}$$

Thus, following the earlier development, we calculate the difference,

$$\mathbf{v}_{n+1} - e^{\mathbf{A}\Delta t}\mathbf{v}_n = e^{\mathbf{A}(n+1)\Delta t}\mathbf{v}(0) + e^{\mathbf{A}(n+1)\Delta t}\int_0^{(n+1)\Delta t} e^{-\mathbf{A}\tau}\mathbf{w}(\tau)\,d\tau$$

$$- e^{\mathbf{A}\Delta t}\left(e^{\mathbf{A}n\Delta t}\mathbf{v}(0) + e^{\mathbf{A}n\Delta t}\int_0^{n\Delta t} e^{-\mathbf{A}\tau}\mathbf{w}(\tau)\,d\tau\right)$$

$$= e^{\mathbf{A}(n+1)\Delta t}\int_{n\Delta t}^{(n+1)\Delta t} e^{-\mathbf{A}\tau}\mathbf{w}(\tau)\,d\tau$$

This integral is similar to Equation 3.6, so it makes sense to define

$$(T_{\mathbf{A}}\mathbf{w})(t) = e^{\mathbf{A}t} \int_{t-\Delta t}^{t} e^{-\mathbf{A}\tau}\mathbf{w}(\tau) \, d\tau \tag{3.10}$$

With this definition, the recurrence formula is identical in form to Equation 3.5:

$$\mathbf{v}_{n+1} = e^{\mathbf{A}\Delta t}\mathbf{v}_n + (T_{\mathbf{A}}\mathbf{w})_{n+1} \tag{3.11}$$

We still have the problem of approximating this integral, and the answer is very similar to Equation 3.7, except that we are now dealing with matrices and vectors and so must be a little more careful with the order in which things are written down.

The simplest approximation to the integral in Equation 3.10 is obtained by assuming that $\mathbf{w}$ is constant in the time interval. In that case, we are faced with integrating the exponential of a matrix. This is, in fact, very similar to integrating an ordinary exponential function. The exponential of a matrix is defined by the usual Taylor series, so we can compute the derivative:

$$De^{\mathbf{A}t} = D\left(\sum_{k=0}^{\infty} \frac{1}{k!}\mathbf{A}^k t^k\right)$$

$$= \sum_{k=1}^{\infty} \frac{1}{k!}\mathbf{A}^k \, k \, t^{k-1}$$

$$= \sum_{\ell=0}^{\infty} \frac{1}{\ell!}\mathbf{A}^{\ell+1} t^\ell$$

$$= \mathbf{A}\sum_{\ell=0}^{\infty} \frac{1}{\ell!}\mathbf{A}^\ell t^\ell$$

$$= \mathbf{A}e^{\mathbf{A}t}$$

From this calculation, we can conclude that

$$\int e^{\mathbf{A}t} \, dt = \mathbf{K} + \mathbf{A}^{-1}e^{\mathbf{A}t}$$

where $\mathbf{K}$ is an arbitrary constant matrix. Using this, and assuming $\mathbf{w}$ is constant in the interval, the integral in Equation 3.10 can be approximated as follows:

$$(T_{\mathbf{A}}\mathbf{w})(t) \approx e^{\mathbf{A}t}\left[\int_{t-\Delta t}^{t} e^{-\mathbf{A}\tau}\, d\tau\right]\mathbf{w}(t)$$

$$\approx e^{\mathbf{A}t}\mathbf{A}^{-1}\left[e^{-\mathbf{A}(t-\Delta t)} - e^{-\mathbf{A}t}\right]\mathbf{w}(t)$$

$$\approx \mathbf{A}^{-1}\left[e^{\mathbf{A}\Delta t} - 1\right]\mathbf{w}(t)$$

Again, just as for the first-order equation, other approximations for this integral are possible, all of which involve some linear combination of the neighboring values, $\mathbf{w}_n$ and $\mathbf{w}_{n+1}$. This time, the linear combination uses matrices instead of constants, but it looks very similar to Equation 3.7:

$$(T_{\mathbf{A}}\mathbf{w})_{n+1} \approx \mathbf{A}^{-1}\left[e^{\mathbf{A}\Delta t} - 1\right](\alpha\mathbf{w}_n + \beta\mathbf{w}_{n+1}) \qquad (3.12)$$

where this time α and β are matrices.

3.3 THE DISCRETE-TIME SIMPLE HARMONIC OSCILLATOR

Equation 3.11 can be used directly to obtain a recurrence relation for the simple harmonic oscillator in the same way in which it was used to obtain the continuous-time solution. However, just as in the continuous-time case, the generalized discrete-time frequency is a complicated matrix $e^{\mathbf{A}\Delta t}$, which is exactly Equation 2.16 with Δt in place of t. This does work and gives the right solutions.

However, there is a simpler solution that requires fewer computations for each calculated point. It is obtained by cascading the two first-order differential equations instead of solving them in parallel and then combining the solutions. The two procedures are equivalent but give different forms for the solution.

The basic equation is

$$(D - z)(D - \overline{z})y = x$$

which, this time, we reduce to two first-order equations as follows:

$$(D - z)y = g$$
$$(D - \overline{z})g = x$$

We already know the discrete-time solutions to each of these equations:

$$y_{n+1} = e^{z\Delta t}y_n + (T_z g)_{n+1} \tag{3.13}$$

$$g_{n+1} = e^{\bar{z}\Delta t}g_n + (T_{\bar{z}}x)_{n+1} \tag{3.14}$$

where T_z and $T_{\bar{z}}$ are both integral operators as defined in Equation 3.6.

The goal now is to use these equations to obtain one recurrence formula that only involves the two previous outputs, y_n and y_{n-1}, and the two previous inputs, x_{n+1} and x_n. In other words, we want to eliminate all reference to the intermediate function, g. This can be done by obtaining a recurrence relation for $T_z g$ from Equation 3.14, then using it in Equation 3.13. Since T_z is a linear operator we can immediately write the recurrence formula,

$$(T_z g)_{n+1} = e^{\bar{z}\Delta t}(T_z g)_n + (T_z T_{\bar{z}}x)_{n+1} \tag{3.15}$$

where the cascading of these two linear operators means

$$(T_z T_{\bar{z}}x)(t) = e^{zt}\int_{t-\Delta t}^{t} e^{-z\tau}(T_{\bar{z}}x)(\tau)\,d\tau$$

$$= e^{zt}\int_{t-\Delta t}^{t} e^{-z\tau}\left(e^{z\tau}\int_{\tau-\Delta t}^{\tau} e^{-\bar{z}\mu}x(\mu)\,d\mu\right)d\tau \tag{3.16}$$

If you don't believe me, you can compute Equation 3.15 yourself by simply making the necessary substitutions and verifying the equality using Equation 3.14.

Now we could use Equation 3.15 to eliminate $(T_z g)_{n+1}$ from Equation 3.13, but that would still leave the $(T_z g)_n$ from Equation 3.15 as part of the equation. We want to eliminate all reference to g. This can be done by using Equation 3.13 for time n instead of $n + 1$:

$$y_n = e^{z\Delta t}y_{n-1} + (T_z g)_n$$

which can be solved for $(T_z g)_n$ and used in Equation 3.15 to give

$$(T_{\bar{z}}g)_{n+1} = e^{\bar{z}\Delta t}\left(y_n - e^{z\Delta t}y_{n-1}\right) + (T_z T_{\bar{z}}x)_{n+1}$$

$$= e^{\bar{z}\Delta t}y_n - e^{(z+\bar{z})\Delta t}y_{n-1} + (T_z T_{\bar{z}}x)_{n+1}$$

Finally, this equation can be used in Equation 3.13 to get the recurrence formula

$$y_{n+1} = \left(e^{z\Delta t} + e^{\bar{z}\Delta t}\right)y_n - e^{(z+\bar{z})\Delta t}y_{n-1} + (T_z T_{\bar{z}}x)_{n+1} \tag{3.17}$$

which, using $z = -d + j\omega$, can be written as

$$y_{n+1} = 2e^{-d\Delta t}\cos(\omega\Delta t)y_n - e^{-2d\Delta t}y_{n-1} + (T_z T_{\bar{z}}x)_{n+1}$$

so we have an equation with only real coefficients. It is the most efficient possible recurrence relation for a general second-order linear differential equation.

3.4 THE SECOND-ORDER APPROXIMATION

The only remaining issue is how to approximate the integral in Equation 3.16. As in Section 3.1.5, the method here is to calculate the integral in Equation 3.16 for the special case $x(t) = \exp(st)$ (a pure tone) and then find a way, by combining adjacent values of the input function, to approximate the integral that works for as wide a range of s as possible.

First, using $x(t) = \exp(st)$ in Equation 3.16 results in the following computation:

$$T_z T_{\bar{z}} e^{st} = e^{zt}\int_{t-\Delta t}^{t} e^{-z\tau}\left(e^{z\tau}\int_{\tau-\Delta t}^{\tau} e^{-\bar{z}\mu}e^{s\mu}\,d\mu\right)d\tau$$

$$= e^{zt}\int_{t-\Delta t}^{t} e^{-z\tau}\frac{e^{(\bar{z}-s)\Delta t}-1}{\bar{z}-s}e^{s\tau}\,d\tau$$

$$= \left(\frac{e^{(\bar{z}-s)\Delta t}-1}{\bar{z}-s}\right)e^{zt}\int_{t-\Delta t}^{t} e^{-z\tau}e^{s\tau}\,d\tau$$

$$= \left(\frac{e^{(\bar{z}-s)\Delta t}-1}{\bar{z}-s}\right)\left(\frac{e^{(z-s)\Delta t}-1}{z-s}\right)e^{st} \qquad (3.18)$$

which is equal to the product of the constants calculated for the first-order case in Equation 3.9, once for z and once for $\bar{z}$.

How can Equation 3.18 best be approximated with only the discrete-time information, x_k? A careful examination of Equation 3.16 reveals that the integral covers two time intervals, from t back to $t - 2\Delta t$. Thus, we might expect some combination of three input values to work. As before, the simplest approximation is to assume that x is constant on this interval. In this case the approximation can be calculated from Equation 3.18 by using $s = 0$:

$$(T_z T_{\bar{z}}x)_{n+1} \approx \frac{e^{\bar{z}\Delta t}-1}{\bar{z}}\frac{e^{z\Delta t}-1}{z}x_{n+1}$$

If we allow the use of the two previous input values instead of just the current one, the general approximation will have the form

$$(T_z T_{\bar{z}}x)_{n+1} \approx \frac{e^{\bar{z}\Delta t}-1}{\bar{z}}\frac{e^{z\Delta t}-1}{z}(\mu x_{n-1} + \alpha x_n + \beta x_{n+1})$$

However, as it turns out, it is enough to use only two terms, or, in other words, assume $\mu = 0$ in this equation. Thus, the approximation we will use is

$$(T_z T_{\bar{z}} x)_{n+1} \approx \frac{e^{\bar{z}\Delta t} - 1}{\bar{z}} \frac{e^{z\Delta t} - 1}{z} (\alpha x_n + \beta x_{n+1}) \qquad (3.19)$$

Now we have the same considerations as we did for the first-order case. Since there are two coefficients, we can force Equation 3.19 (with $x_n = \exp(sn\Delta t)$) to agree with Equation 3.18 for two different values of s. Once again, taking one of these points to be $s = 0$, we obtain the restriction

$$\alpha + \beta = 1$$

The other restriction determines α and β uniquely. It is obtained by setting the squared magnitude of Equation 3.18 equal to the squared magnitude of Equation 3.19 (with $x_n = \exp(ns\Delta t)$), which results in a quadratic equation for α. This second condition leads to a rather complicated equation for α, which is written out in full in the next chapter (Equation 4.7).

Once this algebra is done and α calculated to force a fit at frequency $s = j\pi/2$ (using $\Delta t = 1$), the result is an excellent agreement between theory and approximation, as shown in Figure 3.2, between $s = -j\pi/2$ and $s = +j\pi/2$. The dotted line is the theoretical value, the squared magnitude of Equation 3.18, for $z = -0.01 \pm j(0.1\pi)$. The solid line is the squared magnitude of Equation 3.19. They agree quite accurately right out to $\pm 0.5\pi$ and a little bit beyond; this is about the best that can be done. The conclusion is that the magnitude response of the discrete-time simple harmonic oscillator will be nearly identical to the magnitude response of the continuous-time version it is modeling, as long as the driving function contains no frequencies above half the Nyquist frequency. When other values of z are used, the same sort of close agreement between the theoretical value and the approximation is seen. The plots look very similar regardless of z.

Figure 3.3 shows the phase error of the approximation relative to the theoretically correct value. The plotted phase is the phase of the approximation in Equation 3.19 minus the phase of the integral in Equation 3.18, as a function of the frequency $s = j\phi$. Thus, while the magnitude response is accurate, the phase does not track very well at all.

However, the phase can be approximated much better by a simple change. Notice that Figure 3.3 lies close to the straight line $j\epsilon = s$ where ϵ is the phase error. This implies that changing Equation 3.19 by introducing a unit time delay in the input function will nearly fix the phase tracking problem. The modified equation is

$$(T_z T_{\bar{z}} x)_{n+1} \approx \frac{e^{\bar{z}\Delta t} - 1}{\bar{z}} \frac{e^{z\Delta t} - 1}{z} (\alpha x_{n-1} + \beta x_n) \qquad (3.20)$$

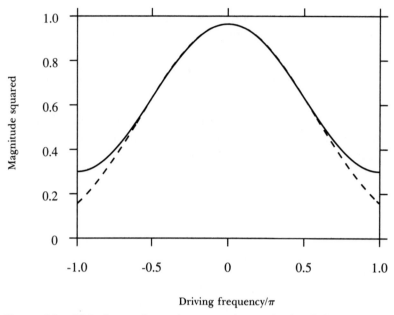

Figure 3.2   This figure shows the squared magnitude of the approximation in Equations 3.18 and 3.19. The theoretically correct curve is dashed. The approximation is the solid line.

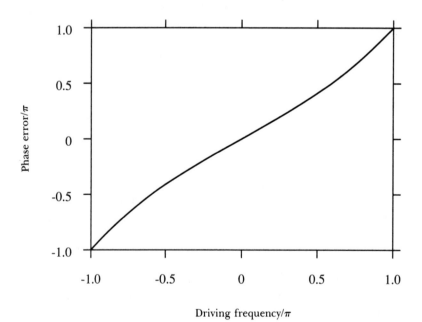

Figure 3.3   In contrast to its accurate magnitude response, the discrete-time simple harmonic oscillator does not have the proper phase response. This plot shows the phase angle of the approximation minus the phase angle of the theoretical value.

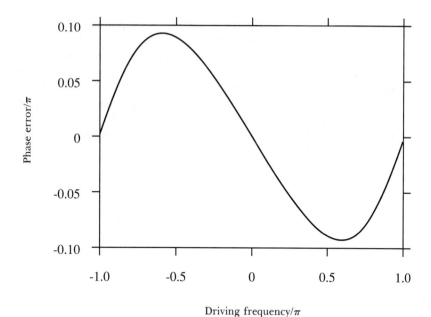

Figure 3.4   After a unit delay is introduced into Equation 3.19 to obtain Equation 3.20, the phase error is dramatically improved. The phase error is always less than $\pi/10$.

The phase error resulting from this equation (with $x_n = \exp(ns\Delta t)$) is plotted in Figure 3.4. This phase error is acceptable in most applications. If better phase tracking is required, the only solution is to keep the frequencies inside a narrow band around zero.

3.5   CONCLUSIONS

As shown in Figure 3.2, the approximation of the integral in Equation 3.19, gives a nearly perfect magnitude match for driving frequencies less than half the Nyquist frequency. What about more general driving functions? As shown in Chapter 8, every function can be thought of as a sum of the basic exponential functions, $t \mapsto e^{j\phi t}$. From Figure 3.2, we can conclude that the integral will be a good approximation for each of these components of x that has $|\phi\Delta t| \leq \pi/2$. In other words, if the forcing function is band-limited to less than half the Nyquist frequency, the magnitude response of the discrete-time simple harmonic oscillator will be nearly the same as that of the continuous-time version, as long as Equation 3.19 is used.

However, the phase of each of these components may be wrong. The actual time-domain waveform produced by the discrete-time oscillator may not match the continuous-time waveform, because of the way the phase errors of the various frequency components add up. If Equation 3.20 is used, these phase errors will be smaller—always less than $\pi/10$, as shown in Figure 3.4. If these phase errors are too great for your application, the only solution is to keep the driving function x limited to a smaller band of frequencies around 0. This can be done by taking sufficiently small Δt, limiting x by filtering, or both.

In any practical situation, you will simply have to construct the required model, using the equations of this chapter, and then compare it to the system being modeled. If the model is not accurate enough, try taking more samples per second or limiting the forcing functions considered.

CHAPTER 4

A Bell and an Organ Pipe

This chapter develops a program that generates waveforms of "bells" or "organ pipes," using only the discrete-time versions of a simple harmonic oscillator developed in Chapter 3. The difference between the sound of a bell and that of an organ pipe is principally whether the system is driven with an impulse, representing a hammer blow, or white noise, representing a turbulent air flow.

The programs developed in this chapter intentionally use the "old style" C programming techniques. These techniques are sufficient to the purposes of this chapter. However, in Chapter 5, old style programming will not suffice. In that chapter, many bells and organ pipes are needed to produce a full bell choir or bank of organ pipes. The old style programming techniques used in this chapter become quite cumbersome in such situations. Old style techniques are sufficient only for simple programs.

4.1 THE EQUATIONS

In Chapter 3 it was shown that a continuous-time harmonic oscillator following the equation

$$y'' - (z + \overline{z})y' + z\overline{z}y = x \tag{4.1}$$

where $z = -d + j\omega$ is the continuous-time frequency, translates to the discrete-time recurrence relation, Equation 3.17,

$$y_{n+1} = (e^{z\Delta t} + e^{\overline{z}\Delta t})y_n - e^{(z+\overline{z})\Delta t}y_{n-1} + (T_z T_{\overline{z}}x)_{n+1} \tag{4.2}$$

where Δt is the time interval between sample points and $T_z T_{\overline{z}}$ is a linear transformation defined by the iterated integral in Equation 3.16. It was also shown that this integral can be accurately approximated by Equation 3.20:

$$(T_z T_{\bar{z}} x)_{n+1} \approx \frac{e^{\bar{z}\Delta t} - 1}{\bar{z}} \frac{e^{z\Delta t} - 1}{z} (\alpha x_{n-1} + \beta x_n) \tag{4.3}$$

where α and β are constants determined by the equations

$$\alpha + \beta = 1$$

$$\left| \frac{e^{\bar{z}\Delta t} - 1}{\bar{z}} \frac{e^{z\Delta t} - 1}{z} \right|^2 \left| \alpha e^{-s\Delta t} + \beta \right|^2 = \left| \frac{e^{(\bar{z}-s)\Delta t} - 1}{\bar{z} - s} \frac{e^{(z-s)\Delta t} - 1}{z - s} \right|^2 \tag{4.4}$$

Both of these equations are obtained by requiring the magnitude of the approximation to match the actual integral. The first equation is for the case of a constant driving force $x(t) = 1$. The second equation is for the driving force $x(t) = \exp(st)$. The value of $s = j\phi$ is chosen for the convenience of the application. As shown in Figure 3.2, a good choice is $s = j\pi/2$.

Equation 4.4 is complicated, but it only needs to be computed once. To save you the trouble of doing all the algebra, I will work it out here. It is advantageous to break it into pieces, especially the factors

$$\kappa_z = \frac{e^{z\Delta t} - 1}{z} \qquad \kappa_{\bar{z}} = \frac{e^{\bar{z}\Delta t} - 1}{\bar{z}}$$

Actually, only the product $\kappa_z \kappa_{\bar{z}}$ is required, either here or in an application. It is calculated as follows:

$$\kappa_z \kappa_{\bar{z}} = \frac{e^{(z+\bar{z})\Delta t} - \left(e^{z\Delta t} + e^{\bar{z}\Delta t} \right) + 1}{z\bar{z}}$$

which, using $z = -d + j\omega$, can be written as

$$\kappa_z \kappa_{\bar{z}} = \frac{e^{-2d\Delta t} - 2e^{-d\Delta t} \cos(\omega\Delta t) + 1}{d^2 + \omega^2} \tag{4.5}$$

The other piece that is difficult to calculate is

$$Q(d, \omega, s) = \frac{e^{(\bar{z}-s)\Delta t} - 1}{\bar{z} - s} \frac{e^{(z-s)\Delta t} - 1}{z - s}$$

$$= \frac{e^{(z+\bar{z}-2s)\Delta t} - \left(e^{(\bar{z}-s)\Delta t} + e^{(z-s)\Delta t} \right) + 1}{z\bar{z} - s(z + \bar{z}) + s^2}$$

which, using $s = j\phi$, can be written as

$$Q(d,\omega,\phi) = \frac{e^{-2(d+j\phi)\Delta t} - e^{-d\Delta t}\left(e^{-j(\omega+\phi)\Delta t} + e^{j(\omega-\phi)\Delta t}\right) + 1}{d^2 + \omega^2 - 2dj\phi - \phi^2}$$

Only the squared magnitude of this quantity is needed. When all the algebra is finished, it reduces to

$$|Q(d,\omega,\phi)|^2 = \frac{\begin{array}{l} 1 + e^{-4d\Delta t} + 2(e^{-3d\Delta t} + e^{-d\Delta t})[\cos((\omega+\phi)\Delta t) + \cos((\omega-\phi)\Delta t)] \\ \quad +2e^{-2d\Delta t}[1 + \cos(2\omega\Delta t) + \cos(2\phi\Delta t)] \end{array}}{(d^2 + \omega^2 - \phi^2)^2 + 4d^2\phi^2}$$

(4.6)

With these calculations done, the equation for α and β can be written as

$$\left|\alpha e^{-j\phi\Delta t} + \beta\right|^2 |\kappa_z \kappa_{\bar{z}}|^2 = |Q(d,\omega,\phi)|^2$$

When the algebra is finished, these equations lead to a quadratic equation for α with the solution

$$\alpha = \frac{1 \pm \sqrt{1 - 2r}}{2} \qquad (4.7)$$

$$r = \left[1 - \left|\frac{Q(d,\omega,\phi)}{\kappa_z \kappa_{\bar{z}}}\right|^2\right]/(1 - \cos(\phi\Delta t))$$

It does not matter which of the signs is chosen in front of the square root. One sign gives α and the other gives β. Choose the minus sign for α to get the phase plot as shown in Figure 3.4.

A special case that will be used in this chapter is when the forcing function is a Dirac delta function, $x(t) = \delta(t)$. In that case the integrals in Equation 3.16 can be calculated directly rather than approximated, which gives

$$(T_z T_{\bar{z}}\delta)((n+1)\Delta t) = e^{z(n+1)\Delta t}\int_{n\Delta t}^{(n+1)\Delta t} e^{-z\tau}e^{\bar{z}\tau}\int_{\tau-\Delta t}^{\tau} e^{-\bar{z}u}\delta(u)\,du\,d\tau$$

$$= e^{z(n+1)\Delta t}\int_{n\Delta t}^{(n+1)\Delta t} e^{(\bar{z}-z)\tau}\left\{\begin{array}{ll} 1 & \text{if } 0 < \tau < \Delta t \\ 0 & \text{otherwise} \end{array}\right\}\,d\tau$$

$$= \left\{\begin{array}{ll} e^{-d\Delta t}\dfrac{\sin(\omega\Delta t)}{\omega} & \text{if } n = 0 \\ 0 & \text{otherwise} \end{array}\right. \qquad (4.8)$$

For programming purposes, Equations 4.2 and 4.3 can be combined and all the coefficients calculated without using any complex numbers. For convenience, the coefficients are renamed and calculated as follows:

$$z = -d + j\omega$$

$$c_1 = e^{z\Delta t} + e^{\bar{z}\Delta t} = 2e^{-d\Delta t}\cos(\omega\Delta t)$$

$$c_2 = e^{(z+\bar{z})\Delta t} = e^{-2d\Delta t}$$

$$b_1 = \beta\kappa_z\kappa_{\bar{z}}$$

$$b_2 = \alpha\kappa_z\kappa_{\bar{z}}$$

With these definitions, the combined Equations 4.2 and 4.3 become

$$y_{n+1} = c_1 y_n - c_2 y_{n-1} + b_1 x_n + b_2 x_{n-1} \tag{4.9}$$

which is easily implemented. The complicated equations for b_1 and b_2 need to be calculated only once. After that, each iteration of Equation 4.9 requires only four real multiplications and three additions.

4.2 A BELL

The program in this section will generate a waveform that sounds like a bell or a tuning fork when it is played through a D/A converter. (A low-pass filter on the output of the D/A converter is desirable to eliminate the unwanted high-frequency portion of the output spectrum. The D/A converter puts out a step function waveform, which contains a lot of energy above the Nyquist frequency.)

The program must be supplied with the time between samples, Δt; the frequency at which the bell rings, ω; and the damping of the bell, $-d$. Changing the frequency ω will change the musical note the bell makes. Changing $-d$ varies the duration of the tone heard from the bell. A large damping term will make the bell sound dull, or even "thudding." A small damping term makes a clear, long-ringing bell. It is convenient to specify the frequency of the bell in Hertz (cycles per second), so the program automatically adjusts the supplied frequency to radians per data point.

The core of the program reproduces Equation 4.9 as follows:

```
y = cl*yl - c2*y2 + scale*pulse;
pulse = 0;
y2 = yl;
yl = y;
```

The mapping between variables in the program and those in Equation 4.9 has been made as smooth as possible. The program variable **y1** is the equation variable y_n, **y2** is y_{n-1}, and so forth. The assignments after the primary equation shift the values, so that **y1** is always the output from the previous iteration and **y2** is the output before that. Impulses are fed into the equation at appropriate times by setting **pulse** equal to the magnitude of the impulse before this program segment is entered. The scale factor **scale** is set equal to $e^{-d\Delta t}\sin(\omega\Delta t)/\omega$. This scale factor is needed only if it is important to retain the proper amplitude response of the oscillator.

This core segment of the program is controlled by a **while** loop that counts down the number of output points requested, as follows:

```
while(number_of_points--)
{
    /* If count_down is zero, it is time for a new
     * impulse. The timer is also re-initialized. */
    if(!count_down--)
    {
        count_down = points_between_strikes;
        pulse = 1;            /* The unit impulse */
    }

    y = c1*y1 - c2*y2 + scale*pulse;
    pulse = 0;
    y2 = y1;
    y1 = y;

    /* Clip the output to fit in a short integer */
    if(y > SHRT_MAX) y = SHRT_MAX;
    else if(y < SHRT_MIN) y = SHRT_MIN;
    /* Write the output to the file in binary form */
    {
        short out = y;
        fwrite(&out, sizeof(short), 1, fp);
    }
}
```

Except for the required declarations and calculations of the coefficients, this is the whole program. There is a program, **waveform**, supplied on the companion disk, that generates both bell and organ waveforms, plots them on your screen, writes them to a specified file, and allows you to change the various constants at will. It is instructive to experiment with this program, changing the frequency and damping to see and hear the different effects.

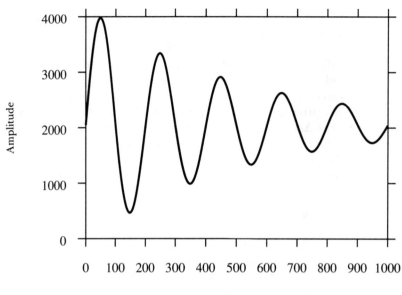

Figure 4.1 The waveform of a simple harmonic oscillator "bell" is plotted. The frequency and damping were chosen to produce a clear picture rather than a good-sounding bell. The envelope of the waveform is primarily responsible for its being recognized as a bell. This waveform has been scaled and shifted into the range from 0 to 4096. This is appropriate for playing through a typical 12-bit D/A converter.

Figure 4.1 is the waveform generated by this program for one choice of damping and frequency. The parameters were chosen to demonstrate the general shape of the bell waveform rather than to generate a realistic bell tone. The feature of this waveform that is principally responsible for making it sound like a bell is the exponentially decaying envelope. The details of the waveform inside this envelope determine the quality of the bell but not the generic definition of a "bell-like sound."

4.3 AN ORGAN PIPE

The difference between an organ pipe and a bell is principally the way the instrument is driven. A bell is struck once and expected to ring for an appreciable amount of time. An organ pipe, on the other hand, is driven by a continuous, turbulent flow of air and stops sounding almost as soon as the air flow is turned off. How can the air driving a real organ pipe be simulated? The principal property of a turbulent airflow is that its spectrum is white—having equal energy at all frequencies—and that the driving force is sustained. The spectrum of an impulse is white, but not sustained. The airflow drive can be simulated by using a random noise generator. It doesn't matter much what the source of the random numbers is, as long as it's white. Gaussian noise might be a better choice, but for this simple example program, the random noise generator supplied with the standard C library is used.

The core of the program for the organ pipe is almost the same as the core of the bell program, except that the approximation of the integral, Equation 4.3, must be used to keep the response of this digital simple harmonic oscillator close to that of a continuous-time system. The core program is

```
y  = c1*y1 - c2*y2 + b1*x1 + b2*x2;
x2 = x1;
x1 = 1 - 2.0*rand()/RAND_MAX;
y2 = y1;
y1 = y;
```

This time, instead of introducing an impulse at appropriate times before this recursion relation is executed, a random number is generated at each iteration.

The function **rand()** generates a random integer between 0 and **RAND_MAX**. Therefore, **x0** will be a random number between -1 and $+1$. The random numbers have been shifted to include a range centered on 0, because otherwise the bias in the random number inputs would generate a bias in the output of the simple harmonic oscillator. While this would not change the sound produced by a real harmonic oscillator, it might change the sound generated by this program, because the output is a two-byte integer with a strictly limited range from -2^{15} to $(2^{15} - 1)$. With a positive bias in the output, there would be more range available below the mean than above.

The **while** loop that controls the organ pipe is similar to the one controlling the bell:

```
while(number_of_points--)
{
    y  = c1*y1 - c2*y2 + b1*x1 + b2*x2;
    x2 = x1;
    x1 = 1 - 2.0*rand()/RAND_MAX;
    y2 = y1;
    y1 = y;

    /* Clip the output to fit in a short integer */
    if(y > SHRT_MAX) y = SHRT_MAX;
    else if(y < SHRT_MIN) y = SHRT_MIN;
    /* Write the output to the file in binary form */
    {
        short out = y;
```

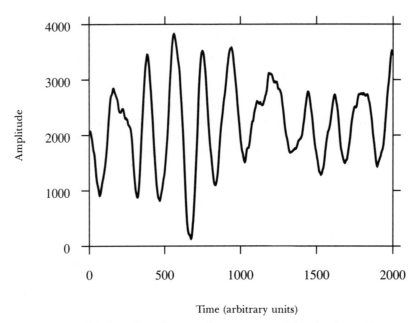

Time (arbitrary units)

Figure 4.2 This is a plot of a waveform generated by the "organ" program of this section. It is not a very good imitation of an organ, but it does demonstrate the large difference made by the driving force.

```
fwrite(&out, sizeof(short), 1, fp);
    }
}
```

Figure 4.2 plots a waveform produced by this "organ" program. This waveform does not sound much like an organ. In fact, it sounds more like the sound produced by blowing across the top of a soda bottle. However, it does demonstrate how important the driving source is to the sound produced by a simple harmonic oscillator.

4.4 SCALING THE WAVEFORM

Since the desired output of these programs is a 16-bit integer, it is important to use the right scaling factor. If the scale is too small, the output will be a constant 0. If the scale is too large, the output will overflow the limits.

The easiest way to calibrate the bell is to use the impulse response of the continuous-time system:

$$y(t) = e^{-dt}\frac{\sin(\omega t)}{\omega}$$

The time t_m at which this impulse response reaches its peak can be calculated by setting the derivative equal to zero:

$$y'(t_m) = e^{-dt_m} \frac{\omega \cos(\omega t_m) - d \sin(\omega t_m)}{\omega} = 0$$

which has the solution

$$t_m = \frac{\arctan(\omega/d)}{\omega}$$

Therefore, the peak value is

$$y(t_m) = \frac{e^{-dt_m}}{\sqrt{d^2 + \omega^2}}$$

The amplitude of the output waveform can be changed at will by varying the amplitude of the impulse hitting the bell. Thus, if a peak amplitude of $2^{15} - 1 = 32,767$ is desired, the amplitude of the pulse should be

$$32,767/y(t_m)$$

instead of 1.

Finding the right factor for the organ-pipe simulation is more complicated. The organ pipe is driven by a new random number in each iteration. This delivers a lot more energy to the system than just an occasional impulse. One way to approach this problem is just to run the program and adjust the scale until the output is the desired amplitude. This can be improved somewhat by using the scale factor developed for the bell, which will take care of variations caused by changes in Δt, d, or ω. Then, once the proper scale factor is found, it will not have to be altered every time one of these variables is changed.

Here is a complete program that produces an organ-like waveform using the techniques developed in this section. This program uses the "old style" of programming. You should not imitate this style. The next chapter shows how to improve on this style in order to obtain a more versatile program.

```
#include <stdio.h>
#include <stdlib.h>
#include <conio.h>
#include <math.h>          /* Contains definition of M_PI */
#include <limits.h>        /* Defines SHRT_MAX and SHRT_MIN */
#include <time.h>          /* Needed for the randomize()
                             macro */
```

```
/* The time between samples in seconds */
#define DT (1.0/32000)

/* The number of seconds' worth of sound in the output
   file */
#define SECONDS 5

/* The frequency.  440 Hertz is a middle A on the piano. */
#define FREQUENCY 440

/* The damping */
#define DAMPING (-0.001)

/* The only argument is name of the file to be written */
void main(int arg_count, char *arg[])
{
    long
        number_of_points = SECONDS/DT;   /* Total number
                                            of points */
    double
        w = FREQUENCY*2*M_PI*DT,   /* Radians per data
                                      point */
        d = DAMPING*DT,            /* Damping per data
                                      point */
        e = exp(d),                /* Damping per data
                                      point */
        c1 = 2*e*cos(w),           /* Difference equation
                                      constants */
        c2 = e*e,
        b1, b2, scale,
        /* The rest are variables for the difference
           equation */
        y1 = 0, y2 = 0, x1 = 0, x2 = 0;
    FILE *fp = fopen(arg[1], "wb");

    if(!fp)
    {
        printf("Could not open the file <%s>\n"
        "You must supply a valid output file name.\n",
        arg[1]); exit(-1);
    }
    /* Compute b1, b2, and scale */
    {
```

```
    double
      t0 = (1 - 2*e*cos(w) + e*e)/(d*d + w*w),
      t = d*d + w*w - M_PI*M_PI,
      t1 = (1 + 2*e*cos(w) + e*e)/sqrt(t*t +
           4*d*d*M_PI*M_PI),
      tm = atan(w/d)/w;

      b2 = (t1 - t0)/(t1 + t0);
      b1 = b2*DT*DT*(t0 + t1)/2;

    scale = 500*sqrt(d*d + w*w)*exp(-d*tm)/(DT*
            RAND_MAX);
}
randomize();              /* Seeds the random number
                             generator */

/* One data point is written to the standard
 * output file per iteration of the main loop */
while(number_of_points--)
{
    double y = c1*y1 - c2*y2 + b1*x1 + b2*x2;
    x2 = x1;
    x1 = scale*(1 - 2.0*rand());
    y2 = y1;
    y1 = y;

    if(y > SHRT_MAX) y = SHRT_MAX;
    else if(y < SHRT_MIN) y = SHRT_MIN;
    {
        short out = y;
        fwrite(&out, sizeof(short), 1, fp);
    }
}
}
```

CHAPTER 5

A Choir of Bells

In this chapter, the simple bell program developed in Chapter 4 is built up into a bell choir capable of playing any score you care to type into an ordinary text file. Several scores that it can play are included on the companion disk.

The code examples of Chapter 4 are difficult to use in the more demanding project of this chapter. A whole new approach to writing these programs is needed. The old "monolithic" style, which uses global variables and built-in constants, must be abandoned. The first order of business is planning the project. Then, a modern, encapsulated programming style is developed to support the many bells needed in the bell choir.

5.1 PLANNING THE PROJECT

The bell choir will be driven by a musical score stored in a disk file. There are two basic events that must be handled by each bell: striking and muting. A bell may be muted at a specific time, allowed to ring until it is inaudible, or struck several times without any muting. An unmuted bell rings for a long time before becoming inaudible, but it will eventually stop sounding. The program should, therefore, check for active bells that are no longer loud enough to be heard and can, therefore, be inactivated to save computation time.

Two basic approaches are possible for storing all the required bells. First, an array of all bells that might be needed could be established before any music is produced. The whole array of bells would exist, even though only a few would be used at any one time. The other approach is to use a linked list of bells, in which case only the currently active bells would actually exist and be part of the list. This section uses the array approach, since each bell requires only a small amount of storage. Each octave contains 12 bells, so a five-octave choir will have 60 bells.

5.2   AN ENCAPSULATED BELL

The program that generated a bell tone in Section 4.2 is not adequate for this new expanded task. In that simple example the time between strikes of the bell was determined ahead of time, as was the frequency and damping of the only bell used. Now there must be many bells, and each bell must be driven by the musical score, not "hard-wired" into the code. What is the best way to meet the new challenge?

5.2.1   C Structures

The C language provides structures, using the keyword **struct**, which are made for just such a task. A structure can be used to keep all the constants and variables required by one bell together, segregated from all the others, and easily accessible by mnemonic names. Moreover, we do not want just one structure, but many—one for each bell in the choir. A **struct** can be used as a template to create as many copies as are required. For example, the structure defined by

```
struct Point {
    float x, y;
};
```

does not cause the compiler to allocate any space for the structure, but it does inform the compiler that any time it encounters a sequence such as

```
struct Point p;
```

it should set aside enough storage space for one copy of the **Point** structure, which in this case is named **p**. The elements of **p** are referenced individually as **p.x** or **p.y**. These elements can be used in any C expression where an ordinary variable can be used.

5.2.2   Type Definitions

The C language provides one more extension to this concept that syntactically makes a user-defined structure appear even more like a built-in type. When the **typedef** keyword is used to define a structure, such as

```
typedef struct {
    float x, y;
} Point;
```

the effect is the same as the first definition of the **Point** structure, except that points can now be declared without using the **struct** keyword. For example, now the point **p** can be declared simply as

```
Point p;
```

which has exactly the same effect as the previous declaration of **p**.

It could be argued that the use of the **typedef** keyword is unnecessary. Its only advantage is that it makes the code that uses the new **Point** structure a little cleaner, easier to read, and easier to write. The same could be said of the whole structure concept, for that matter. We could, in fact, implement all our algorithms in assembler or even machine code without the aid of any of these refinements. However, all these refinements make writing the code easier.

5.2.3 A Structure for the Bell

The structure for each bell holds all the information that is needed to produce the waveform for that bell. One common function manipulates these structures to generate the waveforms for all the bells. It will use no global variables or any static data, which must remain the same between calls. Instead, all the data required for each bell is stored in the **BellControl** structure that we will now introduce, and each bell is defined by one instance of this structure.

The structure for a bell is defined as follows:

```
typedef enum {INACTIVE, ACTIVE, STRUCK} BellStatus;

typedef struct {
    double c1, c2, scale, y1, y2;
    long next_mute_time;
    BellStatus status;
} BellControl;
```

The keyword **enum** is used in C to create an enumerated type, in this case called **BellStatus**. The purpose of an enumerated type is simply to make the code easier to write and easier to read. Each of the elements of an enumerated type is assigned an integer value, beginning at zero by default, and counting up one for each element. Thus, in this case, **INACTIVE** is 0, **ACTIVE** is 1, and **STRUCK** is 2.

When the bell status is **INACTIVE**, the bell is not ringing and will not contribute to the output waveform. When the status is **ACTIVE**, the bell is ringing and will contribute to the output waveform. When the status is **STRUCK**, an impulse will be delivered to the bell the next time a waveform is produced by that bell.

The constant coefficients c_1, c_2, and scale must be calculated by some initialization routine, once for each required bell. The other two variables, y_1 and y_2, are the output from the last iteration and the iteration before that. They should be initialized to zero and will be cleared to zero whenever the bell is muted.

Each time a bell is struck, its next_mute_time element is set to the duration of the note, in terms of the number of sample points of output that should be produced before the bell is muted.

5.2.4   The Plan

The next job is to plan the routines that will be used to create a BellControl structure, produce the bell sound, strike a bell, and mute a bell. In truth, the full specification of these routines is not usually complete until they have all been written. It is difficult to foresee all interactions, and better ways to accomplish the tasks usually come to mind while the routines are being implemented. However, it is important to have some firm plan in mind before just plunging into the writing of the code.

As an example of how ideas can change while the code is being written, I originally intended to keep track of the muting of each bell by using a time-line controlled by the main program. As I was implementing these routines, it occurred to me that it would be much easier to add the next_mute_time element to the BellControl structure and let the bell routines keep track of this detail. After all, the main routine would have had to set up some kind of control structure of its own for each bell that required a muting signal at some future time. That would have meant that there would be two places where information about each bell would be stored. Not only is that less convenient, it makes the program more difficult to write, debug, and alter.

The code is now presented to you as if it had been designed that way in the first place, which you now know is not the case. In its best form, the process of coding a program is a creative task that molds the way you think of the plan and leads to improvements. However, there must be that initial plan, which can be improved.

5.2.5   The Header File

The BellControl structure is defined in the header file bell.inc, included on the companion disk. Prototypes for all the routines that use the BellControl structure or modify its elements in any way are also included in this header file. The C language has no way of enforcing this additional structure; the programmer must act as the enforcer. The advantage of this approach is that if something is going wrong inside the BellControl structure, you will know that the problem must be contained in one of the routines prototyped in this header file.

You may be wondering why the header file is called `bell.inc` instead of the more common `bell.h`. The reason is simple. There are so many header files with the `.h` extension that name conflicts become a real danger. Since these files are incorporated into the programs that use them by means of the preprocessor directive `#include`, I have chosen to give them all the `.inc` extension.

The full `bell.inc` header file, including the definition of `BellControl`, is as follows:

```
#ifndef BELL_INC
#define BELL_INC

typedef enum {INACTIVE, ACTIVE, STRUCK} BellStatus;

typedef struct {
    double c1, c2, scale, y1, y2;
    long next_mute_time;
    BellStatus status;
} BellControl;

BellControl *new_bell(double frequency, double damping,
                      double dt);
/* Allocates a BellControl structure for use by the
 * other routines in this header file.  Returns NULL on
 * error. */

void clear_bell(BellControl *bc);
/* Mutes and inactivates the bell. */

void strike_bell(BellControl *bc, long duration);
/* Strikes the bell with a single impulse.  The duration
 * is the number of data points the bell is allowed to
 * ring. This routine simply sets the appropriate variables
 * in the structure.  It does not produce a waveform. */

void bell(BellControl *bc, double *v, int count);
/* Adds the waveform produced by the referenced bell
 * to the array supplied by the last two arguments. */

void clip(double *v, short *iv, int number);
/* Clips the input vector, v, to 12 bits,
 * putting the result in the 2-byte vector iv. */

#endif
```

Notice the conditional directive on the first line of the header file. This prevents the inclusion of this file more than once in the same source file. Including the same file more than once may lead to errors or warnings from your compiler; at the very least, it will add unnecessary time to the compile cycle. This technique avoids this potential problem. This is particularly useful when one header file includes another one and it is no longer obvious, just from reading the source code, which header files are included.

5.2.6   The Routines

Each `BellControl` structure is allocated and initialized by the `new_bell` routine. This routine takes as arguments the desired frequency of the bell, the damping constant, and the time between sample points. The use of the prefix `new_` is standard in all my routines that allocate new structures, and serves as a reminder of this aspect of the function.

The `new_bell` function is implemented as follows:

```
/* Defines the bell structures and routines */
#include "bell.inc"

/* Prototypes for error_message and error_report */
#include <generic.inc>

#include <stdlib.h>


/* Calculates the maximum value attained by a continuous-
 * time bell of the stated frequency and damping in
 * response to a unit impulse.  Since this routine is
 * only needed for the new_bell function, it is declared
 * static.  This means it is only visible in this file.
 * It cannot be called by any routine outside this file.
 */
static double bell_maximum(double frequency, double
  damping)
{
    double
      w = frequency * 2 * M_PI,
      d = fabs(damping),
      t = atan(w/d)/w,
      r = exp(-d*t)/sqrt(d*d + w*w);

    return(r);
}

/* Allocates and initializes a BellControl structure for
 * a bell of the specified frequency, damping, and sample
```

```
 * interval.   Returns NULL on error.
 */
BellControl *new_bell(double frequency, double damping,
                      double dt)
{
    BellControl *bc = malloc(sizeof(BellControl));
    if(!bc)
    {
        error_message("new_bell:  Could not allocate
                        the space");
        return(NULL);
    }
    memset(bc, 0, sizeof(BellControl));

    /* Now calculate the constants */
    {
        double
            w = frequency * 2 * M_PI,
            e = exp(-fabs(damping) * dt);

        bc->c1 = 2*e*cos(w * dt);
        bc->c2 = e*e;
        bc->scale = e*sin(w*dt)/w;
    }

    /* All bells should be equally loud, which is
     * achieved by setting the scale so that the peak
     * response to a unit impulse will be a preset value
     * determined by the number of bells and the number
     * of bits in the D/A converter.  For a 12-bit D/A
     * converter, 500 turns out to be about right.
     */
    bc->scale *= 500/bell_maximum(frequency, damping);

    return(bc);
}
```

This routine allocates the required space, tests the memory allocation, and initializes the constants. The function **error_message** is one of the routines supplied in the Companion Library. Its prototype is contained in the header file **generic.inc**. This function logs an error message, which will be printed when the **error_report** function is called. Why not just print out an error message and stop? Generally, it is helpful to allow the calling routine to add an error message of its own, explaining what was happening when the error occurred, and perhaps take some other action to work around the error.

5.2.7   Function Prototypes

Notice that the header file **bell.inc** is included. This ensures that the function definitions agree with the prototypes. If they do not, the compiler will generate an error message. When the header file is included in the file that uses these functions, the compiler will be able to check that each of the functions is called with the proper number and type of arguments. This *type-checking* capability, built into the new ANSI standard C, is a great boon to program maintenance. Many bugs, otherwise difficult to find, are automatically trapped by the compiler if function prototypes are always used.

The function **bell_maximum** is only required to help set the scale for each bell, so it is declared **static**, which means it cannot be called by any function outside of the file in which it is defined. This function could be eliminated by combining the two formulas that determine the proper scale to be used, but this way is easier to understand and carries no significant time penalty, since it will only be executed once for each bell that is required.

5.2.8   More Routines

Two small routines that are needed, **clear_bell** and **strike_bell**, are particularly simple:

```
/* Inactivates the bell provided in its argument */
void clear_bell(BellControl *bc)
{
    bc->y1 = 0;
    bc->y2 = 0;
    bc->next_mute_time = 0;
    bc->status = INACTIVE;
}


/* Strikes the bell, producing a unit impulse the
 * next time this bell is used to generate a waveform.
 */
void strike_bell(BellControl *bc, long duration)
{
    bc->status = STRUCK;
    bc->next_mute_time = duration;
}
```

These routines are accomplished through function calls instead of by allowing the main program to alter the **BellControl** structure directly. This practice increases readability and maintainability: It keeps all the routines that manipulate the components of the structure close together in one file, making them easily controlled. If something goes wrong, you will know where to look.

The next (and last) routine is the one that actually produces the waveform. It must be able to activate the bell with a strike, produce the resulting waveform, and mute the bell when the right time comes. The waveform will be produced in an array of type `double`, which is passed to this routine as an argument. Since the bell choir must sum the waveforms from many bells, the new output is added to values already in the array. The main routine must be careful to zero this array before the first bell adds its waveform. The required code is

```c
/* Generates the waveform from the bell specified in its
 * argument, bc.  The argument, count, is the number of
 * points of the waveform requested.  The waveform
 * generated by this bell is added to the waveform array
 * pointed to by its argument, v.  The number of points
 * actually added to the waveform array is the minimum
 * of the argument, count, and the value
 * bc->next_mute_time.
 */
void bell(BellControl *bc, double *v, int count)
{
    /* It saves execution time to declare local variables
     * for these constants.
     */
    double
        c1 = bc->c1,
        c2 = bc->c2,
        y1 = bc->y1,
        y2 = bc->y2;

    if(count > bc->next_mute_time) count =
        bc->next_mute_time;
    bc->next_mute_time -= count;

    /* If the bell is struck, calculate the first point,
     * assuming a unit impulse.  All other points are
     * calculated using the equations for the
     * homogeneous case.
     */
    switch(bc->status)
    {
        case INACTIVE: return;
        case STRUCK:
        {
            double t = c1*y1 - c2*y2 + bc->scale;
            y2 = y1;
            y1 = t;
```

```
            *v += t;
            v++;
            count--;
            bc->status = ACTIVE;
        }
    }

    /* Calculate the homogeneous-case recursion formula
     * for each data point requested.
     */
    for(; count--; v++)
    {
        double t = c1*y1 - c2*y2;
        y2 = y1;
        y1 = t;
        *v += t;
    }

    /* Test bc->next_mute_time to see if it is time to
     * mute the bell.  Also test the values of y1 and
     * y2 to see if the bell is audible. If it is, then
     * these values must be saved in the BellControl
     * structure for future use.
     */
    if(bc->next_mute_time <= 0
    || (fabs(y1) < 1 && fabs(y2) < 1))
        clear_bell(bc);
    else
    {
        bc->y1 = y1;
        bc->y2 = y2;
    }
}
```

Notice how the **next_mute_time** element is used to control the number of waveform points this bell will generate before it is muted. By changing the **count**, which controls the main loop of this routine, the output of the bell is effectively muted at exactly the right time with essentially no overhead.

5.2.9 Questions of Efficiency

This function will be most efficient for long vectors. The section of code that actually generates the waveform of the bell is short, compared to the code that supports it plus the code generated by the compiler to call the function. However, each of these "extra" pieces of code is executed only once per function call. If the calculation loop produces many points per function call, the overhead involved is small per data point produced.

In practice, the length of the vector is determined by the requirements of the music. In most cases, however, the vector will be rather long. For example, if a note is supposed to last one-eighth of a second and the sample rate is 32,000 samples per second, then the vector will contain 4000 points.

Finally, it should be pointed out that some of this "overhead" code would still be necessary even if the bell choir were constructed as a single monolithic monster. No matter how the choir is implemented, the bell must be able to receive the strike and mute commands and must produce output for a length of time specified by the musical score. It is possible that a more efficient program could be written using the old "monolithic" programming style, but the gains would be marginal and would come at the cost of making the program difficult to comprehend, debug, and alter.

5.3 PARSING, PLAYING, AND GRAPHING

The rest of the functions needed to create a bell choir include a parser to read and interpret the musical scores and a **main** routine controlling the whole act. These two sets of routines together are 576 lines long—too much to include as part of the text. Besides, they are somewhat off the main thrust of this book, since they are not directly involved with digital signal processing techniques. However, the files are included on the companion disk in directory **music**. The main routine is contained in the file **choir.c** and the parsing routines in the file **parse.c**. The header files, **bell.inc** and **parse.inc**, are also in that same directory.

The executable file, **choir.exe**, is also in the **music** directory. It is used by providing the input and output file names on the command line as follows:

```
choir score=score_name file=output_file [dt=31.25e-6]
```

where **score_name** is the file name containing the score to be played, **output_file** is the name of the file that will receive the waveform, and the optional specification of **dt** is the time interval between sample points. The default is 32,000 samples per second, which translates to the sample interval above. The open and close brackets surrounding **dt=31.25e-6** are not part of the command line. They are used to indicate that this argument is optional.

The waveform produced by this routine is designed to be played through a 12-bit D/A converter. All the values stored in the disk file are in the range 0 through 4095. They are stored as two-byte integers, low-order byte first. No additional information is stored in this file.

While the choir program is translating a score into a waveform, which can take quite a while, the keyboard is scanned once every time a buffer is written to the disk. If an "x" (case does not matter) is typed, the routine will exit as soon as the current buffer is written. Otherwise, every time a buffer is written to the disk, a "." is printed on the console. Every time a new token is read from the score and executed, that token is written to the console as it appeared in the file. Unrecognized tokens will generate appropriate messages on the console but will not terminate program execution.

Once the waveform is produced, you can play it through a D/A converter or view it graphically on your screen. The program **graph.c** and an executable version of it are included on the companion disk in the **utility** directory. This routine uses the Borland® Graphics Interface (BGI®) and so can plot the waveform on any system that the BGI supports. There is also a program, **play**, in directory **utility**, that can play the waveform through a MetraByte® D/A converter installed on an ISA or EISA bus in an IBM PC/AT compatible computer. If you have access to some other D/A converter, you may be able to alter the **play** routine to suit your circumstances. In any case, you will probably have to change the I/O address to suit your particular installation.

5.4   THE MUSICAL NOTATION

The core of the musical notation used to store a musical score in a disk file is a five-field token that describes a note to be played or a rest in the music. The fields can be expressed as follows, one letter per field,

$$ond, tS$$

The octave field o is optional. If present it can contain some number of + signs, − signs, or an integer. The octave of the previously played note is kept as the default octave for the next note. Each + sign increases the octave by 1, each − sign decreases it by 1. Alternatively, the octave can be expressed in absolute terms with a decimal integer, which may contain either a + or a − sign in its expression. Octave number 0 is the one that contains middle C.

The note field n is mandatory. It must be one of the following: **R, Ab, A, A#, Bb, B, C, C#, Db, D, D#, Eb, E, F, F#, Gb, G, G#**. The first one, R, specifies a rest. The others specify a note as their names imply. Case is ignored when interpreting this (or any other) field.

The duration field d is a floating-point number that specifies the number of beats this note is to sound. If it is absent, the note will be held for the same duration as the most recently played note. If the duration of the first note in the score is not specified, it will be assumed to be one beat.

The delay field t is a floating-point number representing the number of beats that should be counted before the next token in the score is executed. This can be used to play chords, by specifying $t = 0$ for each note of the chord except the last one. If this field is absent, the delay is set to the same value as the duration of the note.

The final field, S, is the staccato field. This field is either empty or contains the letter S, upper or lower case. If it is present, the note will be played staccato style.

There are four additional commands that are not notes. The first sets the tempo. The format is `tempo=200`, which will set the beat duration to 200 milliseconds. The default is 250 milliseconds. No spaces are allowed.

The second command determines the extra time that each bell is allowed to ring. The music produced by the bell choir will sound better, generally, if the bells are allowed to ring slightly longer than specified, so that each chord overlaps the next chord slightly. This is controlled by the keyword `overlap` with the syntax `overlap=0.1`; this value will cause each bell to ring 10 percent longer than specified. This is the default value. Negative overlaps will be treated the same as zero overlap. The overlap will not affect the playing of staccato notes.

The other two commands behave like the muting pedal on a piano. The commands are `pedal` and `nopedal`. The default is `nopedal`. After `pedal`, all following notes, up to the next `nopedal` command, will be played without any muting. Each bell will be allowed to ring until it naturally becomes inaudible, or until the `nopedal` command comes, at which time all currently sounding bells will be muted.

A chord can be played by specifying all the notes of the chord, each with the t field equal to 0, except for the last note of the chord. For example, the notation

```
0c1,0 f1,0 1c1
```

will sound the chord containing middle C, the F in the same octave, and the C in the next higher octave, all for one beat. The next token in the score will take effect one beat after the chord is sounded.

For example, the following line of music from Beethoven's "Ode to Joy"

HYMN TO JOY. 8.7.8.7.D.

WILLIAM J. IRONS, 1812-1883   Arr. from LUDWIG VAN BEETHOVEN, 1770-1827

can be written, using the musical notation of this section, as follows:

```
1b1,0 0d    1b1,0 0d    1c1,0 0d    1d1,0 0d
1d1,0 0d    1c1,0 0e0.5 f#0.5    1b1,0 0g    1a1,0 0d
g1,0 d    g1,0 d    1a1,0 0f#    1b1,0 0g
1b1.5,0 0g    1a0.5,0 0f#    1a2,0 0f#
```

Each line of this transcription corresponds to one bar of the original music, and each chord is separated from the next by three spaces, instead of the single space separating notes of the same chord. Notice that in the second bar, the second chord, the C is held for one full beat while an E and an F# are each played for half a beat.

5.4.1 A Project for the Reader

This musical notation is complete, except for dynamics markings. You can add dynamics yourself as a project. One possibility is to add one more keyword to the notation, perhaps **volume=nnn**, to specify some volume setting. Another possibility is to stick with traditional notation and use @**f** for louder, @**ff** for much louder, @**fff** for very loud, et cetera. The "@" sign is necessary so that the **f** will not be interpreted as the note, **F**. Similarly @**p** would be for quiet, @**pp** for quieter, and @**ppp** for very quiet.

5.4.2 Obtaining Audio Outputs

If at all possible, you should experiment with the music synthesizer, changing various aspects of it and listening to the resulting output. Not only will this help you understand the signal processing and programming techniques involved— it is *fun*. If you can afford to buy a D/A converter for your own computer, that would be ideal. Otherwise, try to find someone close at hand who already has access to one. Some inexpensive D/A converters are now available that may be appropriate. I have not tried any of them.

PART II

Supporting Chapters

*T*his is the "academic" part of the book. By that, I mean that it has a style more like other textbooks; it is not motivated directly by a project. In a sense, I wish this part were not necessary. However, the material in this part did not fit easily into the project-oriented framework of the rest of the book. Furthermore, much of the material in this part is presented quite differently from anything you will find in other books.

There are many theorems stated, some with and some without proof. The proofs that are included are present because it was thought they would be somehow instructive, usually because they illustrate some typical calculations that you might find yourself making in daily practice. Other proofs are omitted completely or only sketched, because the full proofs are rather involved and not particularly helpful to a practicing engineer. However, an understanding of the flavor of a proof is sometimes helpful, even if the full proof is too complicated to present.

In most cases, it is possible to skip over the proofs that are present without missing any essential material. The beginning and ending of each proof is clearly marked. However, the proofs are not difficult, and any effort put forth in reading them will be repaid with a better understanding of the notation and of how computations can be done efficiently.

You can use the material in this part as reference material for the rest of the book, or you may decide to read straight through. Either way, this material makes this book essentially self contained.

Chapters 6 and 7 describe the particulars of the programming style used in this book and the Companion Library, and as such are unique.

Chapter 8 explains the Fourier transform, a standard topic. However, even this is done with a different viewpoint, using P. A. M. Dirac's "bra-and-ket" developed for quantum mechanics. I think this notation makes the Fourier transform theory easier to comprehend.

Chapter 9 explains the discrete Fourier transform, using the bra-and-ket notation to unify this case with the continuous-time case of Chapter 8. Chapter 10.2 explains windowing and its effects on the Fourier transform.

Chapter 11 presents a unified, group-theoretic view of Fourier transforms. Most expositions ignore the connection between Fourier transforms and group theory, preferring instead to present the subject as a series of isolated results. This chapter is for those who aspire to be experts in signal processing. A previous course in group theory is not required.

Chapter 12 develops the fast Fourier transform algorithm using the group-theoretic ideas developed in the previous chapter. The result is an algorithm, included in the Companion Library, capable of calculating the fast Fourier transform of any length. Most available algorithms require 2^n points for some integer n.

Programming Vectors and Matrices

Vectors and matrices are the two most common data structures used in digital signal processing. Efficiency and ease of use are therefore of central importance for these structures. Of course, C provides a structure for vectors and even matrices. Why not just use these structures as supplied? For simple, quick routines that are going to be used for just a short time, and probably only by the developer, using the supplied structures may be the best choice. However, if the goal is to build a large library of routines with an easily remembered interface and built-in error checking, something more is needed.

This chapter develops the vector and matrix structures used in the Companion Library. Section 6.1 explores some of the helpful features of the new ANSI standard for C, especially function prototypes and the resulting type checking. Section 6.2 uses the examples of Section 6.1 to introduce the vector structure used in the Companion Library and to explore some of its advantages. Section 6.3 compares the efficiencies of three different versions of the same function, one using the encapsulated vector structure introduced in Section 6.2 and the other two not. The surprising result is that there is no measurable loss of run-time efficiency. Section 6.4 compares the chosen structure of vectors with an alternative structure. The reasons for the choice made for the Companion Library are carefully explained. Section 6.5 introduces the matrix structure used in the Companion Library and explains its smooth interaction with the previously defined vector structure. Section 6.6 uses the structures introduced in the rest of the chapter to construct a matrix multiplication routine. In Section 6.7, the run-time efficiency of this routine is compared with that of two alternatives. The first alternative is an attempt to speed up the execution while still using the matrix structure developed here, while the other is a special-purpose routine that does not use any fancy structures. As it turns out, the first of these three routines, the highest-level and easiest to write, is also the fastest.

6.1 TOWARD A NEW STANDARD

This section examines some of the advantages embodied in the new ANSI standard C. The biggest change is the availability of function prototypes, as explained in following subsections.

In the "good old days" of C programming, a subroutine that needed a vector argument might have been declared something like this:

```
#define N 50

scale_vector(r, v)
float r;
float *v;
{
    int n = N;
    while(n--) *v++ *= r;
}
```

This routine assumes that all vectors are of type **float** and that all vectors have length **N**. Moreover, the compiler has no way to check that a **float** value is actually passed to the routine in its first argument or that a **float*** (pointer to type **float**) is actually passed in the second argument. All functions were assumed to return an **int**, unless there was explicit direction to the contrary. The compiler simply assumed that the functions were being used correctly. It was entirely up to the programmer to verify function usage. A surprising amount of work was accomplished under these circumstances.

6.1.1 Type Checking

Let's solve one problem at a time. First, the new ANSI standard for C has solved the type checking problem. ANSI C *function prototypes* are highly recommended, although not required. A function prototype for the **scale_vector** routine looks like this:

```
void scale_vector(float r, float *v);
```

The definition of the function occurs later, typically in a different file. The semicolon after the function prototype tells the compiler that this is only a prototype, not a definition. This one line tells the compiler that the function does not return any value, the first argument is of type **float**, and the second argument is a pointer to type **float**. If any of these conditions is violated, the compiler will make an automatic type conversion, if possible, or issue a warning or error message as appropriate. For example, if the program tries to obtain a return value, as in

```
double q = scale_vector(r, v);
```

an error message will be issued by the compiler, because this function does not return a value. On the other hand, if an integer or a **double** is used in the first argument, the compiler will make the necessary type conversion for you without making any complaints. Thus, a code sequence such as

```
double r = 2;
scale_vector(r, v);
```

has the same effect as

```
int r = 2;
scale_vector(r, v);
```

In both cases the value of **r** is translated to type **float** before being passed to the subroutine. However, a code sequence such as

```
double *v = malloc(50*sizeof(double));
.
(do something sensible with v)
.
scale_vector(r, v);
```

will cause the compiler to issue an error message. While a pointer to type **double** has the same structure as a pointer to type **float**, the subroutine will be accessing the stored values as if they were type **float**, usually 4 bytes, while the calling routine has presumably dealt with them as if they were type **double**, usually 8 bytes. The result will be nonsense.

Function prototypes should definitely be used in all cases. Even short throw-away programs benefit from them, because they are easy to write and prevent hard-to-locate bugs. Usually, many function prototypes are grouped together into a file which is #**included** in every file that uses the prototyped functions and in the file that defines them. This allows the compiler to check that all uses of the functions are consistent with their prototypes and that the definitions also agree.

There is one way that the benefits of function prototypes can be obtained without going to the trouble of creating a separate file containing the prototypes. The function definition itself serves as a prototype for all the code following it in the same file. Thus, if a function is to be used only in the current file, and it is defined before it is used (that is, earlier in the file than its first use), then no separate function prototype is required.

6.1.2   Variable Lengths

What if the vectors in the program have unpredictable lengths? Then the length of the vector must be passed as an argument to the subroutine. With this added feature, the example function becomes

```
void scale_vector(float r, float *v, int length)
{
    while(length--) *v++ *= r;
}
```

Notice that it is not necessary to initialize a separate variable to control the loop, because the value of **length**, not a pointer to the value used by the calling routine, is passed on the stack. This means that this subroutine can change its own local copy of the variable without affecting the value in the calling routine.

One final complication is that in many cases the vector elements are not tightly packed in the array. In other words perhaps, for example, only every second or every fifth array element is supposed to be part of the vector. This can happen, for example, when a vector is decimated or when a vector is drawn from a column of a matrix that is stored by rows. It is a common occurrence, common enough that many mathematical subroutine packages make allowances for such cases by adding one more argument to the function, as in the following example:

```
void scale_vector(
    float r, float *v, int length, int spacing)
{
    for(; length--; v += spacing) *v *= r;
}
```

6.2   AN ENCAPSULATED VECTOR

All the objections to the original **scale_vector** function have been eliminated. The compiler can do the type checking and conversion for us; the vector can have arbitrary lengths and arbitrary spacing between elements. However, the simple two-argument function now has 4 arguments to do the same job, and there is no way the subroutine can check the actual array dimension. There is nothing to prevent altering memory locations that are not part of the array we mean to be scaling. Such an error can lead to very difficult debugging problems.

You might think that 4 arguments are not too many. Consider, however, a function call that requires two vectors. Suppose, for example, that one vector is to be scaled by some factor and added to a second vector. This new function would require 7 arguments in all, something like

```
void scale_and_add(float scale,
    float *v1, int length_1, int spacing_1,
    float *v2, int length_2, int spacing_2);
```

Such an approach quickly becomes burdensome at best. Not only is it difficult to remember; it requires a lot of extra typing, is difficult to read, and provides no safeguards on the array bounds.

An approach that solves all these problems is to define a structure that holds all the necessary information. The values in such a structure should be altered only by a small set of "trusted" functions, all kept together in one, or just a few, files. That way, if something goes wrong with the vector, the number of possible locations for the problem will be strictly confined, making the debugging task much easier. Other functions can use the values in the structure freely, but should never alter them. These rules cannot be enforced in C, but must be self-imposed by the individual programmer. A fully *encapsulated* approach would require that only the trusted functions be allowed even to access the structure values directly. Such an approach is cumbersome in C. If this approach appeals to you, try using C++ instead. There is a C++ version of the Companion Library that can be ordered separately. It uses the full power of C++ to make vector and matrix manipulations as easy as the usual arithmetic manipulations of the basic types built into C.

One structure definition that can meet all these goals is the one used in the Companion Library:

```
typedef struct {
    int first,          /* Index to the first element */
        length,         /* Number of elements */
        spacing,        /* Spacing between elements */
        allocated_length;
    float *buffer;      /* Pointer to allocated storage */
} VectorFloat;
```

The pointer **buffer** points to the allocated space, which has total length equal to **sizeof(float)*allocated_length**. Once this pointer is set it is never changed. The **spacing** and **length** components are as explained in the examples in Section 6.1.2. The other component, **first**, is the index to the first element of the vector. Any valid combination of these components will satisfy the equation

$$\text{first} + \text{spacing} * (\text{length} - 1) < \text{allocated\_length}.$$

Because vectors are such common structures in digital signal processing, they must be not only efficient but also convenient. A new vector structure is allocated and initialized by calling the routine, **new_VectorFloat**. The companion routine, **old_VectorFloat**, releases the memory previously allocated. These routines are used as follows:

```
void main(void)
{
    VectorFloat *vf = new_VectorFloat(50);
    float r = 1.5;
    .
    (do some work)
    .
    scale_vector(r, vf)
    .
    (do some more work)
    .
    old_vector(vf);
    .
    .
}
```

In this case, the **new_VectorFloat** function returns a pointer to a newly allocated **VectorFloat** structure containing 50 elements of type **float**, all initialized to zero.

Now the **scale_vector** routine can be rewritten to use this vector structure, as assumed in the example program above. This new interface contains only two arguments in place of the (up to) four required without the vector structure. The function itself can be implemented as follows:

```
void scale_vector(float scale, VectorFloat *vf)
{
    int k = vf->length,      /* The number of elements. */
        step = vf->spacing;  /* Allocating local variables
                              * for frequently used items
                              * saves execution time.   */

    float *c = vf->buffer + vf->first;

    for(; k--; c += step) *c *= scale;
}
```

Notice that in the previous implementation of **scale_vector**, the vector **length** and **spacing** were passed on the stack, while in this implementation these values must be retrieved from the **VectorFloat** structure. Thus, the burden has shifted from the calling routine into the body of the function. Generally, this trade of complexity is advantageous. The calling routine, usually the more complex part of the code, is made easier to write and easier to read. The complications in the function body are easier to understand in the smaller context of the function.

6.3   BUT IS IT EFFICIENT?

The `VectorFloat` structure and associated functions make vector manipulations easier to write and the function interfaces easier to remember, but what about run-time efficiency? Have we sacrificed anything? To answer this question, I wrote three different versions of the `scale_vector` function. The exact code is as follows.

First, there is a header file for the vector routines:

```
typedef struct {
    int first,              /* Index to the first element */
        length,             /* Number of elements */
        spacing,            /* Spacing between elements */
        allocated_length;
    float *buffer;          /* Pointer to allocated storage */
} VectorFloat;

VectorFloat *new_VectorFloat(int length);
void old_VectorFloat(VectorFloat *vf);
```

Next comes the code for vector allocation and deallocation:

```
#include <generic.inc>
#include "vector.inc"  /* Contains the above prototypes */
#include <stdlib.h>
#include <mem.h>
#include <values.h>

VectorFloat *new_VectorFloat(int length)
{
    VectorFloat *nv = malloc(sizeof(VectorFloat));
    long bytes = length*(long)sizeof(float);
    if(!nv)
    {
        error_message("new_VectorFloat---Out of memory");
        return NULL;
    }
```

```
    memset(nv, 0, sizeof(VectorFloat));
    if(bytes > MAXINT)
    {
        error_message(
        "new_VectorFloat---Too many bytes requested");
        old_VectorFloat(nv);
        return(NULL);
    }
    nv->buffer = malloc(bytes);
    if(!nv->buffer)
    {
        error_message(
        "new_VectorFloat---Out of memory");
        old_VectorFloat(nv);
        return(NULL);
    }
    memset(nv->buffer, 0, bytes);
    nv->length = nv->allocated_length = length;
    nv->spacing = 1;
    return nv;
}

void old_VectorFloat(VectorFloat *vf)
{
    if(vf)
    {
        if(vf->allocated_length > 0
        && vf->buffer) free(vf->buffer);

        free(vf);
    }
}
```

Last comes the code to be tested for timing:

```
/* Testing the speed of using VectorFloat versus the
 * speed for the old style without encapsulation.
 */
#include <generic.inc>
#include <stdlib.h>
#include <stdio.h>
#include "vector.inc"
void scale_vector(float scale, VectorFloat *vf)
{
    int k = vf->length,      /* the number of elements */
```

```
        step = vf->spacing;   /* saves execution time */

    float *c = vf->buffer + vf->first;

    for(; k--; c += step) *c *= scale;
}

void old_style_scale(float scale,
    float *v, int length, int spacing)
{
    for(; length--; v += spacing) *v *= scale;
}

void old_style_simple(float scale, float *v, int length)
{
    while(length--) *v++ *= scale;
}

void main(int count, char *arg[])
{
    VectorFloat *vf = NULL;
    float r = 1.5;
    int length = 1000;

    atexit(error_report);
    comline_read(&count, arg, "%d", &length);
    vf = new_VectorFloat(length);
    if(!vf) exit(-1);

    scale_vector(r, vf);
    old_style_scale(
        r, vf->buffer, vf->length, vf->spacing);
    old_style_simple(r, vf->buffer, vf->length);

    old_VectorFloat(vf);
}
```

I timed these three versions for 10 runs each and for vector lengths of 1, 1000, 2000, 3000, 4000, 5000, 6000, 7000, and 8000. The results are shown in Figure 6.1. All three routines were within 2.5 percent of the average. The **old_style_scale** routine required 69.4 ms for a vector of length 8000. The **scale_vector** version took 67.7 ms for the same task, and **old_style_simple** was fastest at only 66 ms. The spread from best to worst in execution time is only 5 percent. For a vector of length 1, the times were 35 μs for the **scale_vector** version and 30 μs for each of the others. This reflects

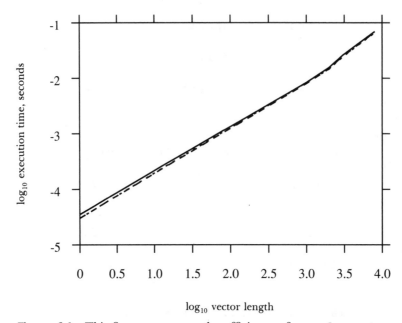

Figure 6.1   This figure compares the efficiency of a **scale_vector** routine using the **VectorFloat** structure with that of two similar routines programmed without the convenience of the structured approach. There is very little difference between the three routines in terms of execution speed. The slowest of the three routines was **old_style_simple**; the structured routine was second. In any case, the differences between the three routines is not significant. The spread between the three amounts to only ±2.5 percent of the total execution time.

the longer setup time required for the encapsulated version. This difference is quickly swamped by the time spent in the calculation loop as the length of the vector grows.

These routines were compiled using Borland's Turbo-C++® version 1.0© compiler, with the optimization set for speed and with all possible optimization choices active. The routines were timed using Borland's Turbo-Profiler® version 1.0©. The reported times are averages over 10 executions of each function. They were run on a 25-MHz 80386-based computer.

6.4   SOME POSSIBLE ALTERNATIVES

There are many possible structures for vectors and matrices. One of the pivotal decisions is whether or not the type information should be included in the structure. The method chosen for the Companion Library requires a new structure for each vector type. There is the **VectorFloat** structure already introduced, **VectorDouble** for double precision (usually eight bytes), **VectorShort** for vectors of two-byte integers, et cetera.

The alternative is to define one structure that will handle all possible vector types. This is done by including the type information in the structure, perhaps as follows:

```
typedef enum {
    CHAR, SHORT, INT, LONG,
    FLOAT, COMPLEX_FLOAT,
    DOUBLE, COMPLEX_DOUBLE,
    LONG_DOUBLE, COMPLEX_LONG_DOUBLE
} ScalarType;

typedef struct {
    ScalarType type;
    .
    .
    void *buffer;
} Vector;
```

where the remainder of the structure is the same as for **VectorFloat**. The **buffer** has to be type **void ***, because the type is not known ahead of time.

Both approaches have advantages and disadvantages, but I think the balance is in favor of not including type information in the structure.

Using the **Vector** structure with the type information included means that each function needs only one interface that will work for all vector types. For example, the prototype

```
void scale_vector(double scale, Vector *v);
```

is the only one needed. The approach chosen for the Companion Library requires a different function for each vector type, so a new function is required for each vector type that will be handled by a given routine:

```
void scale_vector_f(float scale, VectorFloat *vf);
void scale_vector_d(double scale, VectorDouble *vd);
void scale_vector_c(double scale, VectorComplex *vc);
```

This, of course, can be inconvenient. However, it has several advantages that might not be obvious at first. Consider, for example, that the **scale_vector** function must contain a **switch** statement or its equivalent to choose between the subroutines that handle each type of vector. The body of the function will look something like this:

```
void scale_vector(double scale, Vector *v)
{
    (do the error checking)
```

```
    .
    .
switch(v->type)
{
    CHAR:
    SHORT:
    INT:
        error_message("scale_vector:   "
        "not implemented for this type");
        break;
    FLOAT:
        scale_vector_float(scale, v);
        break;
    DOUBLE:
        scale_vector_double(scale, v);
        break;
    LONG_DOUBLE:
        scale_vector_long_double(scale, v);
        break;

    .
    .
    .
    default:
        error_message("scale_vector:   "
        "scalar type not recognized");
}
}
```

This code must be executed each time the function is called. The choice of which function will be executed is delayed until run-time. This increases the function call overhead dramatically and requires that every executable program have all these different functions linked into it, regardless of whether they are all needed or not.

What happens when a new vector type is added? The **switch** statements in every function must be updated to reflect the changes. Modifications must be made to code that was already working.

When a new vector type is added using the **VectorFloat** approach, there is no need to alter working code. The new structure must be defined, and the functions that manipulate it must be added. None of the already working and proven code needs to be modified. All the work goes into writing new functions to be added to the library. Consequently, there is significantly less work required each time a new feature is added to the library.

Suppose, for example, you have defined a set of extended precision routines built around a structure called **ExtendedInt**, and now you want to build a vector of this new type. It is highly unlikely that this new type was allowed for in the original vector routines. You must therefore change the `ScalarType` enumeration, which may require recompiling all the subroutines that use it, and you must modify all the `switch` statements in every function. Then you can write the code to do the actual work.

If the vectors do not contain the type information, all that needs to be done is to define a new vector type called `VectorExtendedInt`. Some of the same vector manipulation routines used for the other vectors will be needed, and probably some that are unique to this new type. This approach maintains the uniformity of the general vector interface without requiring modifications of existing routines.

Including the type information as part of the vector leads to a library of routines that is difficult to maintain. The more routines in the library, the worse the problem becomes. It also leads to larger executable images, because the linker cannot tell ahead of time which vector types will actually be used. All the code to handle all vector types for each function used must be linked into the executable image. A final blow to this approach is the additional execution time overhead of choosing the right piece of code for each function call dynamically.

The `VectorFloat` approach allows the compiler to perform a lot of type checking that must otherwise be included in the functions; it reduces execution overhead by making the choices between different possible code segments at compile and link time; it reduces executable image size by including only the code actually required for the application; and it makes maintaining a library of routines easier.

6.5 MATRICES

Matrices are probably the second most common structures in digital signal processing, after vectors. It is therefore important to have a convenient and efficient matrix structure. Matrix operations frequently require thinking of the matrix as a collection of column (vertical) vectors or as a collection of row (horizontal) vectors. Which view is used depends on the application, and both are frequently needed. The matrix structure chosen for the Companion Library works smoothly with the already defined vector structure, so that both row and column vectors can be extracted from a matrix without moving any of the matrix elements. Other common operations that can be performed without moving the matrix elements include matrix transposition and the extraction of a submatrix. The matrix structure is

```
typedef struct {
    int spacing,         /* Spacing between elements */
        length,          /* Length of the vector */
        allocated_length;
} SubVector;
```

```
typedef struct {
    SubVector column, row;
    int first;
    float *buffer;
} MatrixFloat;
```

The `SubVector` structure keeps track of the row and column vectors, similar to the way the `VectorFloat` structure keeps track of its single vector. One difference is that the `first` index is not included in the `SubVector` structure but instead appears at only one place, in the `MatrixFloat` structure. This is because the first matrix element is always the first element of the first column vector as well as the first element of the first row vector. If the `first` index were kept in two independent places, extra work would be required to make sure they were always the same.

The `allocated_length` is kept so that if the matrix is altered, it may easily be returned to its original structure. The components `allocated_length` and `buffer` are never changed during the life of a matrix.

The row and column vectors are stored in the matrix as follows. First, the `column` and `row` structures are initialized so that the `allocated_length`s and `length`s are both equal to the respective matrix dimensions. The rest of the structure elements are as follows:

$$\texttt{first} = 0;$$

$$\texttt{row.spacing} = 1;$$

$$\texttt{column.spacing} = \texttt{row.length}$$

The pointer `buffer` is initialized to point at `column.length * row.length` elements of type `float`.

Here is an example that will help make this vector structure easier to understand. Let `M` be a matrix structure. Then `M.buffer[M.first]` is the first element of the matrix, in position $(0, 0)$. If the matrix structure has not been changed since it was allocated, then the storage order for the matrix elements of a 5×5 matrix is

$$\begin{pmatrix} 0 & 1 & 2 & 3 & 4 \\ 5 & 6 & 7 & 8 & 9 \\ 10 & 11 & 12 & 13 & 14 \\ 15 & 16 & 17 & 18 & 19 \\ 20 & 21 & 22 & 23 & 24 \end{pmatrix}$$

In other words, the matrix is stored a row at a time. In this matrix, as allocated, the element `M.buffer[0]` has the value 0, `M.buffer[1]` is 1, and so forth.

A matrix structure specifying the submatrix containing only the elements

$$\begin{pmatrix} 6 & 7 & 8 & 9 \\ 11 & 12 & 13 & 14 \\ 16 & 17 & 18 & 19 \end{pmatrix}$$

can be obtained simply by setting the components of **M** as follows:

```
M.first = 6;
M.row.length = 4;
M.column.length = 3;
```

This submatrix may then be used just as the full matrix was used.

Matrix transposition, for example, is very easily accomplished using this structure without moving any of the matrix elements around. The following function accomplishes the transposition of any matrix:

```
void transpose_f(MatrixFloat *mf)
{
    SubVector t = mf->column;
    mf->column = mf->row;
    mf->row = t;
}
```

This operation does not depend on the matrix type, so it would be possible to use the same function for all matrices. However, that approach would require a generic matrix structure, **Matrix**, say, and each use of the function would require type casting, from **MatrixFloat** to **Matrix**, for example. Automatic type checking by the compiler would therefore be circumvented. This is too high a price to pay for the sake of a few generic functions. (In C++ it is possible to use this approach and still enforce type checking.)

Any vector of the matrix can be obtained without moving any matrix elements around. For example, the following function returns a **VectorFloat** structure that points to one of the row vectors of the matrix supplied as an argument:

```
/* Returns a VectorFloat structure that points to the
 * i'th row vector of the argument matrix.  Note that
 * i = 0 returns the first row, i = 1 returns the second,
 * and so forth.
 */
VectorFloat row_vector(MatrixFloat *mf, int i)
{
    VectorFloat r;
```

```
    r.buffer = mf->buffer;
    r.first = mf->first + i * mf->column.spacing;
    r.length = mf->row.length;
    r.spacing = mf->row.spacing;
    r.allocated_length = 0;
    return(r);
}
```

It is important to set **r.allocated_length** to zero. If, by some chance, a pointer to this row vector is constructed and later passed to the **old_VectorFloat** routine, then the structure will be deallocated, but not the buffer. Deallocating the buffer twice, once through such a constructed vector and later (correctly) by calling **old_MatrixFloat**, will most likely cause a disaster. Even worse, the buffer may be deallocated before you are done using it. (That is an unlikely event in standard C, but worth guarding against. In C++, with its automatic destructors, this consideration becomes much more important.)

A similar function can return any required column vector:

```
/* Returns a VectorFloat structure that points to the
 * i'th column vector of the argument matrix.  Note that
 * i = 0 returns the first column, i = 1 returns the
 * second, and so forth.
 */
VectorFloat column_vector(MatrixFloat *mf, int i)
{
    VectorFloat c;
    c.buffer = mf->buffer;
    c.first = mf->first + i * mf->row.spacing;
    c.length = mf->column.length;
    c.spacing = mf->column.spacing;
    c.allocated_length = 0;
    return(c);
}
```

Notice that these two functions are identical, except that **row** and **column** have been interchanged. This means, for example, that either of these two functions could be implemented using the other and the **transpose** function. For example, another possible implementation is

```
VectorFloat column_vector(MatrixFloat *mf, int i)
{
    VectorFloat c;
    transpose(mf);
```

```
    c = row_vector(mf, i);
    transpose(mf);
    return(c);
}
```

This implementation may be a bit slower than the first one, but it has the advantage of reusing the previous code, thus making code maintenance easier. Implemented this way, any change made in the `row_vector` function is automatically manifested in the `column_vector` function also.

As a final example, consider the following function, which returns a matrix structure that points to a submatrix of the one supplied in its argument:

```
/* Returns a MatrixFloat structure pointing to the
 * submatrix of the supplied argument matrix, starting
 * at row r0 and column c0, and ending with row r1 and
 * column c1, inclusive.
 */
MatrixFloat sub_matrix(
    MatrixFloat *mf, int r0, int c0, int r1, int c1)
{
    MatrixFloat reduced = *mf;

    reduced.first = mf->first + c0 * mf->row.spacing
                    + r0 * mf->column.spacing;
    reduced.row.length = c1 - c0 + 1;
    reduced.column.length = r1 - r0 + 1;
    return(reduced);
}
```

6.6 MATRIX MULTIPLICATION

This section develops a matrix multiplication routine, using the matrix and vector structures presented in this chapter. The run-time efficiency of this routine is then compared to that of a matrix multiplication routine that does not use the matrix and vector structures.

A matrix can be viewed as a collection of row vectors, a collection of column vectors, or both. Both views are useful for any given matrix. When two matrices $\mathbf{A}$ and $\mathbf{B}$ are multiplied together, the new matrix $\mathbf{AB}$ is made of numbers obtained by multiplying the row vectors of $\mathbf{A}$ by the column vectors of matrix $\mathbf{B}$. In this section, we will use the notation A^i for the ith row vector of matrix $\mathbf{A}$ and the notation A_j for the jth column vector of matrix $\mathbf{A}$. Thus, A^i_j is the matrix element in row i and column j. It is the ith element of the jth column vector, or, equivalently, the jth element of the ith row vector. Thus, the matrix elements are numbered according to

$$\mathbf{A} = \begin{pmatrix} A_0^0 & A_1^0 & A_2^0 & \cdots & A_m^0 \\ A_0^1 & A_1^1 & A_2^1 & \cdots & A_m^1 \\ A_0^2 & A_1^2 & A_2^2 & \cdots & A_m^2 \\ \vdots & \vdots & \vdots & \ddots & \vdots \\ A_0^n & A_1^n & A_2^n & \cdots & A_m^n \end{pmatrix}$$

Using this notation, the matrix $\mathbf{AB}$ has elements that are computed by the vector products

$$(AB)_j^i = A^i B_j$$

where the product on the right is the usual vector (dot) product, defined as follows:

$$A^i B_j = \sum_{k=0}^N A_k^i B_j^k$$

where N is the number of elements in the vectors, which is the number of rows in matrix $\mathbf{B}$ and the number of columns in matrix $\mathbf{A}$.

Every library of vector and matrix routines will contain functions for multiplying vectors and matrices according to these formulas. Because the vector and matrix structures defined in this chapter work so well together, it is possible to define the matrix product function in terms of repeated vector products. This will, of course, require some additional overhead at run time for calling the vector routines, but it has the advantage of reusing already proven code.

The vector multiplication routine can be implemented as follows:

```
double vector_x_f(VectorFloat *v, VectorFloat *w)
{
    int k = (
        v->length > w->length) ? w->length : v->length,
        v_step = v->spacing,
        w_step = w->spacing;
    float *vc = v->buffer + v->first,
          *wc = w->buffer + w->first;
    double sum = 0;

    for(; k--; vc += v_step, wc += w_step)
        sum += *vc * *wc;
    return(sum);
}
```

The matrix multiplication routine can then be defined as

```c
/* This macro constructs a pointer to the I, J element
 * of the matrix supplied in its first argument.
 */
#define MatrixElement(M, I, J)   \
    ((M).buffer + (M).first      \
     + (I)*(M).column.spacing    \
     + (J)*(M).row.spacing)

int matrix_x_f(
    MatrixFloat *A, MatrixFloat *B, MatrixFloat *AB)
{
    int i;
    /* First check the matrix dimensions */
    if(A->row.length != B->column.length)
    {
        error_message("matrix_x_f---Row length of "
        "A must agree with column length of B");
        return(0);
    }
    if(AB->row.length != B->row.length
    !! AB->column.length != A->column.length)
    {
        error_message("matrix_x_f---Product matrix is "
        "not the right dimensions");
        return(0);
    }
    /* The outer loop iterates through all the row
     * vectors of matrix A.  There are A->column.length
     * such vectors in the matrix.
     */
    i = A->column.length;
    while(i--)
    {
        VectorFloat a = row_vector(A, i);
        /* The inner loop iterates through all the column
         * vectors of matrix B.  There are B->row.length
         * such vectors in the matrix.
         */
        int j = B->row.length;
        while(j--)
        {
            VectorFloat b = column_vector(B, j);
```

```
            *MatrixElement(*AB, i, j)
               = vector_x_f(&a, &b);
        }
    }
    return(1);
}
```

This routine is easily written, easily read, and easily maintained, because it makes repeated use of the already defined and understood functions `row_vector`, `column_vector`, and `vector_x_f`, as well as the carefully constructed matrix structure with appropriate names for its elements.

6.7 EFFICIENCY OF MATRIX MULTIPLICATION

All right, so the function `matrix_x_f` is written in a high-level style that is easily read. Is it efficient? How much of a penalty is there for this high-level programming style in terms of execution time? I did not know the answers to these questions myself until I performed the experiment presented in this section. The results are not what I expected. I wrote two more matrix multiplication routines. One, `matrix_x_L`, retains the full generality of the previous one, but avoids most of the function call overhead by programming the necessary steps in-line. The third routine, `matrix_x_old`, uses the old style programming techniques to achieve what I thought would be the fastest execution time, but at the expense of some generality. It turns out that, for larger matrices, the `matrix_x_f` routine is significantly faster than the other two routines! This result is so surprising that I must show you all the code involved for each routine.

The `matrix_x_L` routine was written to be included in the Companion Library, but the timing comparisons changed my mind. This routine is just as general as `matrix_x_f`, and its interface is identical, but internally it avoids most of the function call overhead.

```
int matrix_x_L(
    MatrixFloat *A, MatrixFloat *B, MatrixFloat *AB)
{
    /* Execution time will be saved by assigning these
     * values to local variables instead of repeatedly
     * dereferencing the pointers.
     */
    int i = A->column.length,
        a_next = A->column.spacing,
        b_next = B->row.allocated_length,
        a_step = A->row.allocated_length,
        b_step = B->column.spacing;
    VectorFloat a = row_vector(A, i-1);
```

```
/* First check the matrix dimensions */
if(A->row.length != B->column.length)
{
    error_message("matrix_x_L---Row length of A "
    "must agree with column length of B");
    return(0);
}
if(AB->row.length != B->row.length
|| AB->column.length != A->column.length)
{
    error_message("matrix_x_L---Product matrix is"
    "not the right dimensions");
    return(0);
}
/* The outer loop iterates through all the row
 * vectors of matrix A.  There are A->column.length
 * such vectors in the matrix.
 */
for(; i--; a.first -= a_next)
{
    /* The inner loop iterates through all column
     * vectors of B.  There are B->row.length such
     * vectors.
     */
    int j = B->row.length;
    VectorFloat b = column_vector(B, j-1);
    for(; j--; b.first -= b_next)
    {
        long double sum = 0;
        int k = a.length;
        float *ap = a.buffer + a.first,
            *bp = b.buffer + b.first;
        for(; k--; ap += a_step, bp += b_step)
            sum += *ap * *bp;

        *MatrixElement(*AB, i, j) = sum;
    }
}
return(1);
}
```

The final version, **matrix_x_old**, uses old-style programming, and is not as general as the other two. Instead of using the matrix structures, it passes pointers to each of the three matrices, plus arguments giving the dimensions of each matrix. The routine assumes that the matrix is set up in a certain way, and so will not work properly if the matrix has been transposed or if it is a submatrix of another matrix. It is even harder to read and comprehend than the `matrix_f_L` version.

```
int matrix_x_old(
float *A, int a_rows, int a_columns,
float *B, int b_rows, int b_columns,
float *AB, int ab_rows, int ab_columns)
{
    int i = a_rows;
    float *a = A + (i - 1)*a_columns;
    float *ab = AB + ab_rows*ab_columns - 1;
    /* First check the matrix dimensions */
    if(a_rows != b_columns)
    {
        error_message("matrix_x_old---Row length of A"
        " must agree with column length of B");
        return(0);
    }
    if(ab_rows != b_rows
    !! ab_columns != a_columns)
    {
        error_message("matrix_x_old---Product matrix is"
        " not the right dimensions");
        return(0);
    }
    /* The outer loop iterates through all the row
     * vectors of matrix A.  There are A->column.length
     * such vectors in the matrix.
     */
    for(; i--; a -= a_columns)
    {
        int j = b_columns;
        float *b = B + j - 1;
        for(; j--; b--)
        {
            long double sum = 0;
            int k = a_columns;
            float *ap = a,
                  *bp = b;
            for(; k--; ap++, bp += b_columns)
                sum += *ap * *bp;

            *ab-- = sum;
```

```
        }
    }
    return(1);
}
```

Although this last routine is the most difficult to read and the least general, I thought it would be the fastest, since it uses no function calls, accomplishing everything in-line. It also avoids unnecessary pointer arithmetic, such as the repeated calculations in the **MatrixElement** macro, using instead only the necessary increments, as in the statement ***ab-- = sum**. However, it is not the fastest routine. The timings were as shown in Table 6.1, where n is the dimension of the square matrix, so n^2 is the number of matrix elements, and the times are given in milliseconds. Figure 6.2 plots the $\log_{10}$ of the execution time versus the $\log_{10}$ of the number of matrix elements, n^2.

It is surprising that the highest-level routine, **matrix_x_f**, is also the fastest for larger matrix sizes. The 90×90 matrix multiplication required 9.4 and 9.6 seconds for the other two routines, but only 7.6 for **matrix_x_f**, saving 1.8 and 2 seconds, respectively. This is a significant, although not dramatic, saving of execution time.

I timed these three routines using Borland's Turbo-Profiler. All three of the routines are in one disk file, all compiled by Borland's Turbo-C++ compiler with all optimizations turned on, and no debug information included in the object file. The main routine simply creates three matrices and calls each of the three multiplication routines. The profiler was set to time each of the three lines calling each of these three functions.

What is the lesson? Is optimization possible? Certainly, optimization is important, but it is also frequently contrary to the expectations of even the most seasoned programmers. The only sure path is to use a profiler such as Borland's and improve only those areas where your program is spending most of its time. Design your program carefully, choosing the most efficient algorithms

Table 6.1 Timing for Matrix Multiplications

n^2	matrix_x_f	matrix_x_L	matrix_x_old
25	2.81	2.26	2.33
100	14.92	14.43	14.49
225	44.08	46.87	46.58
400	98.51	108.51	107.78
900	309.07	360.49	355.89
1600	706.49	848.57	834.88
3600	2299.00	2845.90	2789.60
4900	3613.00	4515.40	4418.30
6400	5349.90	6742.20	6599.00
8100	7572.80	9597.10	9389.30

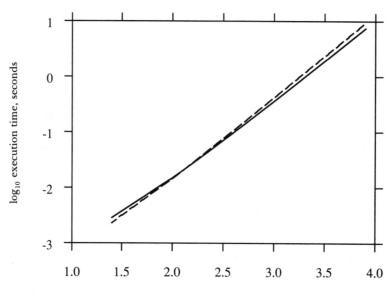

Figure 6.2   This plot shows the execution time for a matrix multiplication as a function of the number of matrix elements for each of the three routines presented in the text. The surprising result is that, except for low-dimension matrices, the high-level routine, `matrix_x_f` (the solid line), is also the fastest routine by a significant margin.

possible, but don't automatically attempt to gain execution speed at the expense of readability. It may be counterproductive!

Evidently, the encapsulated programming style adopted in this book costs little or nothing in terms of execution time for typical operations of digital signal processing, while at the same time it makes the function interfaces cleaner and easier to remember. It also results in a uniform and more general structure for vectors and matrices. Any code you write that properly uses the full sense of these structures will work properly with any routine in the Companion Library. In short, code written to the standard in this book enhances reusability, improves maintainability, and does not extract a performance penalty.

The Function Interface Standard

All functions in the Companion Library and all routines presented in the text share a common interface standard. This standard has some impact on the efficiency of the programs, but, more importantly, it affects the efficiency of the programmer. Where there was a conflict, I chose to make the functions easier to remember and easier to use. Many parts of the standard—for example, the conventions on capitalization—are arbitrary, in the sense that another standard would serve equally well. The standard has been worked out to make the memorization task easier. For example, when a function requires both an input and an output vector, the input is first, followed by the output, in the argument list. This rule is always followed. The opposite rule would work just as well. However, if there were no rule at all, it would be more difficult to keep the argument sequence in mind. The only purpose of the standard is to make the programmer's job easier, in part by enhancing readability of the code.

7.1 HEADER FILES AND FUNCTION PROTOTYPES

Every routine in the Companion Library has a function prototype in one of the header files, using the modern ANSI standard style. The header files have names like `numeric.inc`. The three-letter file extension is chosen as an abbreviation for `include`. The usual convention in the C language for header files is `.h`; the `.inc` extension is used for the Companion Library to avoid name conflicts with other libraries.

Some of the header files depend on others, but you do not have to keep track of these dependencies. For example, `numeric.inc` requires both `matrix.inc` and `vector.inc`, so it automatically includes these files; you do not need to include them separately. However, doing so will not cause a problem. Each header file defines a macro constant that can be used to determine whether or not it has been included. For example, `numeric.inc` begins with

```
#ifndef NUMERIC_INC
#define NUMERIC_INC
 .
 .
 .
#endif
```

so that at most one copy of this file will be included, no matter how many times `#include numeric.inc` appears in your code.

7.2   SOME EXAMPLES FROM THE LIBRARY

The interface standard is best explained with a few examples from the Companion Library. The vector and matrix structures were both introduced in Chapter 6. The naming of these structures reflects the standard adopted for the names of all structures in the library. For example, `VectorFloat` has the first letter of each component word capitalized. This is the trademark of structure types in this library. A new structure of this type is allocated and initialized by calling the routine `new_VectorFloat`. The prefix `new_` in front of the structure type is always used for this purpose; such a function returns a pointer to the referenced structure. The matching routine that disposes of a previously allocated vector is `old_VectorFloat`. As with the allocation routines, the prefix `old_` is always used this way. The prototypes for these routines are

```
VectorFloat *new_VectorFloat(int length);
void old_VectorFloat(VectorFloat *v);
```

This is typical of all such pairs of routines. The allocation routine takes the necessary arguments, specifying in this case only the length of the vector. It returns a pointer to the new structure. On failure, a `NULL` pointer is returned. The deallocation routine takes only a pointer to the structure being released. It does not need to return a value, since failure is unlikely.

The fast Fourier transform routine is similar. As explained in Chapter 12, the algorithm can benefit significantly by precomputing the required roots of unity and the factorization of the length of the vectors to be transformed. The results of these computations is stored in a structure declared in the header file `numeric.inc` with the name `FFT`. An `FFT` structure is allocated by a call to `new_FFT`, deallocated by a call to `old_FFT`, and used by calling one of the functions `fft`, `fft_pair`, or `fft_real`. The prototypes for these functions are as follows:

```
FFT *new_FFT(int length);
void old_FFT(FFT *control);
```

```
int fft(FFT *control,
    VectorComplex *f, VectorComplex *dft);
int fft_pair(FFT *control,
    VectorDouble *f1, VectorComplex *df1,
    VectorDouble *f2, VectorComplex *df2);
int fft_real(FFT *control,
    VectorDouble *f, VectorComplex *dft);
```

As before, the **new_FFT** routine returns a **NULL** pointer if there is an error. The deallocation routine does not return a value, since an error is unlikely. The other three routines all return 0 if there is an error. Otherwise, they all return a 1.

The FFT routines illustrate a new convention: Any routine that requires precomputed information accepts a pointer to the information as its first argument.

Notice also that these routines follow the input–output rule previously stated: The input vector is followed by the output vector in the argument list. In the case of **fft_pair**, there are two sets of input and output vectors. The output vector **df1** depends only on the input vector **f1**, so these two are neighbors on the argument list. The other option would be to put both the input vectors first, then both the output vectors. It seems more natural to order the arguments as stated above.

Sometimes a library routine returns a value that cannot serve as an error indicator. For example, the function **vector_x_f** calculates the dot product of two vectors. Its prototype is

```
double vector_x_f(VectorFloat *u, VectorFloat *v);
```

In this case, it is not possible to indicate error conditions by the return value. However, errors must be signaled if, for example, the two vectors are not of the same length. In such cases the program will be terminated with an appropriate error message.

These examples demonstrate most of the standard interface. The following rules spell out the interface standard more precisely.

1. Structure types are named with initial capitals for each word in the structure name, for example **VectorComplex**. (Strictly speaking the **FFT** structure name violates this convention. However, since **FFT** is an acronym for Fast Fourier Transform, common usage dictates all caps. The words *do* have their initials capitalized, and *then* they are abbreviated to their initials.)

2. New structures are allocated and initialized by calling the function named for the structure type with a prefix **new_**, for example **new_VectorComplex**.

3. Previously allocated structures are deallocated by the function named for the structure type with a prefix **old_**, for example **old_VectorComplex**.

4. Except for the two previous items, all library routines contain only lower-case letters and underscores in their names. The underscores are used instead of capitals to separate words.

5. Functions requiring precomputed structures, such as the FFT routines, accept pointers to these structures as their first argument.

6. When a function has an input and an output argument, the output argument follows the input argument.

7. With very few exceptions, if the function returns zero, there has been an error. When this is not practical, the offending function will terminate the program if an error is encountered, with an appropriate error message.

8. Enumeration constants, use initial caps to separate words. This is the same rule as for structure names, but context should make clear which is which.

9. Macro constants defined in the header files are all caps.

10. Macros that are not simply constants use initial caps in the same way as structures and enumeration types. The difference is made obvious by their use in the source code.

11. Variables follow the same standard as function names.

12. All detected errors are reported using the **error_message** and **error_report** pair of functions explained in Section 7.3.

13. Header files all use **.inc** for the file extension.

14. Header files that require other header files automatically include the needed files.

15. Header files define macro constants based on their file name and use these to inhibit processing the same header file more than once. For example, **numeric.inc** defines the macro constant **NUMERIC_INC**.

These rules are rather arbitrary. However, some set of rules is essential for any large collection of related functions as an aid to memory and, therefore, ease of use.

In order to include the header files properly, the compiler has to know where to find them. Since header files automatically include any other header files that are required, some convention for where the header files are located is necessary. Fortunately, this is already taken care of for us. All the header files are included with a statement such as

```
#include <numeric.inc>
```

The angle brackets surrounding the file name to be included indicate that the compiler should "look for the header file in the standard locations." Most C compilers allow you to define your own standard locations. For example, Borland's Turbo-C "Directory" option allows a list of directories that are searched for the header files. If your compiler does not allow such a list, just put the header files for the Companion Library in the same directory as all the other standard header files. There is no chance of name conflicts, because of the `.inc` extension used.

ERROR REPORTING AND CONTROL

Programming errors are frequently difficult to track down. To aid the debugging effort, all routines in the Companion Library use a common error reporting scheme, which your programs should use as well: When an error is encountered, an appropriate error message is added to a chain of error messages kept by the pair of error-reporting functions **error_message** and **error_report**.

These functions are used as follows:

```
void error_message(char *message);
```

will place the string pointed to by **message** on a chain of error messages. A call to

```
void error_report(void);
```

prints all the error messages on the console screen. Once a message is printed by calling **error_report**, it is removed from the chain of messages. It is a good idea to include the **error_report** function in the exit code, perhaps as simply as by including the line

```
atexit(error_report);
```

as early as possible in your program. For those unfamiliar with **atexit**, it is an ANSI standard C library routine with prototype in **stdlib.h**. Its argument is a pointer to a function that will be called before the program exits. Any kind of code can be included in this routine, but usually it is reserved for some kind of clean-up. For example, if graphics are being used, the exit routine might switch to text mode, then call the **error_report** function.

Most of the Companion Library routines return a 0 or **NULL** to indicate an error. However, this is not always possible, since these are sometimes valid returns. The behavior of the routines in the Companion Library when an error is encountered can be controlled by changing the global variable **error_option**, declared in **generic.inc**. Normally, when an error is encountered, the library routine adds an error message to the list and returns an error code. However, executing the line

```
error_option = ErrorExit;
```

changes the behavior. With this setting, the library routines will exit after an error instead of returning. The appropriate error messages will be added to the error list before exiting. The behavior is returned to normal by setting

```
error_option = ErrorReturn;
```

Many of the library routines use other library routines as subroutines. It can be confusing to get an error message from a library routine you did not call directly. For this reason, the library routines always set **error_option** to **ErrorReturn** before calling subroutines. The previous value of **error_option** is restored before the library routine returns control to your program. In practice, this is accomplished by incrementing **error_option** before calling subroutines and decrementing after returning. It therefore also serves as a count of the depth of calls into the library. The value of **ErrorReturn** is 1, and the value of **ErrorExit** is 0.

7.4   COMPLEX NUMBERS

Complex numbers are awkward to handle in C, because there is no provision for them in the basic language and types are not extensible (as they are in C++, for example). It is important to provide convenient but efficient means of handling complex arithmetic. A function for each elementary operation would not be acceptable in signal processing, because of the function call overhead. The Companion Library, therefore, includes a set of macros to handle the basic operations and functions to handle the more complicated, less frequently used operations.

Each of the complex types is defined by one of the structures

```
typedef struct {float x, y; } ComplexFloat;
typedef struct {double x, y; } Complex;
typedef struct {long double x, y; } ComplexLongDouble;
```

These types are defined in **numeric.inc**.

7.5   MACROS

The macros for manipulating complex numbers illustrate the general rules followed by all macros in the Campanion Library. All macros begin with a capital letter, which is **C** for the complex number macros, such as **Cmul**, **Csum**, and **Cinv** (for complex inverse). These and other macros are explained in the library documentation, but take, for example, **Cmul**, which is defined as

```
#define Cmul(a, b, ab)
```

```
{                                                                      \
    long double tEMp = (a).x * (b).x - (a).y * (c).y;                  \
    (ab).y = (a).x * (b).y + (a).y * (b).x;                            \
    (ab).x = tEMp;                                                     \
}
```

There are three things we want to point out here. First, the strange name **tEMp** is chosen with initial and final letters lower-case and all the rest upper-case so that it will be unlikely to conflict with any variable you may have defined elsewhere in your function. In particular, you will get some kind of error message if you call this macro with the arguments **Cmul(tEMp, b, ab)**, since this will generate a conflict in the usage of **tEMp**. All temporary variables in macros are defined using this strange ordering of upper- and lower-case letters.

Second, the use of **tEMp** allows this macro to be used with any combination of arguments, such as **Cmul(a, b, b)**, **Cmul(a, b, a)**, or even **Cmul(a, a, a)**. The use of **tEMp** reduces the efficiency of the macro slightly (or maybe not at all if you have a good optimizer), but it makes the macro usable in all circumstances. Otherwise, several macros would be required to take care of each of the above three possibilities.

Third, these macros can be used equally well with complex structures or with pointers to complex structures. That is the reason for the parenthesis around the arguments in the body of the macros. For example, the following code fragment is legal:

```
#include <complex.inc>

void demo_function(Complex *a)
{
    Complex d = {1.0, -1.0};
    Cmul(d, *a, *a);
}
```

The **Cmul** macro in this example expands into

```
{
    long double tEMp = (d).x * (*a).x - (d).y * (*a).y;
    (*a).y = (d).x * (*a).y + (d).y * (*a).x;
    (*a).x = tEMp;
}
```

The construction **(*a).x** is equivalent to **a->x**. According to the ANSI standard, we could equally well write the macros to use pointers instead of structures directly, but this does not work with some compilers. If **cd** is a structure of type **ComplexDouble**, for example, then, according to the ANSI standard, **&cd** is supposed to be a pointer of type **ComplexDouble**. Then the first line of the macro could be

```
long double tEMp = (a)->x * (b)->x - (a)->y * (b)->y;
```

which should work if called with `Cmul(&d, a, a)` in the above function, but it will generate an error from some compilers.

7.6   VECTORS

Vectors, explained in Chapter 6, are the most frequently used structures in digital signal processing. The vector structures are defined in the header file `vector.inc`. There is one vector structure for each scalar type, plus the `GenericVector` structure, defined as

```
typedef struct {
    int first,          /* Index to the first element */
        length,         /* Number of elements */
        spacing,        /* Spacing between logical elements */
        allocated_length;
    char *buffer;
} GenericVector;

typedef struct {
    int first,          /* Index to the first element */
        length,         /* Number of elements */
        spacing,        /* Spacing between elements */
        allocated_length;
    double *buffer;     /* Pointer to allocated storage */
} VectorDouble;

typedef struct {
    int first,          /* Index to the first element */
        length,         /* Number of elements */
        spacing,        /* Spacing between elements */
        allocated_length;
    Complex *buffer;    /* Pointer to allocated storage */
} VectorComplex;
```

The `spacing` information is included for vectors that are not packed tightly. This commonly occurs in two circumstances. First, a vector can be decimated by simply changing its `spacing` and perhaps its `first` components. Second, any row or column vector of a matrix can be represented using these structures. The `first` component is used instead of shifting the `buffer` pointer, so that `buffer` can be left always pointing at the first allocated element.

The `GenericVector` structure is used to manipulate a vector without any special knowledge about what type of vector elements are being used. For example, the `GenericVector` structure can be used for a function that returns the structure to its original state, for example, the library function

```
void expand_vector(GenericVector *v)
{
    v->first = 0;
    v->length = allocated_length;
    v->spacing = 1;
}
```

Functions like this can be used wherever specific knowledge of the vector type is not required. For example, there is one library routine for the allocation of each vector type, but most of the work in each case is accomplished by a single subroutine that handles all cases as follows:

```
GenericVector *new_GenericVector(int length, long bytes,
char *module_name)
{
    GenericVector *v = malloc(sizeof(GenericVector));
    if(!v)
    {
        char message[strlen(module_name) + 40];
        sprintf(message,
        "%s---Out of memory", module_name);
        error_message(message);
        return NULL;
    }
    if(bytes > MAXINT)
    {
        char message[strlen(module_name) + 40];
        sprintf(message,
            "%s---Requested too many bytes: %ld",
            module_name, bytes);
        error_message(message);
        free(v);
        return(NULL);
    }
    memset(v, 0, sizeof(GenericVector));
    v->buffer = malloc(bytes);
    if(!v->buffer)
    {
        char message[strlen(module_name) + 40];
        sprintf(message,
```

```
                "%s---Out of memory", module_name);
        error_message(message);
        free(v);
        return(NULL);
    }
    memset(v->buffer, 0, bytes);
    v->length = v->allocated_length = length;
    v->spacing = 1;
    return v;
}


VectorFloat *new_VectorFloat(int length)
{
    long bytes = (long)length*sizeof(float);
    return (VectorFloat *)new_GenericVector(
        length, bytes, "new_VectorFloat");
}


VectorDouble *new_VectorDouble(int length)
{
    long bytes = (long)length*sizeof(double);
    return (VectorDouble *)new_GenericVector(
        length, bytes, "new_VectorDouble");
}


VectorComplex *new_VectorComplex(int length)
{
    long bytes = (long)length*sizeof(Complex);
    return (VectorComplex *)new_GenericVector(
        length, bytes, "new_VectorComplex");
}
```

This approach guarantees that all the vectors will be allocated identically. However, if a new vector type is ever created that requires special handling, that can also be accomplished easily.

Other vector operations require one function for each vector type. For example:

```
void scale_vector_f(double x, VectorFloat *v)
{
    int step = v->spacing, n = v->length;
    float *c = v->buffer + v->first;

    for(; n--; c += step) *c *= x;
}
```

```
void scale_vector_d(double x, VectorDouble *v)
{
    int step = v->spacing, n = v->length;
    double *c = v->buffer + v->first;

    for(; n--; c += step) *c *= x;
}
```

In such cases the function name is modified with a postfix _f for type **float**, _d for type **double**, et cetera. The complete set of postfixes is as follows:

Type	Postfix
short	s
int	i
long	l
float	f
double	d
long double	ld
ComplexFloat	Cf
Complex	C
ComplexLongDouble	Cl

This list is similar to the list of postfixes that a C++ compiler automatically adds to overloaded function names. They are used in much the same way here as they are in C++. However, a C++ compiler adds one of these codes for each argument of the function, while in the library, these modifiers are used only as necessary, not usually one per argument.

Fourier Transforms, Uncertainty, and Convolutions

This chapter covers the continuous-time Fourier transform and the related topics of the uncertainty principle and convolutions. The space of square integrable functions, $\mathcal{L}_2$, is explained and used to state the Fourier transform and other theorems in this chapter.

The purpose of the Fourier transform is to describe a specific signal in terms of its frequency components. The Fourier transform can be defined for both continuous-time signals and for discrete-time signals. The continuous-time case is the subject of this chapter, whereas Chapter 9 covers the discrete-time case.

Both of these two chapters on Fourier transforms are essential material for digital signal processing. However, not all of the material is strictly required for the project in Part III. You might want to skip to Part III now, and use the rest of Part II as reference material.

There are four principal ideas and results in this chapter. The first and most fundamental of these is the notion of a *set of orthogonal functions*, found in Section 8.3, which is basic to all numeric transforms, not only the Fourier transform. The second is the *Fourier transform theorem* itself, which is properly called the Plancherel theorem (Section 8.5). The third central point is the *Parseval theorem*, which, as a special case, shows that the Fourier transform coefficients represent the energy density of the original waveform as a function of frequency (Section 8.9). The fourth and final central result is the *uncertainty principle*. Two Sections, 8.10 and 8.11, are specifically devoted to this result, because of its importance.

Section 8.14, the last section of the chapter, is devoted to the notion of convolutions and the interplay between convolutions and Fourier transforms. This section is central to understanding the relationship between the frequency response of a filter and its impulse response.

8.1 INTRODUCTION TO FOURIER TRANSFORMS

Some continuous-time signals can be written directly in terms of their frequency components. For example,

$$x(t) = \cos(\nu t) = \frac{e^{j\nu t} + e^{-j\nu t}}{2} \tag{8.1}$$

contains the two complex frequencies, ν and $-\nu$. How many other signals can be written this way? Any sum of finitely many terms, like Equation 8.1, defines a function in terms of its frequency components, but this is only a small part of the answer. The continuous-time frequencies cover the real axis, so the way to write the formula in the general case is to use a sum that covers all these possible frequencies. Such a sum is represented by an integral and can be expressed as

$$x(t) = \int_{-\infty}^{+\infty} a(\omega)e^{j\omega t}\, d\omega \tag{8.2}$$

This is not a complete answer either, because we do not know what restrictions on the function $a(\omega)$ will make this integral converge. We also do not know, given a function expressed in different terms, whether it can be written this way or not.

The first difficulty is a real one, because the formula Equation 8.2 does not converge for some choices of the amplitude function that might seem reasonable at first glance. For example, what about the case $a(\omega) = 1$ for all ω? Such a signal would have equally strong frequency components for all frequencies. However, when this is tried in Equation 8.2, the result is

$$x_1(t) = \int_{-\infty}^{+\infty} e^{j\omega t}\, d\omega$$

$$= \lim_{L\to\infty} \int_{-L}^{L} e^{j\omega t}\, d\omega$$

$$= \lim_{L\to\infty} \frac{e^{jLt} - e^{-jLt}}{jt}$$

$$= \lim_{L\to\infty} \frac{2\sin(Lt)}{t} \tag{8.3}$$

which is clearly not defined except in the special case $t = 0$. (However, Equation 8.20 (page 136) shows that this limit actually exists, in a sense made clear later, and is equal to $2\pi\delta(\omega)$, where δ is the Dirac delta function discussed in the next paragraph.)

On the other hand, what about Equation 8.1? How can this relationship be expressed using Equation 8.2? No ordinary choice of $a(\omega)$ will do the job. We must choose

$$a(\omega) = \frac{\delta(\omega - \nu) + \delta(\omega + \nu)}{2}$$

where $\delta(x)$ is the Dirac delta function. This "function," more properly called a distribution, is zero everywhere except where its argument is zero, and there its value is infinite. It represents an ideal impulse. This distribution was used in Section 2.6 to obtain the impulse response of a simple harmonic oscillator. As was mentioned in Section 2.6, the proper definition of the Dirac delta function is as follows:

Definition 8.1   *The Dirac delta function,* $\delta(t)$, *is that distribution for which*

$$\int_a^b f(\tau)\delta(\tau)\,d\tau = f(0) \tag{8.4}$$

for any interval $[a, b]$ *containing 0 and for any function* f *that is continuous on that interval.*

Using the above choice of $a(\omega)$ in Equation 8.2 gives the result

$$x(t) = \int_{-\infty}^{+\infty} \frac{\delta(\omega - \nu) + \delta(\omega + \nu)}{2} e^{j\omega t}\,d\omega$$

$$= \frac{e^{j\nu t} + e^{-j\nu t}}{2}$$

$$= \cos(\nu t)$$

Evidently the theory of Fourier transforms is not as elementary as might be hoped. The full theory has been worked out rigorously and requires an understanding of group theory as well as some fairly advanced complex analysis. In fact, it has been extended to non-Abelian groups, where it is called *harmonic analysis*. The interested reader might consult the book [1] by Bachman, which is a fine book that presents the basic theory concisely. It does, however, require a solid grounding in basic modern mathematics.

Luckily, from a practical point of view, most engineers can proceed without a full understanding of the theory of Fourier transforms, because every real-world signal is continuous and has compact support, (that is, it is zero outside some fixed interval of finite length), which guarantees the existence of its Fourier transform. However, we must be careful when manipulating these symbols formally.

8.2   THE BRA-AND-KET NOTATION

The basic concepts behind Fourier transforms are actually simple and beautiful. However, they are difficult to grasp using the ordinary integral notation of most expositions, because the messy-looking integrations effectively bury the basic concepts from view. I am therefore taking an unusual approach here by introducing P. A. M. Dirac's bracket notation, otherwise known as the *bra-and-ket* notation. This notation is common in quantum mechanics courses, but, is not usually introduced at an elementary level, nor is it commonly used in electrical engineering. However, Gabor made good use of this notation in his work, for example [4]. I hope its use here will help clarify the central issues.

The bracket notation is quite general, capable of handling the complicated expressions of quantum mechanics involving vector-valued and matrix-valued functions. However, the bracket notation needed for Fourier transforms on the real line is quite simple, being in some ways a degenerate special case that does not reveal the full generality of the notation. For the purposes of this chapter a *ket* is an ordinary function, $f(t)$, but it is written as $|f\rangle$. A *bra* is similarly written as $\langle f|$, but this time it is the complex conjugate of the function $f(t)$. Of course, if f is a real-valued function, then these two versions are the same. In general, a ket should be thought of as something quite distinct from a bra.

Of course, if the bra-and-ket notation were only another way to write functions, it would be useless. Any new notation must make writing formulas easier, not more complicated. The bra-and-ket notation simplifies writing certain integral expressions that are pervasive in Fourier analysis. In this chapter, for any two functions f and g, the concatenation of a bra and a ket means

$$\langle f\,|\,g\rangle = \int_{-\infty}^{+\infty} \overline{f}(t)g(t)\,dt$$

where $\overline{f}$ means the complex conjugate of the function f. This integral is often called the *inner product* of the two functions f and g.

In Chapter 11, several other realizations of the bracket are defined. For example, if the two functions f and g are defined only on the set of integers, $\mathcal{Z}$, then the bracket becomes

$$\langle f\,|\,g\rangle_{\mathcal{Z}} = \sum_{k=-\infty}^{+\infty} \overline{f}(k)g(k)$$

Despite these and other differing interpretations of the bracket in various settings, the statement of the Fourier transform theorem is nearly identical in all settings when the bracket notation is used.

You should think of the above integral or sum (respectively) as the result of a bra and a ket operating on each other. The study of Fourier analysis involves many such integrations, so the bracket notation significantly simplifies writing the necessary formulas and makes them formally the same in all settings.

8.3 THE ORTHOGONALITY THEOREM

How does this notation help with Fourier analysis? The following theorem, neatly expressed using the bracket notation, is the core of Fourier analysis. As we shall see, the bracket notation makes all the resulting formulas much easier to write and easier to understand. First, a definition:

Definition 8.2 Orthogonal Functions   *Let f and g be two functions of one real variable with complex range. If the inner product is zero,*

$$\langle f \,|\, g \rangle = 0$$

then f and g are said to be orthogonal to each other.

This is just like the definition of orthogonal vectors, except that the inner product is defined using the bracket instead of the dot product of two vectors.

Theorem 8.1 Orthogonality of Exponentials   *The following formula,*

$$\langle e^{j\mu t} \,|\, e^{j\nu t} \rangle = 2\pi\delta(\nu - \mu)$$

holds for any two real numbers, ν and μ. In other words, the two exponentials are orthogonal if $\mu \neq \nu$.

Before discussing in what sense this theorem is true, let's look at its implications for Fourier analysis. First, consider Equation 8.2, which defines a function $x(t)$ as a sum (integration) of other functions of time $e^{j\omega t}$, with coefficients $a(\omega)$. This function, $a(\mu)$, can be recovered from x using Theorem 8.1, as follows:

$$\langle e^{j\mu t} \,|\, x \rangle = \int_{-\infty}^{+\infty} e^{-j\mu t} x(t)\, dt$$

Using Equation 8.2 for $x(t)$ gives

$$= \int_{-\infty}^{+\infty} e^{-j\mu t} \int_{-\infty}^{+\infty} a(\omega) e^{j\omega t}\, d\omega\, dt$$

Interchanging the order of integration (strictly speaking, we should prove in each case whether or not the order of integration can be interchanged; however, the intention here is to convey the general concept, not to maintain rigorous formality), gives

$$= \int_{-\infty}^{+\infty} a(\omega) \int_{-\infty}^{+\infty} e^{-j\mu t} e^{j\omega t} \, dt \, d\omega$$

which, using the bracket notation, can be written as

$$= \int_{-\infty}^{+\infty} a(\omega) \langle e^{j\mu t} | \, e^{j\omega t} \rangle \, d\omega$$

By Theorem 8.1, this becomes

$$= \int_{-\infty}^{+\infty} a(\omega) 2\pi \delta(\omega - \mu) \, d\omega$$

$$= 2\pi a(\mu)$$

This proves that $a(\mu)$ can be calculated by

$$a(\mu) = \frac{1}{2\pi} \langle e^{j\mu t} | x \rangle$$

This is almost the full statement of the Fourier transform. Starting with a function x of time, a function a of frequency can be calculated. This function can then be used to obtain x again, using Equation 8.2. In other words, a function of time $x(t)$ can be "transformed" into a function of frequency, $a(\mu)$. As we shall see later, the inverse transform also exists, taking $a(\mu)$ back to $x(t)$.

8.4   PREPARATIONS

The full statement of the Fourier transform is Theorem 8.4 on page 117. However, some preparations are necessary for a full understanding of the theorem and for the proof of the uncertainty principle, Theorem 8.11.

Section 8.4.1 introduces the function notation used throughout the remainder of the book. Section 8.4.2 introduces the space of square integrable functions, $\mathcal{L}_2$, and section 8.4.3 shows how the square integrable functions may be multiplied or added together to produce a result that is still square integrable.

8.4.1   Function Notation

Sometimes a single letter such as f is used to represent a function of time or of frequency. Other times, an expression such as $e^{j\omega t}$ is used to represent a function of time—or is it a function of frequency? Actually, it is a function of both time and frequency. Which one is being used as the variable must be understood from context. However, especially with the bra-and-ket notation, this can be confusing. Notice also the symmetry between frequency ω and time t in this function. These variables are essentially indistinguishable. To eliminate these ambiguities, we introduce some notation, as follows. The function χ_ω is a function of time, defined by

$$\chi_\omega(t) = e^{j\omega t} \tag{8.5}$$

Similarly, the function χ_t is a function of frequency, defined by

$$\chi_t(\omega) = e^{j\omega t} \tag{8.6}$$

Of course, these functions are not really different. The only difference is how the variables are named. For example, is χ_3 a function of time or of frequency? There is no way to tell. There is no need to distinguish one from the other. We could write

$$\chi_3(t) = e^{j3t}$$

or just as easily

$$\chi_3(\omega) = e^{j3\omega}$$

Thus, the notation does not completely eliminate the ambiguity. The context in which the function is used usually makes it clear.

Using these definitions, Theorem 8.1 can be restated as

$$\langle \chi_\mu | \chi_\nu \rangle = 2\pi\delta(\mu - \nu) \tag{8.7}$$

In this case, it is clear that the integral defining the bracket is over time:

$$\langle \chi_\mu | \chi_\nu \rangle = \int_{-\infty}^{+\infty} \overline{\chi}_\mu(t)\chi_\nu(t)\, dt$$

However, if the equation is written as

$$\langle \chi_t | \chi_s \rangle = 2\pi\delta(t - s) \tag{8.8}$$

then, probably, integration over frequency is implied, in which case the integration is

$$\langle \chi_t | \chi_s \rangle = \int_{-\infty}^{+\infty} \overline{\chi}_t(\omega)\chi_s(\omega)\, d\omega$$

In one sense, there is really no difference between these two formulas. A simple renaming of the variables changes one into the other. However, in Chapter 9, these two equations are explored further in more general settings, in which case the essential differences are made clear. Some discussion of these differences now will help clarify the situation.

Equation 8.7 involves integration over time, and, to distinguish it from Equation 8.8, we write the bracket as follows:

$$\langle \chi_\mu | \chi_\nu \rangle_{\Re} = \int_{-\infty}^{+\infty} \overline{\chi}_\mu(t) \chi_\nu(t) \, dt$$

The subscript $\Re$ stands for the set of real numbers, in this case time, from $-\infty$ to $+\infty$. On the other hand, Equation 8.8 does not involve integration over time. Rather, it is an integration over the functions χ_ω. The set of all these functions, called *characters* of $\Re$ (explained in chapter 9), is denoted by $\widehat{\Re}$. Thus, the bracket in this case is properly written with the subscript:

$$\langle \chi_t | \chi_s \rangle_{\widehat{\Re}} = \int_{-\infty}^{+\infty} \overline{\chi}_t(\omega) \chi_s(\omega) \, d\omega$$

In this chapter, these differences might appear pedantic, because the actual formula in each case is almost the same. Because of this, the subscript will not be used for the rest of this chapter. As a general comment, I would like to point out that the meanings of operators and other notations are *overloaded* in many settings in order to avoid baroque constructions. For example, in the C language, the **+** operator is overloaded. It can be used to add integers of type **char**, **short**, **int**, and **long**. It can be used to add floating-point numbers of type **float**, **double**, or **long double**. This is a use of overloading that is so familiar that you probably don't even think about it. But it is real overloading. Just think of the different machine code that the compiler must generate in each case. In C++, this same operator can be overloaded even more to mean practically anything desired. However, for readability and usability, any additional overloading should have a meaning that is closely related to the original meaning of the operator, albeit in a new setting.

It is just the same for mathematical notation. Most of the time, ambiguities in the notation can be resolved easily from context. Unlike overloading allowed for a compiler, mathematical notation is sometimes allowed to contain true ambiguities that cannot be separated by the immediate context. In such cases, it is up to the author to make the precise meaning plain to the reader. Overloading of mathematical notation is just as useful, and even essential, as is overloading of operators in computer languages.

8.4.2 Square Integrable Functions

We are almost ready to state the Fourier transform theorem, but one more piece of the puzzle must be put in place first. Not every function has a Fourier transform. Some restrictions must be placed on the functions to be considered, or the theorem cannot be properly stated. The easiest restriction to use is that the functions must be *square integrable.*

Definition 8.3 Square Integrable: *A complex-valued function $f(t)$ of one real variable is called square integrable if*

$$\langle f \mid f \rangle = \int_{-\infty}^{+\infty} \mid f(t) \mid^2 dt$$

is defined and finite.

It is also convenient to identify two functions that are the same except for a "small" set of points. What is a "small" set of points? Certainly, any one point makes a "small" set. Any finite number of points is also a "small" set. The precise definition is that the set should have *measure* 0. So, what is the measure of a set?

Definition 8.4 Characteristic Function: *Let $S \subset \Re$ be a set of real points. The characteristic function of the set S is defined by*

$$h_S(t) = \begin{cases} 1 & \text{if } t \in S \\ 0 & \text{otherwise} \end{cases}$$

For the purposes of this book, the measure of a set can be defined as the integral of its characteristic function:

Definition 8.5 Measure: *The measure of a set $S \subset \Re$ is defined to be the integral*

$$\int_{-\infty}^{+\infty} h_S(t) \, dt$$

of its characteristic function.

Any finite set of points has measure 0. Any interval $[a, b]$, on the other hand, has measure $b - a$. Any set that contains a nontrivial interval must also have a positive (nonzero) measure. If two functions are different only on a set of measure zero, then it is usually convenient to "identify them," ignoring these differences. Two identified functions behave identically in almost any formula. For example, they have the same integral.

Definition 8.6 *Let f and g be two functions. If the set of points*

$$\{x \in \Re \mid f(x) \neq g(x)\}$$

has measure 0, then we say

$$f = g \quad almost\ everywhere$$

In other texts, you might see this shortened to

$$f = g \quad a.e.$$

Now we can define a set of functions, $\mathcal{L}_2(\mathfrak{R})$, all of which possess Fourier transforms:

Definition 8.7 *$\mathcal{L}_2(\mathfrak{R})$ is the set of all complex-valued functions of one real variable that are square integrable. Any two functions f and $g \in \mathcal{L}_2(\mathfrak{R})$ that are equal almost everywhere are actually considered to be the same element of $\mathcal{L}_2(\mathfrak{R})$ (they are identified with each other). This set is frequently written simply as $\mathcal{L}_2$ for brevity.*

For example, suppose $f \in \mathcal{L}_2$ is not equal to 0. Since we are identifying functions that are equal almost everywhere, this implies that $|f|^2$ is strictly positive on a set of nonzero (positive) measure. From this fact, it is easy to prove that the integral

$$\langle f|f \rangle = \int_{-\infty}^{+\infty} |f|^2\, dt > 0$$

is strictly positive. In other words, all nonzero functions in $\mathcal{L}_2$ have a strictly positive *norm*, defined by $\langle f|\, f \rangle$.

How many square integrable functions are there? It is easy to find functions that do not satisfy this restriction. There are no nonzero constant functions in $\mathcal{L}_2$, because

$$\langle 1 \mid 1 \rangle = \int_{-\infty}^{+\infty} dt$$

is not defined. Even the functions χ_ω are not square integrable, because their inner products do not converge in the usual sense.

You might start thinking that $\mathcal{L}_2$ is a very small set of functions. However, this is not true. Every real-world signal is square integrable. Every observed signal has finite duration and finite variation (takes on only finite values). This is enough to guarantee that it is in $\mathcal{L}_2$. This is easily proved, for if f is a function that is bounded by $|f| \leq B$ and is nonzero only on the interval $[a, b]$, it is in $\mathcal{L}_2$, because

$$\langle f \mid f \rangle = \int_{-\infty}^{+\infty} \bar{f}(t) f(t)\, dt$$

$$= \int_{a}^{b} |f(t)|^2\, dt$$

$$\leq \int_a^b B^2 \, dt$$

$$\leq (b - a)B^2$$

which guarantees that the integral exists.

8.4.3   Adding and Multiplying Functions in $\mathcal{L}_2$.

The set of functions $\mathcal{L}_2$ has three additional important properties:

1.   The sum of any two square integrable functions is square integrable.
2.   The product of any two square integrable functions is square integrable.
3.   The convolution of any two square integrable functions is square integrable.

In other words, all the usual algebraic manipulations may be performed without leaving the set of square integrable functions. These facts can be proved using the two inequalities stated in this section:

Theorem 8.2 Cauchy–Schwarz *Inequality: For any two functions g and h $\in \mathcal{L}_2$,*

$$\left| \langle g \mid h \rangle \right|^2 \leq \langle g \mid g \rangle \langle h \mid h \rangle$$

This inequality can be used to show that the product of any two square integrable functions is again square integrable. Just as important, as it stands, it claims that the inner product (bracket) of any two square integrable functions exists. In other words, if $\langle g \mid g \rangle$ and $\langle h \mid h \rangle$ exist, then so does $\langle g \mid h \rangle$.

Theorem 8.3 Minkowski's Inequality: *For any two functions f and g $\in \mathcal{L}_2$,*

$$\langle f + g \mid f + g \rangle^{1/2} \leq \langle f \mid f \rangle^{1/2} + \langle g | g \rangle^{1/2}$$

This is actually a special case of the Minkowski inequality, but it is the only one needed in this book. This version implies that the sum of any two square integrable functions is again square integrable. The claim about convolutions will be discussed in Section 8.14.

8.5   THE FOURIER TRANSFORM THEOREM

Theorem 8.4 Plancherel Theorem: *For every square integrable function f $\in \mathcal{L}_2$, its Fourier transform*

$$\hat{f}(\omega) = \frac{1}{\sqrt{2\pi}} \langle \chi_\omega | f \rangle = \frac{1}{\sqrt{2\pi}} \int_{-\infty}^{+\infty} e^{-j\omega t} f(t) \, dt$$

exists and is itself square integrable.

For any function $\hat{f} \in \mathcal{L}_2$, the inverse Fourier transform

$$f(t) = \frac{1}{\sqrt{2\pi}}\langle \overline{\hat{f}} \mid \chi_t \rangle = \int_{-\infty}^{+\infty} \hat{f}(\omega)e^{j\omega t}\, d\omega$$

exists and is itself square integrable.

The inverse Fourier transform of the Fourier transform of any function in $\mathcal{L}_2$ is equal to the original function almost everywhere.

The Fourier transform of the inverse Fourier transform of any function in $\mathcal{L}_2$ is equal to the original function almost everywhere.

The $1/\sqrt{2\pi}$ factors are used in both the Fourier transform and the inverse Fourier transform in this theorem, because putting the factor here makes the squared magnitude of the Fourier transform coefficients, $|\hat{f}(\omega)|^2$, proportional to the energy density of the function at frequency ω in the same ratio $|f(t)|^2$ is proportional to the energy density at time t. Theorem 8.6 states this fact formally. Other authors might choose to place the factors $\sqrt{2\pi}$ elsewhere. I like them this way, but other approaches are equivalent. The factors have to be used somewhere.

8.6   THE SQUARE PULSE

A square pulse is a good example, because it illustrates how the Fourier transform process returns a function that may differ at a few points from the original function and also because it is an important example for digital signal processing. A digital-to-analog converter, for example, puts out a sequence of square pulses, not a smoothly varying waveform.

The square pulse centered on time 0 is defined by

$$h_\tau(t) = \begin{cases} 1 & \text{if } |t| \leq \tau \\ 0 & \text{otherwise} \end{cases} \tag{8.9}$$

This function is obviously square integrable. Its Fourier transform can be calculated as follows:

$$\begin{aligned}
\widehat{h_\tau}(\omega) &= \frac{1}{\sqrt{2\pi}}\langle \chi_\omega \mid h_\tau \rangle \\
&= \frac{1}{\sqrt{2\pi}} \int_{-\infty}^{+\infty} e^{-j\omega t} h_\tau(t)\, dt \\
&= \frac{1}{\sqrt{2\pi}} \int_{-\tau}^{\tau} e^{-j\omega t}\, dt
\end{aligned}$$

$$= \frac{e^{-j\omega\tau} - e^{j\omega\tau}}{-j\omega\sqrt{2\pi}}$$

$$= \frac{2\sin(\omega\tau)}{\sqrt{2\pi}\,\omega} \tag{8.10}$$

Calculating the inverse Fourier transform of $\widehat{h_\tau}$ is a little trickier but can be done, with the use of standard integral tables, as follows:

$$\frac{1}{\sqrt{2\pi}}\langle\widehat{\overline{h_\tau}}|\chi_t\rangle = \frac{1}{\sqrt{2\pi}}\int_{-\infty}^{+\infty} e^{j\omega t}\widehat{h_\tau}(\omega)\,d\omega$$

$$= \frac{1}{\sqrt{2\pi}}\int_{-\infty}^{+\infty} e^{j\omega t}\frac{2\sin(\omega\tau)}{\sqrt{2\pi}\omega}\,d\omega$$

$$= \frac{1}{\pi}\int_{-\infty}^{+\infty} (\cos(\omega t) + j\sin(\omega t))\frac{\sin(\omega\tau)}{\omega}\,d\omega$$

$$= \frac{1}{\pi}\int_{-\infty}^{+\infty} \left(\cos(\omega t)\frac{\sin(\omega\tau)}{\omega} + j\sin(\omega t)\frac{\sin(\omega\tau)}{\omega}\right)d\omega$$

The imaginary part of this integral is zero, because the imaginary part of the integrand is odd. Thus, the formula becomes

$$\frac{1}{\sqrt{2\pi}}\langle\widehat{\overline{h_\tau}}|\chi_t\rangle = \frac{1}{\pi}\int_{-\infty}^{+\infty} \cos(\omega t)\frac{\sin(\omega\tau)}{\omega}\,d\omega$$

$$= \frac{1}{\pi}\int_{-\infty}^{+\infty} \cos\left(\frac{ut}{\tau}\right)\frac{\sin(u)}{u}\,du$$

where the last step was made by making the substitution $u = \omega\tau$. This is a standard integral that can be found in most tables of definite integrals. The value is

$$\frac{1}{\sqrt{2\pi}}\langle\widehat{\overline{h_\tau}}|\chi_t\rangle = \begin{cases} 1 & \text{if } |t| < \tau \\ \frac{1}{2} & \text{if } t = \pm\tau \\ 0 & \text{if } |t| > \tau \end{cases} \tag{8.11}$$

This is not exactly the original function, h. It is different at two points, $t = \pm\tau$. This is the kind of difference to expect between the original function and the function returned by taking the Fourier transform followed by the inverse Fourier transform. The discrepancies, if they exist, are always at points of discontinuity.

8.7 SOME CAUTIONS

Theorem 8.1 is central to Fourier transforms, but it must be understood in a context that has not been fully explained. The Fourier transform theorem provides just the context in which Theorem 8.1 is needed. The inverse Fourier transform of a transformed function,

$$\hat{x}(\omega) = \frac{1}{\sqrt{2\pi}} \langle \chi_\omega \mid x \rangle$$

can be calculated according to

$$\frac{1}{\sqrt{2\pi}} \langle \hat{x} | \chi_t \rangle = \frac{1}{\sqrt{2\pi}} \int_{-\infty}^{+\infty} \hat{x}(\omega) e^{j\omega t} \, d\omega$$

$$= \frac{1}{\sqrt{2\pi}} \int_{-\infty}^{+\infty} \frac{1}{\sqrt{2\pi}} \langle \chi_\omega | x \rangle \frac{e^{j\omega t}}{\sqrt{2\pi}} \, d\omega$$

$$= \frac{1}{2\pi} \int_{-\infty}^{+\infty} \int_{-\infty}^{+\infty} x(u) e^{j\omega u} \, du \, e^{j\omega t} \, d\omega$$

and here is the tricky part. The next step is to interchange the order of the integrals. This is not, in general, a valid operation. Sometimes the order of the integrals makes a difference in the final value, or even in whether the integrals converge. In this case, the integrals may be interchanged if the resulting non-standard integral is interpreted using Theorem 8.1. Assuming that this is valid, the calculation can continue as follows:

$$\frac{1}{\sqrt{2\pi}} \langle \hat{x} | \chi_t \rangle = \frac{1}{2\pi} \int_{-\infty}^{+\infty} x(u) \int_{-\infty}^{+\infty} e^{-j\omega u} e^{j\omega t} \, d\omega \, du$$

$$= \frac{1}{2\pi} \int_{-\infty}^{+\infty} x(u) \langle \chi_u | \chi_t \rangle \, du$$

which by Theorem 8.1 and Equation 8.7 is

$$= \int_{-\infty}^{+\infty} x(u) \delta(t - u) \, du$$

$$= x(t)$$

which is what the Fourier transform theorem claims is true.

However, interchanging the integrals must be done with caution and the right justifications, according to various theorems. For example, the integral in

Theorem 8.1 does not converge in any ordinary sense, as the following computation of it demonstrates:

$$
\int_{-\infty}^{+\infty} e^{j\nu t} e^{-j\mu t}\, dt = \lim_{L\to\infty} \int_{-L}^{L} e^{j(\nu-\mu)t}\, dt
$$

$$
= \lim_{L\to\infty} \frac{e^{j(\nu-\mu)L} - e^{-j(\nu-\mu)L}}{j(\nu-\mu)}
$$

$$
= \lim_{L\to\infty} \frac{2\sin[(\nu-\mu)L]}{\nu-\mu}
$$

This integral is infinite if $\nu = \mu$; otherwise, it does not converge, but rather oscillates. These questions will not be investigated further in this book, but it is important to remember that caution must be exercised. Otherwise, it is easy to "prove" that $0 = 1$.

8.8 MORE ABOUT THE BRA AND KET

Dirac's bra-and-ket notation not only makes writing formulas easier, it makes the manipulation of complex expressions easier as well. The properties of the bracket notation discussed in this section are all direct results of its definition. One of the central properties is *linearity*. Linearity was defined in Section 2.1. Reiterating, an operator $\mathcal{L}$ is linear if

$$
\mathcal{L}(ax + by) = a\mathcal{L}(x) + b\mathcal{L}(y)
$$

for any constants a and b and any functions x and y. We say the operator is *real-linear* if this equation is true for real constants a and b. We say it is *complex-linear* if the formula is true for complex constants a and b. Any complex-linear operator is also real-linear, but the converse is not in general true. As the following theorem proves, the bracket is complex-linear in the ket, but only real-linear in the bra.

Theorem 8.5 *For any three functions f, g, $h \in \mathcal{L}_2$ and any complex constants a and b, the ket is complex-linear:*

$$
\langle f | ag + bh \rangle = a\langle f | g \rangle + b\langle f | h \rangle \tag{8.12}
$$

The bra is real-linear:

$$
\langle ag + bh | f \rangle = \overline{a}\langle g | f \rangle + \overline{b}\langle g | h \rangle \tag{8.13}
$$

Complex conjugation inverts the bracket:

$$\langle f|g \rangle = \overline{\langle g|f \rangle} \tag{8.14}$$

Proof   The proof of this theorem comes directly from the definition. To prove Equation 8.12, calculate from the definition as follows:

$$\langle f|ag + bh \rangle = \int_{-\infty}^{+\infty} \overline{f}(t)[(ag(t) + bh(t)] \, dt$$

$$= a \int_{-\infty}^{+\infty} \overline{f}(t)g(t) \, dt + b \int_{-\infty}^{+\infty} \overline{f}(t)h(t) \, dt$$

$$= a\langle f|g \rangle + b\langle f|h \rangle$$

as asserted. Equation 8.13 can be proved by applying Equation 8.14 to Equation 8.12, or directly from the definition similarly to the above calculation. Proving Equation 8.14 is also straightforward:

$$\overline{\langle f|g \rangle} = \overline{\int_{-\infty}^{+\infty} \bar{f}(t)g(t) \, dt}$$

$$= \int_{-\infty}^{+\infty} \overline{\bar{f}(t)g(t)} \, dt$$

$$= \int_{-\infty}^{+\infty} \overline{g}(t)f(t) \, dt$$

$$= \langle g|f \rangle \qquad\qquad ///$$

Because the Fourier transform and the inverse Fourier transform can be expressed in terms of the bracket notation, this theorem also proves that both directions of the Fourier transform are complex-linear.

8.9   EQUAL POWERS AND OTHER PROPERTIES

Another useful property of Fourier transforms is a special case of what is known as the *Parseval formula*:

Theorem 8.6 Parseval: *For any two functions f, $g \in \mathcal{L}_2$, with Fourier transforms $\hat{f}$ and $\hat{g}$,*

$$\langle f|g \rangle = \langle \hat{f}|\hat{g} \rangle$$

Proof This theorem is proved by writing out the integrals, rearranging the order of integration, and using Theorem 8.1. The calculation is as follows:

$$\langle \hat{f} \mid \hat{g} \rangle = \int_{-\infty}^{+\infty} \overline{\hat{f}(\omega)} \hat{g}(\omega) \, d\omega$$

$$= \int_{-\infty}^{+\infty} \overline{\langle \chi_\omega \mid f \rangle} \langle \chi_\omega \mid g \rangle \, d\omega$$

$$= \frac{1}{2\pi} \int_{-\infty}^{+\infty} \overline{\int_{-\infty}^{+\infty} \overline{\chi_\omega(t)} f(t) \, dt} \int_{-\infty}^{+\infty} \overline{\chi_\omega(u)} g(u) \, du \, d\omega$$

$$= \frac{1}{2\pi} \int_{-\infty}^{+\infty} \int_{-\infty}^{+\infty} \chi_\omega(t) \bar{f}(t) \, dt \int_{-\infty}^{+\infty} \overline{\chi_\omega(u)} g(u) \, du \, d\omega$$

which, when the integrals are rearranged, becomes

$$= \frac{1}{2\pi} \int_{-\infty}^{+\infty} \int_{-\infty}^{+\infty} \bar{f}(t) g(u) \int_{-\infty}^{+\infty} \overline{\chi_\omega(u)} \chi_\omega(t) \, d\omega \, du \, dt$$

which can be written as

$$= \frac{1}{2\pi} \int_{-\infty}^{+\infty} \int_{-\infty}^{+\infty} \bar{f}(t) g(u) \int_{-\infty}^{+\infty} \overline{\chi_u(\omega)} \chi_t(\omega) \, d\omega \, du \, dt$$

$$= \frac{1}{2\pi} \int_{-\infty}^{+\infty} \int_{-\infty}^{+\infty} \bar{f}(t) g(u) \langle \chi_u \mid \chi_t \rangle \, du \, dt$$

which, by Equation 8.7, is

$$= \int_{-\infty}^{+\infty} \int_{-\infty}^{+\infty} \bar{f}(t) g(u) \delta(u - t) \, du \, dt$$

$$= \int_{-\infty}^{+\infty} \bar{f}(t) g(t) \, dt$$

$$= \langle f \mid g \rangle$$

which proves the theorem. ///

When the Parseval formula is applied with $f = g$, the "equal power" theorem is obtained:

Theorem 8.7 Equal Powers: *For any function $f \in \mathcal{L}_2$ with Fourier transform $\hat{f}(\omega) = \langle \chi_\omega \mid f \rangle / \sqrt{2\pi}$,*

$$\langle f \mid f \rangle = \langle \hat{f} \mid \hat{f} \rangle$$

This theorem implies that the magnitude-squared Fourier coefficient, $|\hat{f}(\omega)|^2$, can be thought of as the energy density at frequency ω. This is because

$$\langle f \mid f \rangle = \int_{-\infty}^{+\infty} |f(t)|^2 \, dt$$

is proportional to the energy in the original waveform, and the theorem shows that it is also equal to

$$\langle \hat{f} \mid \hat{f} \rangle = \int_{-\infty}^{+\infty} \left| \hat{f}(\omega) \right|^2 \, d\omega$$

Just as $|f(t)|^2$ is proportional to the energy density at time t, so $\left| f(\omega) \right|^2$ is proportional to the energy density at frequency ω. Translating either of these two values to actual energy densities requires knowledge of the equipment used to sample the waveform. At a minimum, the resistance in the circuit must be known.

The next theorem lists three properties of the Fourier transform that are often used in practice.

Theorem 8.8 *For any function $f \in \mathcal{L}_2$*

$$\langle \chi_\omega \mid Df \rangle = j\omega \langle \chi_\omega \mid f \rangle \qquad (8.15)$$

$$\langle \chi_\omega \mid f_\tau \rangle = e^{-j\omega\tau} \langle \chi_\omega \mid f \rangle \qquad (8.16)$$

$$\langle \chi_\omega \mid e^{j\mu t} f \rangle = \langle \chi_{\omega-\mu} \mid f \rangle \qquad (8.17)$$

where $f_\tau(t) = f(t - \tau)$ is the translation of f in time, and Df is the derivative of f with respect to time.

Equation 8.16 says that a time translation transforms into a phase shift. Equation 8.17 shows that multiplying a function by a pure tone shifts the frequencies of its transform.

Proof   Equation 8.15 is proved by an integration by parts, as follows:

$$\langle \chi_\omega \mid Df \rangle = \int_{-\infty}^{+\infty} \overline{\chi}_\omega(t) Df(t)\, dt$$

$$= \int_{-\infty}^{+\infty} D\left[\overline{\chi}_\omega(t) f(t)\right]\, dt - \int_{-\infty}^{+\infty} \left[D\overline{\chi}_\omega(t)\right] f(t)\, dt$$

The first of these two integrals is zero, because

$$\lim_{t \to \pm\infty} f(t) = 0$$

which is true of any function $f \in \mathcal{L}_2$. If this were not true, the function could not be square integrable. Since $\chi_\omega(t)$ is bounded, the product, $\overline{\chi}_\omega(t) f(t)$, also approaches 0 as $t \to \pm\infty$. Thus, the equation reduces to

$$\langle \chi_\omega \mid Df \rangle = -\int_{-\infty}^{+\infty} \left[D\overline{\chi}_\omega(t)\right] f(t)\, dt$$

$$= j\omega \int_{-\infty}^{+\infty} \overline{\chi}_\omega(t) f(t)\, dt$$

$$= j\omega \langle \chi_\omega \mid f \rangle$$

which proves Equation 8.15.

Equation 8.16 is proved by a simple substitution, as follows:

$$\langle \chi_\omega \mid f_\tau \rangle = \int_{-\infty}^{+\infty} \overline{\chi}_\omega(t) f(t - \tau)\, dt$$

which, by the substitution $u = t - \tau$, becomes

$$= \int_{-\infty}^{+\infty} \overline{\chi}_\omega(u + \tau) f(u)\, du$$

$$= \int_{-\infty}^{+\infty} \overline{\chi}_\omega(u) e^{-j\omega\tau} f(u)\, du$$

$$= e^{-j\omega\tau} \langle \chi_\omega \mid f \rangle$$

which proves the formula.   ///

The last equation is the inverse version of Equation 8.16 and can be proved using the same technique.

8.10   THE UNCERTAINTY RELATION

Nearly everyone has heard of the Heisenberg uncertainty principle of quantum mechanics. It says that the product of the uncertainty in position and the uncertainty in momentum is always greater than or equal to a particular constant. The uncertainty relation is also true for signal processing. One practical consequence is this: an accurate determination of the frequency content of a signal requires a long measuring time. An equivalent statement is: A short-duration signal contains a wide range of frequencies.

The difference between these two points of view is that the first is analytic and the second is constructive. The analytic view asks what is needed to make a particular measurement. The constructive view considers what is required to build a waveform with a desired property. For example, if a transmitter must contain its radiation within a specified band, then the uncertainty principle asserts there is a fundamental limit on how fast it can change frequencies and still meet its bandwidth limitations.

These facts are both results of the same inequality that relates properties of a function and its Fourier transform. They are results of the way the quantities and their uncertainties are defined. The first step is to define exactly what is meant by the time of a signal, $\langle t \rangle$, its uncertainty Δt, the frequency of a signal, $\langle \omega \rangle$, and its uncertainty $\Delta \omega$. Once these are defined, the uncertainty principle is easily stated as the inequality

$$\Delta t \Delta \omega \geq \frac{1}{2}.$$

There is no possibility of improving this fundamental inequality, unless you accept some new definition of frequency, time, or uncertainty. (You may find some journal articles that claim to have improved upon this fundamental limit. There has actually been a fair amount of activity in this direction in certain communities. However, look closely and you will find either a mistake, a new definition of frequency, or a new definition of uncertainty. If these new definitions suit your purposes, then by all means use them. However, it can be confusing, unless the new definition is clearly stated and its consequences explored.)

Given a waveform f, at what time did it occur? Suppose, for example, this waveform is a short bell tone or the shot of a gun. No matter how short the sound is, it occupies a finite stretch of time, so the time it occurred cannot be stated with absolute certainty. The usual definition of the time of occurrence is the power-weighted average time

$$\langle t \rangle = \frac{\int_{-\infty}^{+\infty} t |f(t)|^2 \, dt}{\int_{-\infty}^{+\infty} |f(t)|^2 \, dt}$$

The denominator normalizes the average. This type of calculation is frequent enough to warrant its own notation:

Definition 8.8 Expectation Value: *For any operator A defined on $\mathcal{L}_2$ and any function $f \in \mathcal{L}_2$ for which the integral $\langle f \mid Af \rangle$ is defined, the expectation value of A is defined by*

$$\langle A \rangle_f = \frac{\langle f \mid Af \rangle}{\langle f \mid f \rangle}$$

The notion of an *operator* has not been precisely defined, but some examples will be sufficient in helping to explain it. The multiplication operator, which maps a function $f(t)$ to the function $tf(t)$ has already been considered. Another operator is differentiation, D, which maps a function from f to Df. It turns out that these operators are central in importance to proving the uncertainty relation.

The time assigned to a function is $\langle t \rangle_f$. What is the uncertainty in this assignment of time? The standard deviation Δt is the usual measure of uncertainty. It can be defined by its variance:

$$\Delta t^2 = \langle (t - \langle t \rangle)^2 \rangle_f$$

The following identity is frequently helpful in both applications and theoretical development:

Theorem 8.9 *For any linear operator A on $\mathcal{L}_2$ and for any function $f \in \mathcal{L}_2$, the variance of A can be calculated by either of the expressions in the equality*

$$\left\langle \left(A - \langle A \rangle\right)^2 \right\rangle_f = \langle A^2 \rangle_f - \langle A \rangle_f^2$$

Proof This theorem is proved by some direct calculations, as follows:

$$\left\langle \left(A - \langle A \rangle\right)^2 \right\rangle_f \langle f \mid f \rangle = \int_{-\infty}^{+\infty} \bar{f}(t) \left(A - \langle A \rangle\right)^2 f(t) \, dt$$

$$= \int_{-\infty}^{+\infty} \bar{f}(t) \left(A^2 - A\langle A \rangle - \langle A \rangle A + \langle A \rangle^2\right) f(t) \, dt$$

Since A is assumed to be linear, this reduces to

$$= \int_{-\infty}^{+\infty} \bar{f}(t) \left(A^2 - 2\langle A \rangle A + \langle A \rangle^2 \right) f(t)\, dt$$

$$= \left(\langle A^2 \rangle_f - 2\langle A \rangle_f \langle A \rangle_f + \langle A \rangle_f^2 \right) \langle f \mid f \rangle$$

$$= \left(\langle A^2 \rangle_f - \langle A \rangle_f^2 \right) \langle f \mid f \rangle$$

which proves the theorem.   ///

The uncertainty in time, Δt, has been defined. What about the uncertainty in frequency, $\Delta \omega$? The most obvious way to find $\Delta \omega$ is by making the same calculation as required for Δt but using the Fourier transform $\hat{f}$ in place of f. The formula is

$$\Delta \omega^2 = \langle \omega^2 \rangle_{\hat{f}} - \langle \omega \rangle_{\hat{f}}^2$$

Among all possible linear operators on $\mathscr{L}_2$, the class of *Hermitian* operators is particularly important. All observable quantities in quantum mechanics are represented by Hermitian operators, as are all operators of interest in linear signal processing. One of the important properties of Hermitian operators is that they have real expectation values. The formal definition is as follows:

Definition 8.9   Hermitian Operators: *An operator H on $\mathscr{L}_2$ is called Hermitian if, for any two functions f and $g \in \mathscr{L}_2$ for which the integrals are defined, the following equality holds:*

$$\langle f \mid Hg \rangle = \langle Hf \mid g \rangle$$

For example, the operator that multiplies by time is Hermitian:

$$\langle f \mid tg \rangle = \langle tf \mid g \rangle$$

This is proved practically as soon as the equation is written down. This is also true for every real constant, but not for a complex constant multiplier, because of Equation 8.13. Differentiation, D, is not Hermitian, but the operator jD is

Hermitian, which can be proved by an integration by parts almost identical to the one used to prove Equation 8.15, as follows:

$$\langle f \mid jDg \rangle = \int_{-\infty}^{+\infty} \bar{f}(t) jDg(t)\, dt$$

$$= \int_{-\infty}^{+\infty} jD\left(\bar{f}(t)g(t)\right) dt - \int_{-\infty}^{+\infty} \left(jD\bar{f}(t)\right)g(t)\, dt$$

$$= -\int_{-\infty}^{+\infty} \left(jD\bar{f}(t)\right)g(t)\, dt$$

$$= \int_{-\infty}^{+\infty} \overline{\left(jDf(t)\right)}g(t)\, dt$$

$$= \langle jDf \mid g \rangle$$

which proves jD is a Hermitian operator.

The fact that Hermitian operators have real expectation values is important to the proof of the uncertainty relationship. It is also easily proved by formal manipulation of the brackets.

Theorem 8.10   *The expectation value of a Hermitian operator H is real,*

$$\langle H \rangle_f \in \Re$$

for any $f \in \mathcal{L}_2$.

Proof   By Equation 8.14,

$$\overline{\langle f \mid Hf \rangle} = \langle Hf \mid f \rangle$$

and, since H is Hermitian,

$$= \langle f \mid Hf \rangle$$

which proves $\langle f \mid Hf \rangle$ is real. The expectation value $\langle H \rangle$ is therefore also real, because $\langle f \mid f \rangle$ is real.   ///

Theorem 8.11   Uncertainty Principle: *For any function $f \in \mathcal{L}_2$, the product of the uncertainty in time and uncertainty in frequency satisfies the inequality*

$$\Delta\omega\Delta t \geq \frac{1}{2}$$

This is a special case of a more general theorem. The more general theorem is actually easier to prove than this particular case, because it uses notation that is easier to handle in the proof. The general theorem is:

Theorem 8.12 Let H and K be two Hermitian operators, and let $f \in \mathcal{L}_2$ be any square integrable function. Then the product of the uncertainties in H and K satisfy the inequality

$$\Delta H \Delta K \geq \frac{1}{2} \left| \langle HK - KH \rangle_f \right|$$

In other words, the product of the uncertainties of H and K is always at least as large as half the expectation value of the *commutator* of these two operators. If H and K commute with each other,

$$HK = KH,$$

then the commutator is 0. If two observables (read that as "Hermitian operators") commute, then they can both be measured simultaneously with arbitrarily fine precision. If they do not commute, then there is a lower limit on how accurately they can be simultaneously measured, as stated in the theorem.

In the special case of Theorem 8.11, the required observables are

$$H f(t) = t f(t)$$

whose expectation value is the time of occurrence, and

$$K f(t) = -j D f(t)$$

whose expectation value is the frequency. This fact is proved by using the Parseval theorem, theorem 8.6, as follows. The expectation of $-jD$ is defined by

$$\langle -jD \rangle_f = \frac{\langle f \mid -jDf \rangle}{\langle f \mid f \rangle}$$

The Parseval theorem shows that the numerator can be written as

$$\langle f \mid -jDf \rangle = \langle \hat{f} \mid -j\widehat{Df} \rangle$$

Which, according to equation 8.15 is equal to

$$= \langle \hat{f} \mid \omega \hat{f} \rangle$$

Another application of the Parseval theorem to the denominator proves:

$$\langle -jD \rangle_f = \frac{\langle f \mid -jDf \rangle}{\langle f \mid f \rangle} = \frac{\langle \hat{f} \mid \omega \hat{f} \rangle}{\langle \hat{f} \mid \hat{f} \rangle} = \langle \omega \rangle_{\hat{f}}$$

As shown above, both of these operators are Hermitian, so they can be used in Theorem 8.12 Because these operators do not commute, there is a limit to the accuracy with which they can be simultaneously measured.

The proofs of Theorems 8.11 and 8.12 are given here for the sake of completeness. The interested reader should have no trouble following the proofs. If you are not interested, you can now skip to Section 8.11 without missing any material needed later.

Proof of Theorem 8.11   The special case is proved from the more general theorem by using the operator H that multiplies by t, $Hf(t) = tf(t)$, and the operator $K = -jD$, the differentiation operator. In that case, $\langle H \rangle_f = \langle t \rangle_f$, and $\langle K \rangle_f = \langle -jD \rangle_f = \langle \omega \rangle_{\hat{f}}$ by Equation 8.15. With these operators, the left-hand side of the inequality is $\Delta t \Delta \omega$ as required. The right-hand side can be calculated by noting that

$$(HK - KH)f(t) = -(jtD - jDt)f(t)$$
$$= -jtDf(t) + jD(tf(t))$$
$$= -jtDf(t) + jf(t) + jtDf(t)$$
$$= jf(t)$$

Thus, the left-hand side of the inequality becomes

$$\langle HK - KH \rangle_f = \langle j \rangle_f = j$$

Putting this back into the inequality proves Theorem 8.11.   ///

Proof of Theorem 8.12   The proof of this theorem is a little bit tricky. The key is to use the Cauchy–Schwarz inequality, Theorem 8.2, with a choice of functions that will give ΔH and ΔK on the right-hand side. The way to do this is

$$g(t) = \left(H - \langle H \rangle_f \right) f(t)$$

and

$$h(t) = \left(K - \langle K \rangle_f \right) f(t)$$

This gives the desired variances, because, for example,

$$\langle g \mid g \rangle_f = \langle (H - \langle H \rangle_f) f \mid (H - \langle H \rangle_f) f \rangle$$

and, since H is Hermitian, so is $H - \langle H \rangle_f$, and this can be written as

$$= \langle f \mid (H - \langle H \rangle_f)^2 f \rangle$$

$$= \left\langle (H - \langle H \rangle_f)^2 \right\rangle_f \langle f \mid f \rangle$$

$$= \Delta H^2 \langle f \mid f \rangle$$

by the definition of ΔH.

That takes care of the right-hand side of the Cauchy–Schwarz inequality. The left-hand side, from which the lower bound of the uncertainty will come, is

$$\langle g \mid h \rangle = \langle (H - \langle H \rangle_f) f \mid (K - \langle K \rangle_f) f \rangle$$

and, since $H - \langle H \rangle_f$ is Hermitian, this can be written as

$$= \langle f \mid (H - \langle H \rangle_f)(K - \langle K \rangle_f) f \rangle$$

$$= \langle f \mid (HK - \langle K \rangle_f H - \langle H \rangle_f K + \langle H \rangle_f \langle K \rangle_f) f \rangle$$

$$= \langle f \mid HK f \rangle - \langle K \rangle_f \langle f \mid H f \rangle$$

$$\quad - \langle H \rangle_f \langle f \mid K f \rangle$$

$$\quad + \langle H \rangle_f \langle K \rangle_f \langle f \mid f \rangle$$

$$= \left(\langle HK \rangle_f - \langle K \rangle_f \langle H \rangle_f \right) \langle f \mid f \rangle$$

by the definition of the expectation. Putting this into the Cauchy–Schwarz inequality,

$$|\langle g \mid h \rangle|^2 \le \langle g \mid g \rangle \langle h \mid h \rangle$$

gives the equation

$$\left| \left(\langle HK \rangle_f - \langle K \rangle_f \langle H \rangle_f \right) \langle f \mid f \rangle \right|^2 \le \Delta H^2 \Delta K^2 \langle f \mid f \rangle^2$$

Since $\langle f \mid f \rangle$ is real and positive, its square can be canceled from both sides of this equation, giving

$$\left| \left(\langle HK \rangle_f - \langle K \rangle_f \langle H \rangle_f \right) \right|^2 \le \Delta H^2 \Delta K^2 \qquad (8.18)$$

The uncertainty relation is obtained from Equation 8.18 by evaluating the imaginary part of the expression inside the absolute value on the left-hand side. The real part cannot be evaluated, but it is not required, as we will show. Since H and K are Hermitian, their respective expectations are real. However, HK is not necessarily Hermitian. It can be written as the sum of a Hermitian operator and an *anti-Hermitian* operator, as follows:

$$HK = \frac{1}{2}(HK + KH) + \frac{1}{2}(HK - KH)$$

The first of these is Hermitian, because

$$\langle f \mid (HK + KH)f \rangle = \langle f \mid HKf \rangle + \langle f \mid KHf \rangle$$

and, since H and K are both Hermitian, this can be written:

$$= \langle Hf \mid Kf \rangle + \langle Kf \mid Hf \rangle$$

and again, because the operators are Hermitian,

$$= \langle KHf \mid f \rangle + \langle HKf \mid f \rangle$$

$$= \langle (KH + HK)f \mid f \rangle$$

which is exactly what is needed to prove that $HK + KH$ is Hermitian. A similar calculation proves that $HK - KH$ is anti-Hermitian, meaning

$$\langle f \mid (HK - KH)f \rangle = -\langle (HK - KH)f \mid f \rangle$$

Since $\langle f \mid g \rangle = \overline{\langle g \mid f \rangle}$, this proves that $\langle f \mid (HK - KH)f \rangle$ is imaginary.

We can use these facts in Equation 8.18, by observing that the squared magnitude of a complex number is equal to the sum of the squares of its real and imaginary parts and is therefore greater than or equal to the square of the imaginary part alone. Ignoring the real part of the expression, we have proved

$$\frac{1}{4} \left| \langle HK - KH \rangle \right|^2 \le \left| \left(\langle HK \rangle_f - \langle K \rangle_f \langle H \rangle_f \right) \right|^2$$

Combining this with Equation 8.18 proves the inequality of the theorem.   ///

8.11 MINIMUM UNCERTAINTY

The uncertainty principle is more than just a statement of how carefully things can be measured. It actually says that any signal that occupies a very short time must have a correspondingly wide spectrum, and conversely, long-duration signals may have narrow spectrums. As an example of this behavior of signals, the Gaussian-modulated pulse is examined in this section. The Gaussian-modulated waveform is, in fact, the only one for which the uncertainty product achieves the lower bound stated in Theorem 8.11. This fact can be proved by examining the conditions under which both the Cauchy–Schwarz inequality becomes an equality, and, simultaneously, the inequality encountered in the proof of Theorem 8.12 is an equality. When these conditions are written down properly, a differential equation results, the only solution of which is the Gaussian-modulated waveform presented in this section.

The Gaussian distribution,

$$\phi_\sigma(t) = \frac{e^{-t^2/2\sigma^2}}{\sqrt{2\pi}\sigma} \tag{8.19}$$

is the only function that has the same functional form as its Fourier transform. The facts we shall need about the Gaussian distribution are collected together in the following:

Theorem 8.13   *For any real $\sigma > 0$, the following equations are true:*

$$\int_{-\infty}^{+\infty} \phi_\sigma(t - \tau)\, dt = 1$$

$$\int_{-\infty}^{+\infty} t\phi_\sigma(t - \tau)\, dt = \tau$$

$$\int_{-\infty}^{+\infty} (t - \tau)^2 \phi_\sigma(t - \tau)\, dt = \sigma^2$$

$$\widehat{\phi_\sigma}(\omega) = \frac{1}{\sigma}\phi_{1/\sigma}(\omega)$$

All of these equations can be proved by direct calculation. The last one requires some knowledge of entire functions and the residue theorem.

The Gaussian distribution can be used to construct a waveform with the minimal uncertainty product stated in Theorem 8.11. The method is to choose a function $f \in \mathscr{L}_2$ such that $|f|^2 = \phi_\sigma$. This is easily accomplished by choosing

$$f_{\sigma,\mu}(t) = \sqrt{\phi_\sigma(t)}\, e^{j\mu t}$$

$$= (8\pi)^{1/4}\sqrt{\sigma}\, \phi_{\sqrt{2\sigma}}(t)e^{j\mu t}$$

which is a Gaussian-modulated waveform. Any frequency can be chosen for μ, because the magnitude of the complex exponential is always 1. With this choice for the function, we can calculate

$$\left| f_{\sigma,\mu}(t) \right|^2 = \phi_\sigma(t)$$

independent of μ. Therefore, by Theorem 8.13,

$$\Delta t^2 = \left\langle (t - \langle t \rangle_f)^2 \right\rangle_{f_{\sigma,\mu}} = \sigma^2$$

The uncertainty in frequency, $\Delta\omega$, can be calculated most easily by taking the Fourier transform of $f_{\sigma,\mu}$ and computing in the frequency domain. The Fourier transform of $f_{\sigma,0}$ can be calculated by using Theorem 8.13:

$$\widehat{f_{\sigma,0}}(\omega) = \frac{(2\pi)^{1/4}}{\sqrt{\sigma}} \phi_{1/\sqrt{2\sigma}}(\omega)$$

The transform in the cases with $\mu \neq 0$ can be obtained from this by using Equation 8.17:

$$\widehat{f_{\sigma,\mu}}(\omega) = \frac{1}{\sqrt{2\pi}} \langle \chi_\omega \mid f_{\sigma,\mu} \rangle$$

$$= \frac{1}{\sqrt{2\pi}} \langle \chi_{\omega-\mu} \mid f_{\sigma,0} \rangle$$

$$= \widehat{f_{\sigma,0}}(\omega - \mu)$$

It is now a simple matter to compute $\Delta\omega$, because the magnitude squared of $\widehat{f_{\sigma,\mu}}$ can be written in terms of the Gaussian distribution as follows:

$$\left| \widehat{f_{\sigma,\mu}} \right|^2 = \phi_{1/2\sigma}(\omega - \mu)$$

With this equation and Theorem 8.13, the calculation goes as follows:

$$\Delta\omega^2 = \left\langle \omega^2 - \langle \omega \rangle^2 \right\rangle_{\widehat{f_{\sigma,\mu}}}$$

$$= \int_{-\infty}^{+\infty} (\omega^2 - \langle \omega \rangle^2) \left| \widehat{f_{\sigma,\mu}}(\omega) \right|^2 d\omega$$

$$= \int_{-\infty}^{+\infty} (\omega^2 - \langle \omega \rangle^2) \phi_{1/2\sigma}(\omega - \mu) \, d\omega$$

$$= \left(\frac{1}{2\sigma} \right)^2$$

which means

$$\Delta\omega = \frac{1}{2\sigma}$$

by Theorem 8.11:

$$\Delta\omega\Delta t = \frac{1}{2}$$

8.12 SOME EXTENSIONS

Many of the common functions that we want to be able to use with Fourier transforms are not square integrable. Luckily, Theorem 8.4 can be extended to include these cases, but only if nonstandard functions, like the Dirac delta function, are introduced. The details of these expansions to the Fourier transform theorem will not be discussed in this book, but some examples will be useful.

The cosine function is not square integrable. We can, however, take its Fourier transform by using Theorem 8.1, as follows:

$$\langle \chi_\omega \mid \cos(\mu t)\rangle = \langle \chi_\omega \mid \frac{e^{j\mu t} + e^{-j\mu t}}{2}\rangle$$

$$= \frac{1}{2}\langle \chi_\omega \mid \chi_\mu + \chi_{-\mu}\rangle$$

$$= \frac{1}{2}\left(\langle \chi_\omega \mid \chi_\mu\rangle + \langle \chi_\omega \mid \chi_{-\mu}\rangle\right)$$

$$= \pi\left(\delta(\mu - \omega) + \delta(\mu + \omega)\right)$$

The Dirac delta function is not square integrable either, but its Fourier transform can be determined easily:

$$\hat{\delta}(\omega) = \frac{1}{\sqrt{2\pi}}\langle \chi_\omega \mid \delta\rangle$$

$$= \frac{1}{\sqrt{2\pi}}\int_{-\infty}^{+\infty} e^{-j\omega t}\delta(t)\, dt$$

$$= \frac{1}{\sqrt{2\pi}} \tag{8.20}$$

The Dirac delta function evidently has equally strong frequency components for all possible frequencies. This answers the question that was raised in Equation 8.3. When that equation was first explored, we did not have the machinery necessary for finding the answer.

8.13   THE TRANSFER FUNCTION

The *transfer function* of a differential equation is the frequency response of the equation in response to a unit impulse. The simplest example is a first-order linear equation. The general first-order linear equation is

$$Dx(t) - zx(t) = f(t)$$

Taking the Fourier transforms on both sides gives the equation

$$\langle \chi_\omega \mid Dx \rangle - \langle \chi_\omega \mid zx \rangle = \langle \chi_\omega \mid f \rangle$$

which is valid, because the bracket is linear in its second component. The second term on the left-hand side is just z times the Fourier transform of x. According to Equation 8.15, the first term on the left-hand side is $j\omega \langle \chi_\omega \mid x \rangle$. Therefore, the equation is transformed into

$$j\omega \langle \chi_\omega \mid x \rangle - z \langle \chi_\omega \mid x \rangle = \langle \chi_\omega \mid f \rangle$$

This can be solved algebraically for the Fourier transform of x:

$$\hat{x}(\omega) = \frac{\hat{f}(\omega)}{j\omega - z}$$

This equation shows that $\hat{x}$ has a pole at $j\omega = z$. In any real-world system, the real part of z is negative, providing damping on the system. Thus, the denominator will never actually be zero for real values of ω. This equation can be used to solve for the original function x, but more frequently the interest is in plotting the frequency response of the system. For that purpose, it is ordinarily assumed that $\left| \hat{f}(\omega) \right| = 1$, a condition that is obtained by $f(t) = \sqrt{2\pi}\delta(t)$.

A more interesting example is the simple harmonic oscillator:

$$D^2 x - (z + \bar{z})Dx + |z|^2 x = f$$

Taking Fourier transforms on both sides of this equation gives

$$-\omega^2 \hat{x}(\omega) - (z + \bar{z})j\omega \hat{x}(\omega) + |z|^2 \hat{x}(\omega) = \hat{f}(\omega)$$

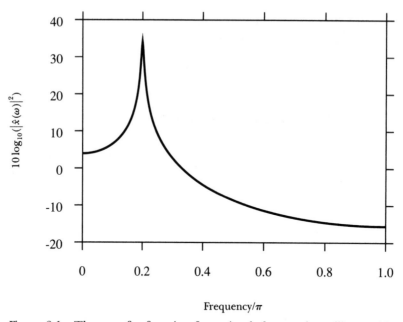

Figure 8.1   The transfer function for a simple harmonic oscillator with $z = -0.01 + j\,0.2\pi$. In this plot, the frequency axis is labeled so that 1 is the Nyquist frequency, π radians per data point. The vertical axis is in decibels, $10\log_{10}(|\hat{x}|^2)$.

The left-hand side can be factored, just like the original differential equation. Doing this and solving for $\hat{x}$ results in

$$\hat{x}(\omega) = \frac{\hat{f}(\omega)}{(j\omega - z)(j\omega - \bar{z})}$$

Figure 8.1 is a plot of $|\hat{x}(\omega)|^2$, assuming $|\hat{f}(\omega)|^2 = 1$ for a particular choice of z. The peak is at frequency $\omega = \pm 0.2\pi$. Only one peak appears in the figure, because only the positive frequency axis is plotted. Since only the magnitude of the transform is being plotted, the negative half of the axis is a perfect reflection of the positive half. This function is often called the "transfer function" of the differential equation.

8.14   CONVOLUTIONS

In Section 8.4.3, the Cauchy–Schwarz and Minkowski inequalities were stated and used to show that $\mathcal{L}_2$ is an *algebra*, meaning that functions in $\mathcal{L}_2$ can be added or multiplied together and the resulting function is still a member of $\mathcal{L}_2$.

There is another notion of multiplication of functions in $\mathcal{L}_2$ besides the usual (pointwise) multiplication everyone is comfortable with. The *convolution* of two functions in $\mathcal{L}_2$ is again a function in $\mathcal{L}_2$.

Since there are two notions of multiplication of functions in $\mathcal{L}_2$, it is sometimes necessary to explicitly state which is being used. *Pointwise* multiplication of two functions f and g is defined by

$$(fg)(t) = f(t)g(t)$$

The convolution of two functions is defined as follows:

Definition 8.10   Convolution: *For any two functions f and $g \in \mathcal{L}_2$, the convolution of f and g is defined by*

$$f * g(t) = \int_{-\infty}^{+\infty} f(u)g(t - u)\, du$$

It is not obvious that the convolution of two square integrable functions is always square integrable, but this is easily proved as part of the following:

Theorem 8.14   *For any three functions f, g, and $h \in \mathcal{L}_2$ and any complex constants a and b, the convolution operation is closed on $\mathcal{L}_2$:*

$$f * g \in \mathcal{L}_2 \tag{8.21}$$

Convolution is commutative:

$$f * g = g * f \tag{8.22}$$

Convolution distributes over addition and is linear:

$$f * (ag + bh) = af * g + bf * h \tag{8.23}$$

The Dirac delta function is the identity for convolution:

$$f * \delta = f \tag{8.24}$$

The Fourier transform of the convolution is the product of the Fourier transforms of the convolved functions:

$$\widehat{f * g}\,(\omega) = \sqrt{2\pi}\,\widehat{f}(\omega)\widehat{g}(\omega) \tag{8.25}$$

Proof   Equation 8.21 can be proved by using Equation 8.25. If Equation 8.25 is true, then by the Plancherel theorem, Theorem 8.4, both of the functions $\hat{f}(\omega) = \langle \chi_\omega \mid f \rangle / \sqrt{2\pi}$ and $\hat{g}$ are elements of $\mathcal{L}_2$, and therefore so is the product, $\hat{f}\hat{g}$, because of the Cauchy–Schwarz inequality, Theorem 8.2. Since $f * g$ is the inverse Fourier transform of $\hat{f}\hat{g}$, then, again by Theorem 8.4, $f * g \in \mathcal{L}_2$.

Equation 8.22 can be proved by a simple change of variables and is left for the reader to pursue.

Equation 8.23 is proved practically as soon as the necessary integral equations are written down.

Equation 8.24 is easily proved using the definition of the Dirac delta function.

Equation 8.25 can be proved as follows:

$$\widehat{f * g}\,(\omega) = \frac{1}{\sqrt{2\pi}} \langle \chi_\omega \mid f * g \rangle$$

$$= \frac{1}{\sqrt{2\pi}} \int_{-\infty}^{+\infty} \overline{\chi}_\omega(t) f * g(t)\,dt$$

$$= \frac{1}{\sqrt{2\pi}} \int_{-\infty}^{+\infty} \overline{\chi}_\omega(t) \int_{-\infty}^{+\infty} f(u)g(t - u)\,du$$

Interchanging the order of integration gives

$$= \frac{1}{\sqrt{2\pi}} \int_{-\infty}^{+\infty} f(u) \int_{-\infty}^{+\infty} \overline{\chi}_\omega(t)g(t - u)\,dt\,du$$

Making the substitution $v = t - u$ gives

$$= \frac{1}{\sqrt{2\pi}} \int_{-\infty}^{+\infty} f(u) \int_{-\infty}^{+\infty} \overline{\chi}_\omega(v + u)g(v)\,dv\,du$$

$$= \frac{1}{\sqrt{2\pi}} \int_{-\infty}^{+\infty} f(u) \int_{-\infty}^{+\infty} \overline{\chi}_\omega(v)\overline{\chi}_\omega(u)g(v)\,dv\,du$$

$$= \frac{1}{\sqrt{2\pi}} \int_{-\infty}^{+\infty} f(u)\overline{\chi}_\omega(u)\,du \int_{-\infty}^{+\infty} \overline{\chi}_\omega(v)g(v)\,dv$$

$$= \frac{1}{\sqrt{2\pi}} \langle \chi_\omega \mid f \rangle \langle \chi_\omega \mid g \rangle$$

$$= \sqrt{2\pi}\,\hat{f}(\omega)\hat{g}(\omega)$$

which proves the theorem.   ///

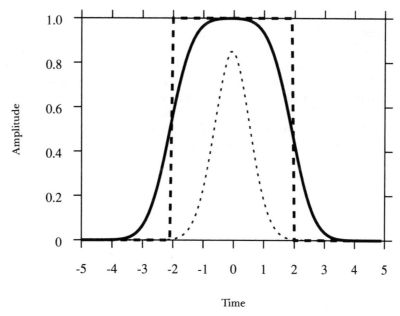

Figure 8.2 Convolution operation tends to smear out a function. In this example the original square pulse (dashed line) is convolved with a Gaussian distribution (dotted line), which gives the heavy solid line.

Convolutions are widely used in digital signal processing. Every linear, time-invariant system is described completely by its impulse response. Given the impulse response $\mathcal{F}(t)$ of such a system, its response to an arbitrary input $x(t)$ is $\mathcal{F} * x(t)$. This is explored thoroughly in Chapter 13. Equation 8.25 shows that the frequency response of this system is precisely $\hat{\mathcal{F}}(\omega)$.

Calculating the convolution is a computationally intensive task if the impulse response is long. In fact, for long impulse responses, the fastest way to calculate a convolution is by using the *fast Fourier transform* algorithm (see Chapter 12) and Equation 8.25. First, the transform of x is calculated; then, it is multiplied by the transform of $\mathcal{F}$, giving $\hat{\mathcal{F}}\hat{x}$. Then, according to Equation 8.25, the inverse transform is exactly $\mathcal{F} * x(t)/\sqrt{2\pi}$.

Convolution tends to "smear" a sharp-edged function. For example, consider the case of a Gaussian convolved with a square impulse: $\phi_\sigma * h_\tau$, where h_τ is defined by Equation 8.9. The convolution can be calculated as follows:

$$\phi_\sigma * h_\tau(t) = \int_{-\infty}^{+\infty} \phi_\sigma(u) h_\tau(t-u) \, du$$

$$= \int_{t-\tau}^{t+\tau} \phi_\sigma(u) \, du$$

This function will be close to 1 if the interval $[t - \tau, t + \tau]$ contains most of the central peak of the Gaussian distribution. It gradually trails off to zero as the interval moves away from the central peak. Figure 8.2 illustrates this process. The heavy dashed line is the original step function. The lighter dotted line is the original Gaussian distribution. The heavy solid line is the convolution of the step function and the Gaussian. The convolution retains the overall character of the original step function, but the sharp edges are smeared, rather like eroded hillsides. This property of convolutions can be quite useful for constructing functions with certain desired shapes.

Discrete Fourier Transforms

Fourier transforms, explained in Chapter 8, are useful for theoretical work and practical calculations. However, the continuous-time Fourier transform cannot be used directly for digital signal processing. The values of discrete-time signals are known only at the discrete sample times, and only finitely many such sample points can be used or known at any time. The discrete Fourier transform (DFT for short) must work within these restrictions, yet still provide knowledge of the frequency domain analogous to the information provided by the continuous-time, infinite-duration Fourier transform of Chapter 8.

The mathematics behind Fourier transforms, and discrete Fourier transforms in particular, is called *harmonic analysis*. Harmonic analysis is the study of functions defined on groups. The name for this branch of mathematics is derived from the very cases needed for signal processing. It is the study of the harmonic content of functions or signals. Harmonic analysis shows how every function defined on a group can be written in terms of a distinguished set of functions on the group, called its *characters*. In Chapter 8, the group was $\Re$, the real numbers, and the characters were the exponentials, $\exp(j\omega t)$. In all cases required for digital signal processing, the characters turn out to be exponentials.

This chapter presents the central ideas behind the discrete Fourier transform and details the most important cases, without getting involved in any proofs. Section 9.1 informally introduces the main concepts, just as Section 8.1 did for the continuous-time case. Section 9.2 explains the Fourier transform for the four cases most often required for signal processing. The striking similarities of these four cases are not accidental. Chapter 11 explains the fundamentals of harmonic analysis and explains how these four cases of the Fourier transform are all connected to each other and to the case of Chapter 8. Dirac's bracket notation makes the connections between the various cases much easier to see.

9.1 THE CENTRAL IDEAS

Chapter 8 explains the continuous-time, infinite-duration Fourier transform. The Fourier transform is calculated by integrating a known function from $-\infty$ to $+\infty$. In this chapter, four other cases are considered. One variation is discrete-time: the function is known only at discrete sample points, but for all time. The second variation retains the continuous time of Chapter 8, but the function is defined only on a given finite interval of time. The third variation combines discrete time and finite duration. The fourth variation is for two-dimensional signals, such as pictures, that contain $N \times M$ pixels.

9.1.1 Orthogonal Functions

How is the Fourier transform in each of these cases related to the other cases? How can a Fourier transform be defined consistently in such widely varying situations? What are the central ideas that unify all these cases?

The basic purpose of a Fourier transform is to express a function or signal in terms of its individual frequency components. Those "frequency components" are themselves functions, $\{\chi_\ell \mid \ell \in L\}$, indexed over some set L. The function of interest, f, can be written as a sum of these frequency components for some set of complex numbers $\{a_\ell\}$:

$$f = \frac{1}{\kappa} \sum_{\ell \in L} a_\ell \chi_\ell$$

The constant κ depends only on the underlying group, not on the function. It is these coefficients that are called the Fourier transform of f, frequently represented as

$$\hat{f}(\ell) = \frac{1}{\kappa} a_\ell$$

For the case covered in Chapter 8, there are so many of these frequency components that the sum must be replaced by an integral. The frequency components are

$$\chi_\omega(t) = e^{j\omega t}$$

and the original function can be expressed in terms of its Fourier transform according to the formula

$$f(t) = \frac{1}{\sqrt{2\pi}} \langle \overline{\hat{f}} \mid \chi_t \rangle = \frac{1}{\sqrt{2\pi}} \int_{-\infty}^{+\infty} \hat{f}(\omega) e^{j\omega t} \, d\omega$$

In all cases, the Fourier transform is a way of expressing the original function as a sum of the "frequency component" functions. These "frequency component functions" must satisfy four conditions:

1. They must relate to our usual notion of a frequency.
2. They must be mutually orthogonal in some sense, so that the transform is easily calculated.
3. Every function of interest must be expressible in terms of these "frequency components."
4. The Fourier transform coefficient $\hat{f}(\omega)$ should be proportional to the energy density at frequency ω.

In Chapter 8, the orthogonality condition was expressed by the formula Theorem 8.1:

$$\langle \chi_\omega \mid \chi_\mu \rangle = \kappa^2 \delta(\mu - \omega) \tag{9.1}$$

where $\kappa^2 = 2\pi$ and δ is the Dirac delta function. In the discrete cases, the Dirac delta function must be replaced by the *discrete delta function*, defined by

$$\delta(m) = \begin{cases} 1 & \text{if } m = 0 \\ 0 & \text{otherwise} \end{cases}$$

Otherwise the formula does not change, except that the interpretation of the bracket depends on the group, that is, the particulars of the case.

9.1.2 An Example

An explicit calculation of a simple case will help get these ideas across. Suppose Equation 9.1 holds for some chosen set of functions χ_ℓ with a finite index set L. Also, suppose f is a function that can be written in terms of these "frequency components" as

$$f = \frac{1}{\kappa} \sum_{\ell \in L} a_\ell \chi_\ell \tag{9.2}$$

Then the Fourier transform of f can be calculated directly from f as follows:

$$\hat{f}(m) = \frac{1}{\kappa} \langle \chi_m \mid f \rangle$$

$$= \frac{1}{\kappa} \langle \chi_m \mid \frac{1}{\kappa} \sum_{\ell \in L} a_\ell \chi_\ell \rangle$$

Because the bracket is linear, the sum can be brought outside:

$$= \frac{1}{\kappa^2} \sum_{\ell \in L} a_\ell \langle \chi_m \mid \chi_\ell \rangle$$

which, according to Equation 9.1, is

$$= \frac{1}{\kappa^2} \sum_{\ell \in L} a_\ell \kappa^2 \delta(\ell - m)$$

$$= a_m$$

Thus, as long as the frequency functions are orthogonal, the transform is unique and computable if it exists.

Many transforms used in physics and engineering are based on the central concept of a complete set of orthogonal functions. The orthogonality condition is expressed in Equation 9.1. The chosen set of orthogonal functions is *complete* if every function of interest can be expressed in terms of them, as in Equation 9.2, or more generally as an integral.

9.1.3   Enough Functions

But how can we be sure that every function of interest can be expressed using the frequency components? What are the right "frequency component" functions? It turns out that both questions are answered in the same breath by harmonic analysis. The "frequency components" are called the *characters* of the (commutative) group on which the functions are defined. These characters are both mutually orthogonal and sufficient to express every function as a sum of the characters. The study of these characters is taken up in Chapter 11. In that chapter, harmonic analysis is used to provide a unified view of all Fourier transforms. In this chapter, only the special cases of most interest to digital signal processing are stated.

9.1.4   Summary

The central idea, therefore, is to find a set of mutually orthogonal "frequency component" functions that are sufficient to represent all functions of interest. Of course, we would like all the different cases to be somehow related to each other; the key to that is choosing the right "frequency component" functions. There should be some notion of a convolution in each of these cases, and something like Theorem 8.14 on page 139 should hold, relating the transform of a convolution to the product of the transforms of each function. Moreover, the Parseval formula, Theorem 8.6, on page 122 is essential to a normal interpretation of a Fourier transform. Something similar must hold for all other cases also. Finally, the uncertainty relation and the minimum-uncertainty packet should have a counterpart in each case.

9.2 THE FOURIER TRANSFORM IN FOUR CASES

The Fourier transform acts on a class of functions defined on some domain, producing as its output a class of functions on some other domain. The case studied in Chapter 8 has $\Re$ as the original domain and $\hat{\Re}$ as the transform domain, where the notation $\hat{\Re}$ means the domain of frequencies. In general, the Fourier transform can be defined for any domain G that is an *Abelian group*. The domain of the transformed functions is $\hat{G}$, which is always related to the "frequencies" available for the original domain G. These notions will be made precise in Chapter 11. In this chapter, these issues are skirted in favor of an intuitive approach to understanding the various cases of the Fourier transform that are important in practice.

The domains studied in this chapter are the following:

1. $G = \mathcal{Z}/N\mathcal{Z}$, the group of integers modulo N, a fixed integer
2. $G = \mathcal{Z}$, the group of all integers
3. $G = \mathcal{Z}/N\mathcal{Z} \times \mathcal{Z}/M\mathcal{Z}$, a two-dimensional group representing a picture with $N \times M$ pixels
4. $G = \Re/\mathcal{Z}$, the group of real numbers modulo 1, which is essentially the same as $G = S^1$, the unit circle. This is the Fourier transform on a fixed interval, say $[0, 1]$ on the real line.

In this chapter, these four cases are studied in relative isolation; how they are related will be examined somewhat in Section 10.1. In Chapter 11, the general theory is developed, and there the underlying unity of all these cases becomes evident.

9.2.1 One Dimension, N Points: $G = \mathcal{Z}/N\mathcal{Z}$

The simplest case is $G = \mathcal{Z}/N\mathcal{Z}$, the group of integers modulo N. This group is usually represented by the integers $0, 1, 2, \ldots, N - 1$. It is convenient here and elsewhere to define a new exponential function,

$$\psi_a(t) = e^{j2\pi at}$$

This is purely a matter of convenience, since clearly it could also be written as

$$\psi_a(t) = \chi_{2\pi a}(t)$$

using the previous definition of χ_x :

$$\chi_x(t) = e^{jxt}$$

The formulas are easier to read with the new definition. This does introduce one more piece of notation to remember, but I think the trade-off is worthwhile in this case.

In Chapter 8, the bracket notation was introduced. This bracket notation extends to all cases of the Fourier transform. For each Abelian group G, there is a notion of integration on the group, and the bracket can be defined by

$$\langle f \mid g \rangle_G = \int_G \overline{f}(t)g(t)\,dt$$

Chapter 11 explains how the notion of integration can be extended to functions on Abelian groups. For the purposes of this chapter, the definition of the bracket in each case is simply stated. In this case the bracket reduces to a summation:

$$\langle f \mid g \rangle_{\mathbb{Z}/N\mathbb{Z}} = \sum_{k=0}^{N-1} \overline{f}(k)g(k)$$

In fact, for all discrete groups, integration reduces to a simple summation such as this.

Theorem 9.1   Fourier Transform on $\mathbb{Z}/N\mathbb{Z}$: *For any integer $N > 0$ and any function f defined on the group $G = \mathbb{Z}/N\mathbb{Z}$, the Fourier transform of f is defined by*

$$\hat{f}(a) = \frac{1}{\sqrt{N}}\langle \psi_{a/N} \mid f \rangle_G$$

$$= \frac{1}{\sqrt{N}}\sum_{k=0}^{N-1} f(k)\overline{\psi}_{a/N}(k) \qquad \text{for any } a \in \mathbb{Z}/N\mathbb{Z}$$

For any function $\hat{f}$ defined on $\mathbb{Z}/N\mathbb{Z}$, the inverse Fourier transform is defined by

$$f(g) = \frac{1}{\sqrt{N}}\langle \overline{\psi}_{g/N} \mid \hat{f} \rangle_{\hat{G}}$$

$$= \frac{1}{\sqrt{N}}\sum_{a=0}^{N-1} \hat{f}(a)\psi_{a/N}(g) \qquad \text{for any } g \in \mathbb{Z}/N\mathbb{Z}$$

The inverse Fourier transform of the Fourier transform of any function on $\mathbb{Z}/N\mathbb{Z}$ is equal to the original function.

The Fourier transform of the inverse Fourier transform of any function on $\mathbb{Z}/N\mathbb{Z}$ is equal to the original function.

Notice that the statement and formulation of this theorem are almost identical to those of Theorem 8.4. This is no accident. There are three differences:

1. The scale factor in this case is $1/\sqrt{N}$ instead of $1/\sqrt{2\pi}$.
2. No mention of "equality almost everywhere" is needed, because the points are discrete. The value of the function at every point is important.
3. Because the group is finite, every function is automatically square integrable, so there is no restriction of that type required.

This summarizes all the differences to be found between any two cases of the Fourier transform. The bracket notation makes the formulas in all cases nearly identical.

For $G = \mathbb{Z}/N\mathbb{Z}$, there are only N distinct functions $\psi_{a/N}$, for $0 \le a < N$. These functions are orthogonal.

Theorem 9.2   *Let N be an integer larger than 1. Then, for any two integers $0 \le a < N$ and $0 \le b < N$, the following formula holds:*

$$\langle \psi_{a/N} \mid \psi_{b/N} \rangle_G = N\delta(b - a)$$

where δ is the delta function

$$\delta(\ell) = \begin{cases} 1 & \text{if } \ell = 0 \\ 0 & \text{otherwise} \end{cases}$$

Compare the statement of this theorem with theorem 8.1. The only differences are that $\sqrt{2\pi}$ is replaced by N, that the delta function is now the discrete delta function, and that the bracket is a sum instead of an integral.

Proof: The proof of this formula is taken in two cases. First, if $b = a$, then

$$\overline{\psi}_{a/N}(k)\psi_{b/N}(k) = 1 \qquad \text{for all } k$$

and there are N terms in the sum, so the case $b = a$ is proven.

Now assume that $b \neq a$. Then we can write the equation as

$$\langle \psi_{a/N} \mid \psi_{b/N} \rangle_G = \sum_{k=0}^{N-1} \overline{\psi}_{a/N}(k)\psi_{b/N}(k)$$

$$= \sum_{k=0}^{N-1} e^{j2\pi(b-a)k/N}$$

A change of variables, $\ell = k - m$, gives

$$= \sum_{\ell=0}^{N-1} e^{j2\pi(b-a)(\ell+m)/N}$$

which is the same, because it still sums all the Nth roots of unity.

$$= \sum_{\ell=0}^{N-1} e^{j2\pi(b-a)\ell/N} e^{j2\pi(b-a)m/N}$$

$$= e^{j2\pi(b-a)m/N} \sum_{\ell=0}^{N-1} \overline{\psi}_{a/N}(\ell)\psi_{b/N}(\ell)$$

$$= e^{j2\pi(b-a)m/N} \langle \psi_{a/N} \mid \psi_{b/N} \rangle_G$$

In other words, the original bracket is equal to itself times the exponential out in front of this last expression. Since $b \neq a$, there is an integer m for which the exponential is not 1, proving that the original sum must be 0.   ///

9.2.2   One Dimension, Countably Many Points: $G = \mathcal{Z}$

In this case, the group $G = \mathcal{Z}$ is infinite, and questions about the convergence of infinite sums arise. We will mostly sidestep these questions, but it is important to realize that the discrete delta function must, for this reason, give way to the Dirac delta function once more. This case is sort of a mix of the two cases $G = \mathfrak{R}$ and $G = \mathcal{Z}/N\mathcal{Z}$. The bracket, as in the previous case, reduces to a sum:

$$\langle f \mid g \rangle_{\mathcal{Z}} = \sum_{k=-\infty}^{+\infty} \overline{f}(k)g(k)$$

In this theorem, $\mathcal{L}_2(\mathcal{Z})$ stands for the set of all square summable sequences (or functions, it is the same notion). These sequences are double-ended, going from $-\infty$ to $+\infty$. The sequence a_k is square summable if

$$\langle a \mid a \rangle_{\mathcal{Z}} = \sum_{k=-\infty}^{+\infty} |a_k|^2$$

exists and is finite. This is very similar to the requirement in Chapter 8 that the functions be square integrable. The only difference is that in this case, the functions are defined only at integer values, so the integration is replaced by a sum. It turns out that the frequencies available on this group naturally map to the group $\Re/Z$ of the reals modulo 1. This group can be represented by any interval of unit length, for example $[0, 1)$, or $[-1/2, 1/2)$. In both cases, the square brace is used if the corresponding endpoint is to be included in the set, the round brace if it is not. The bracket in this case is defined by

$$\langle f \mid g \rangle_{\Re/Z} = \int_0^1 \overline{f}(t) g(t) \, dt$$

The notation $\mathcal{L}_2(\Re/Z)$ stands for the set of all square integrable functions on $\Re/Z$. The Fourier transform in this case is as follows.

Theorem 9.3   *For any sequence $f \in \mathcal{L}_2(Z)$, the Fourier transform,*

$$\hat{f}(\theta) = \langle \psi_\theta \mid f \rangle_Z$$

$$= \sum_{k=-\infty}^{+\infty} f(k) \overline{\psi}_\theta(k)$$

exists and is a member of $\mathcal{L}_2(\Re/Z)$.
    For any function $\hat{f} \in \mathcal{L}_2(\Re/Z)$, the inverse Fourier transform,

$$f(m) = \langle \overline{\psi}_m \mid \hat{f} \rangle_{\Re/Z}$$

$$= \int_0^1 \hat{f}(\theta) \psi_m(\theta) \, d\theta$$

exists and is a member of $\mathcal{L}_2(Z)$.
    The inverse Fourier transform of the Fourier transform of any function in $\mathcal{L}_2(Z)$ is equal to the original function.
    The Fourier transform of the inverse Fourier transform of any function in $\mathcal{L}_2(\Re/Z)$ is equal to the original function almost everywhere.

In this case, it is difficult to prove directly that the functions ψ_θ are mutually orthogonal, because the infinite sum is

$$\langle \psi_\theta \mid \psi_\phi \rangle_Z = \sum_{k=-\infty}^{+\infty} \overline{\psi}_\theta(k) \psi_\phi(k)$$

This sum cannot be evaluated directly. In fact, if $\theta = \phi$, each term in the sum is 1, so it diverges to infinity.

However, the functions used for the inverse Fourier transform in this case can be shown to be mutually orthogonal by direct calculation, because the integral is over a finite interval:

$$\langle \psi_m \mid \psi_k \rangle_{\Re/Z} = \int_0^1 \overline{\psi}_m(z)\psi_k(z)\,dz$$

$$= \int_0^1 e^{j2\pi(k-m)z}\,dz$$

$$= \begin{cases} 1 & \text{if } k = m \\ 0 & \text{otherwise} \end{cases}$$

because k and m are integers.

9.2.3 Finite Duration: $G = \Re/Z$

This is really just the inverse of the case $G = Z$, but it is stated here to emphasize the duality. The only difference between Theorem 9.4 in this section and Theorem 9.3 in the previous section is the positions where the complex conjugates are used.

Theorem 9.4 *For any function $f \in \mathcal{L}_2(\Re/Z)$ the Fourier transform*

$$\hat{f}(m) = \langle \psi_m \mid f \rangle_{\Re/Z}$$

$$= \int_0^1 f(x)\overline{\psi}_m(x)\,dx$$

is defined and is a member of $\mathcal{L}_2(Z)$.

For any sequence $\hat{f} \in \mathcal{L}_2(Z)$, the inverse Fourier transform,

$$f(x) = \langle \psi_x \mid \hat{f} \rangle_Z$$

$$= \sum_{k=-\infty}^{+\infty} \hat{f}(k)\overline{\psi}_x(k)$$

exists and is a member of $\mathcal{L}_2(\Re/Z)$.

The inverse Fourier transform of the Fourier transform of any function in $\mathcal{L}_2(\Re/Z)$ is equal to the original function almost everywhere.

The Fourier transform of the inverse Fourier transform of any function in $\mathcal{L}_2(Z)$ is equal to the original function.

9.2.4 Two Dimensions, $N \times M$: $G = \mathbb{Z}/N\mathbb{Z} \times \mathbb{Z}/M\mathbb{Z}$

Two-dimensional Fourier transforms are commonly needed in picture processing. There is no essential difference between the two-dimensional case and the one-dimensional case. The group $G = \mathbb{Z}/N\mathbb{Z} \times \mathbb{Z}/M\mathbb{Z}$ is exactly what is required for a two-dimensional transform with N points in one direction and M points in the other. The elements of this group are written as (g, h), where $g \in \mathbb{Z}/N\mathbb{Z}$ and $h \in \mathbb{Z}/M\mathbb{Z}$.

As for other discrete groups, integration reduces to summation. In this case, the bracket is

$$\langle f \mid g \rangle_{\mathbb{Z}/N\mathbb{Z} \times \mathbb{Z}/M\mathbb{Z}} = \sum_{l=0}^{N-1} \sum_{k=0}^{M-1} \overline{f(l,k)} g(l,k)$$

As for all finite groups, every function is square integrable, because integration is defined by a finite summation.

Since the group is now "two-dimensional," it is clear that the exponentials used for the other cases must be generalized somewhat. It turns out that the required generalization is quite simple. The functions needed in this case are, in a sense, products of the exponentials used before. Specifically, let f be a function on $\mathbb{Z}/N\mathbb{Z}$ and let g be a function defined on $\mathbb{Z}/M\mathbb{Z}$. Then the "product function" $f \times g$ defined on $\mathbb{Z}/N\mathbb{Z} \times \mathbb{Z}/M\mathbb{Z}$ is the function defined by

$$(f \times g)(l, k) = f(l)g(k)$$

For example, the "product" $\psi_{a/N} \times \psi_{b/M}$ is defined by

$$(\psi_{a/N} \times \psi_{b/M})(l, k) = \psi_{a/N}(l)\psi_{b/M}(k)$$

$$= e^{j2\pi al/N} e^{j2\pi bk/M}$$

$$= e^{j2\pi(alM + bkN)/NM}$$

Theorem 9.5 *For any function f defined on $\mathbb{Z}/N\mathbb{Z} \times \mathbb{Z}/M\mathbb{Z}$, the Fourier transform is defined by*

$$\hat{f}(a, b) = \frac{1}{\sqrt{NM}} \langle \psi_{a/N} \times \psi_{b/M} \mid f \rangle_{\mathbb{Z}/N\mathbb{Z} \times \mathbb{Z}/M\mathbb{Z}}$$

$$= \frac{1}{\sqrt{NM}} \sum_{l=0}^{N-1} \sum_{k=0}^{M-1} \overline{\psi}_{a/N}(l)\overline{\psi}_{b/M}(k) f(l, k)$$

For any function $\hat{f}$ defined on $\mathbb{Z}/N\mathbb{Z} \times \mathbb{Z}/M\mathbb{Z}$, the inverse Fourier transform is defined by

$$
\begin{aligned}
f(q,r) &= \frac{1}{\sqrt{NM}} \langle \overline{\psi}_{q/N} \times \overline{\psi}_{r/M} \mid \hat{f} \rangle_{\mathbb{Z}/N\mathbb{Z} \times \mathbb{Z}/M\mathbb{Z}} \\
&= \frac{1}{\sqrt{NM}} \sum_{a=0}^{N-1} \sum_{b=0}^{M-1} \psi_{q/N}(a)\psi_{r/M}(b)\hat{f}(a,b)
\end{aligned}
$$

The inverse Fourier transform of the Fourier transform of any function is equal to the original function.

The Fourier transform of the inverse Fourier transform of any function is equal to the original function.

This case is similar to Theorem 9.1, because in both cases there are only finitely many points. This fact removes all questions of convergence of the integrals or sums.

CHAPTER 10

Windowing the Data

Sometimes an experiment yields a very limited amount of data, which must be used carefully to get the maximum amount of information. For example, a very short impulse response might be recorded with a high-speed A/D converter and still yield only a few data points. In other situations, the problem is just the opposite — there is so much data that it cannot, or should not, be used all at once. For example, in speech processing, the digitized speech waveform is analyzed in short segments, so that the time evolution of the waveform can be observed. In both cases, the data must be handled with care. It turns out that the data should seldom be used as originally obtained. Usually a better result is obtained if the data points are tapered off toward the edges of the data window. This process is called *windowing* the data. The window shape has a significant impact on the final results. The effects of various windowing options are explored in this chapter. This chapter is essential reading for Part III.

RESTRICTIONS TO FINITE TIME

Theorem 11.8 of Chapter 11 covers all cases of the Fourier transform simultaneously. Of course, in digital signal processing, the only cases that can be used directly are those that have finitely many group elements. Only a finite number of data points can be used, or even obtained, in any finite duration of time. Often, however, the theory has been worked out using the group $G = \Re$ or maybe $G = S^1$, and the question arises: What information does the finite Fourier transform give about what the infinite transform would have been if it could have been calculated?

Suppose a function f defined on $\Re$ is known only for a finite stretch of time, say $[0, 1]$. Can the Fourier transform on this interval provide any information about the Fourier transform of f on $\Re$? In general, the answer is no. For example, the function could be constant, perhaps 0, on the interval and still have an essentially arbitrary Fourier transform when viewed as a function on $\Re$.

However, there are two cases in which progress can be made. First, if the function is zero at all points outside the measurement interval, the Fourier transform on that interval certainly carries all the required information.

Second, suppose the function is changing over time, perhaps for an indefinite period of time. Progress is possible in this case if the goal is to obtain a picture of the evolution of this function in time. In this case, the function can be windowed into a finite interval and the transform calculated in that window.

10.1.1   Restriction to an Interval

In the first case, assuming the function is zero outside of some interval, it is enough to consider only the case of the interval $[0, 1]$, because all other intervals can be transformed into this one by scaling and translation. Then the Fourier transform of f is

$$\hat{f}(\omega) = \frac{1}{\sqrt{2\pi}} \int_{-\infty}^{+\infty} f(t) e^{-j\omega t} \, dt = \frac{1}{\sqrt{2\pi}} \int_{0}^{1} f(t) e^{-j\omega t} \, dt$$

because f is zero outside of this interval. This is almost the same as the case $G = \Re / \mathcal{Z}$ in Theorem 9.4, but there are two differences: First, the scale is wrong. Second, and more significant, when $G = \Re / \mathcal{Z}$, the only frequencies required are the ones with $\omega = 2\pi k$ for integers $k \in \mathcal{Z}$. However, at these frequencies the two transforms agree except for a scale factor.

Even though the Fourier transform values at the frequencies $2\pi k$ contain all the information about the function, in this case they cannot be used to reconstruct the function without the ancillary information that it is zero outside of the unit interval $[0, 1]$. This is because all these frequencies have periods that are submultiples of 1. That means that the function reconstructed from only these frequencies will repeat itself forever with period 1. However, on the unit interval the reconstructed function agrees exactly with the original function. When the whole function is reconstructed using all frequencies, the in-between frequencies do not change the shape of the function on the interval but only force it to zero outside the interval.

10.1.2   Padding the Data

"Padding" a data set before taking the Fourier transform is a common practice in signal processing. Usually this term means simply extending a vector of data by adding zeros. Then, when the Fourier transform is calculated, more frequencies are available. Certainly this process cannot add information to the data set. If the signal is known to be zero, or imagined to be zero outside of the original data set, then such an extension may be sensible. However, it is only a way of interpolating between data points in the frequency domain. No new information can be extracted by adding arbitrary data points to the original information. Keep this in mind when evaluating the spectra in various publications. If padding was used, the resulting spectrum appears to contain more information than it really does. The result may be misleading.

10.2 WINDOWING

In the second case, where the primary interest is the time evolution of the function, some kind of windowing must be done in order to localize the function in time before the transform is taken. After windowing, this case is the same as the first one. The only question is what window should be used. Typically some time interval T, at which the Fourier transforms are to be taken, is determined. Then the function f is translated in time by the formula

$$f_{kT}(t) = f(t - kT)$$

and the window h is applied centered on time 0:

$$g_k(t) = h(t)f_{kT}(t) = h(t)f(t - kT)$$

Then the Fourier transform is taken:

$$\widehat{g_k}(\omega) = \widehat{h f_{kT}}(\omega)$$

which, by Equation 8.25, page 139 is

$$\widehat{g_k}(\omega) = \sqrt{2\pi}\,\widehat{h} * \widehat{f_{kT}}(\omega)$$

This formula reminds us that the choice of the window function determines not only the time-domain piece of the function that is used, but also its frequency-domain interpretation. According to Section 8.11, the minimum-uncertainty wave packet is a Gaussian-modulated exponential. In fact, that is the only functional form that can give the minimal uncertainty product. In this sense, the optimal choice of the window function is a Gaussian, $h = \phi_\sigma$, where σ is chosen to give the desired restriction in time. However, there are at least two problems with this choice. First, it is an infinitely long window, and so cannot be used directly. Second, it is not a partition of unity.

10.2.1 Three Window Functions

Three different window functions are explored in this chapter. They are the Gaussian window, the cosine-squared window, and the super-Gaussian window of order 6. The actual functions are defined as follows. The cosine-squared window is

$$\Lambda_T(t) = \begin{cases} \cos^2(\pi t/2T) & \text{for } |t| \leq T \\ 0 & \text{otherwise} \end{cases}$$

where T is the time spacing used between windows. The Gaussian window is

$$\Gamma_{T,\sigma}(t) = \begin{cases} \exp\left(\dfrac{-t^2}{2\sigma^2}\right) & \text{for } |t| \leq T \\ 0 & \text{otherwise} \end{cases}$$

where σ is the chosen standard deviation. The super-Gaussian window is defined by

$$\Omega_{T,\nu,\kappa}(t) = \begin{cases} \exp\left(\dfrac{-|t|^\nu}{\kappa}\right) & \text{for } |t| \leq T \\ 0 & \text{otherwise} \end{cases}$$

where ν is usually an integer, called the order of the distribution, and κ is chosen to give the desired standard deviation. Figure 10.1 compares these three window functions, each 100 points long, each with a standard deviation of 14.21 (after squaring the window function). The standard deviation of the cosine-squared window is set by its length. The other two windows were adjusted to have the same standard deviation numerically. Notice that this means that for the Gaussian window, σ is approximately $14.21\sqrt{2}$ (see section 8.11), but its actual value is chosen so that the calculated standard deviation on the 100 discrete points of the window is exactly 14.21. The super-Gaussian plotted in Figure 10.1 is order 6.

10.2.2   Uncertainty Product for Cosine-Squared Window

The cosine-squared window has the distinct advantage of being a partition of unity, in the sense that when it is translated by T and added to itself, the overlap adds to 1, as illustrated in Figure 10.2. This is exactly the sort of behavior required in such applications as filtering by repeated applications of a Fourier transform and its inverse. But how close is it to the optimal (in the sense of minimal uncertainty) Gaussian window? According to Theorem 8.11, the minimal product is

$$\Delta\omega\Delta t \geq \frac{1}{2}$$

To calculate this for the cosine-squared window, each of the values $\Delta\omega$ and Δt must be calculated.

The definition of Δt is

$$\Delta t^2 = \left\langle t^2 - \langle t \rangle^2 \right\rangle_{\Lambda_T} \tag{10.1}$$

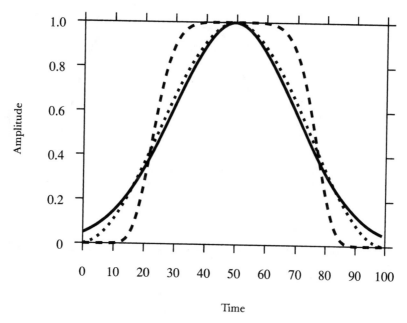

Figure 10.1   This figure compares three window functions. The solid line is the Gaussian window, $\Gamma_{100,\sigma}$; the dotted line is the cosine-squared window, Λ_{100}; and the dashed line is the super-Gaussian of order 6, $\Omega_{100,6,\kappa}$. The calculated standard deviation for these 100-point-long discrete windows is 14.21 data points in all three cases.

but since $\langle t \rangle = 0$, this reduces to

$$= \langle t^2 \rangle_{\Lambda_T}$$

$$= \langle \Lambda_T \mid t^2 \Lambda_T \rangle / \langle \Lambda_T \mid \Lambda_T \rangle \tag{10.2}$$

It is possible to calculate $\Delta\omega$ by using the same formula on the transformed window. However, it is easier to calculate $\Delta\omega$ as was done in the proof of Theorem 8.11, Equation 8.15:

$$\Delta\omega^2 = \langle -D^2 \rangle_{\Lambda_T}$$

$$= \langle \Lambda_T \mid -D^2 \Lambda_T \rangle / \langle \Lambda_T \mid \Lambda_T \rangle$$

and, since jD is a Hermitian operator, this can be written as

$$= \langle jD\Lambda_T \mid jD\Lambda_T \rangle / \langle \Lambda_T \mid \Lambda_T \rangle \tag{10.3}$$

The first step is to calculate $\langle \Lambda_T \mid \Lambda_T \rangle$. This and all other calculations are most

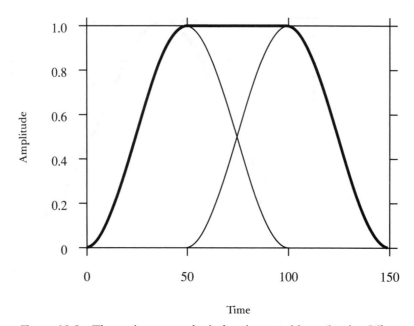

Figure 10.2   The cosine-squared window is a partition of unity. When one window is shifted by half its length relative to another, and the two are added, the overlapping part adds to 1. This is exactly what is needed for digital filtering using the FFT.

conveniently done by using $T = \pi/2$, in which case

$$\Lambda(t) = \Lambda_{\pi/2}(t) = \begin{cases} \cos^2(t) & \text{if } |t| \leq \pi/2 \\ 0 & \text{otherwise} \end{cases}$$

where the subscript has been dropped for convenience. Afterwards, the general results can be obtained by scaling. Using this notation, we can calculate

$$\langle \Lambda \mid \Lambda \rangle = \int_{-\infty}^{+\infty} \Lambda^2(t)\, dt$$

$$= \int_{-\pi/2}^{+\pi/2} \cos^4(t)\, dt$$

$$= \frac{3\pi}{8} \tag{10.4}$$

Equation 10.3 is actually easier to calculate than Equation 10.2, although it requires calculating the derivative,

$$D\Lambda(t) = \begin{cases} -2\cos(t)\sin(t) & \text{if } |t| \leq \pi/2 \\ 0 & \text{otherwise} \end{cases}$$

which, when used in the numerator of Equation 10.3, gives

$$\langle jD\Lambda \mid jD\Lambda \rangle = \int_{-\pi/2}^{+\pi/2} 4\cos^2(t)\sin^2(t)\,dt$$

$$= \frac{\pi}{8}$$

Combining this result with Equation 10.4 gives

$$\Delta\omega^2 = \frac{1}{3}$$

in the special case $T = \pi/2$. In the general case, this must be scaled as follows:

$$\Delta\omega^2 = \frac{1}{3}\left(\frac{\pi}{2T}\right)^2$$

which gives, finally,

$$\Delta\omega = \frac{\pi}{2\sqrt{3}T} \tag{10.5}$$

Now, to calculate Δt from Equation 10.2, the numerator is

$$\langle \Lambda \mid t^2\Lambda \rangle = \int_{-\pi/2}^{+\pi/2} t^2 \cos^4(t)\,dt$$

which, after one integration by parts, reduces to

$$= \frac{3\pi^3}{32} - 2\int_{-\pi/2}^{+\pi/2}\left[\frac{3t^2}{8} + \frac{t\sin(2t)}{4} + \frac{t\sin(4t)}{32}\right]dt$$

Each of these integrals is in the standard tables:

$$\langle \Lambda \mid t^2\Lambda \rangle = \frac{\pi^3}{32}$$

Combining this with Equation 10.4 gives

$$\Delta t^2 = \frac{\pi^2}{12}$$

in the special case $T = \pi/2$, which becomes

$$\Delta t^2 = \left(\frac{2T}{\pi}\right)^2 \frac{\pi^2}{12}$$

in the general case. Taking the square root gives

$$\Delta t = \frac{T}{\sqrt{3}} \tag{10.6}$$

Combining Equations 10.6 and 10.5 gives

$$\Delta\omega\Delta t = \frac{\pi}{6} \approx 0.5236 \tag{10.7}$$

which is barely more than the minimum uncertainty of 0.5 obtained by a Gaussian window. Thus, the cosine-squared window has a lot in its favor:

1. It is easy to calculate.
2. It provides a naturally finite window.
3. It is a partition of unity with a 50 percent overlap.
4. It has close to the theoretically optimum uncertainty product of $\frac{1}{2}$.

10.3   UNCERTAINTY PRODUCTS FOR FINITE WINDOWS

Of course, in practice the windows used always have finitely many points, so let's compare the truncated Gaussian and super-Gaussian windows with a cosine-squared window of the same number of points and same standard deviation in time. The cosine-squared window is completely determined by the number of points. The points are placed under the cosine function, so the end points of the window are not zero. The window values are determined by

$$\Lambda_N(k) = \sin^2\left(\frac{\pi}{N}(k + 0.5)\right)$$

where k runs from 0 through $N - 1$. The solid line in Figure 10.3 is the 10-point cosine-squared window, and the dashed line is the 9-point cosine-squared window. Both windows are partitions of unity when shifted by 5 points.

Figures 10.4 and 10.5 show the magnitude of the Fourier transform of the three 100-point windows plotted in Figure 10.1. The solid line in Figure 10.4 is the transformed Gaussian, and the dotted line is the transformed cosine-squared window. Figure 10.5 is the transform of the super-Gaussian window, which is the dashed line in Figure 10.1. In all cases, the plots are defined by

$$y = 10\log_{10}\left(|\hat{h}(\pi x)|^2\right)$$

so are in a decibel scale. These transformed windows are used to calculate $\Delta\omega$ in each case.

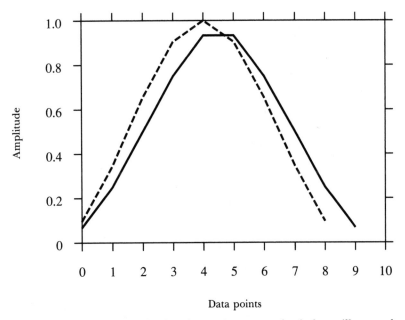

Figure 10.3 The 9- and 10-point cosine-squared windows illustrated here demonstrate some fine points involved in programming these and other window functions.

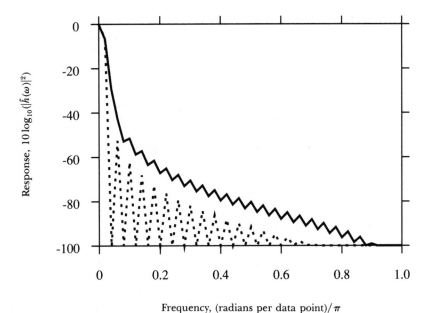

Figure 10.4 The magnitudes of the Fourier transforms of the 100-point Gaussian and cosine-squared windows are plotted. The dotted line is for the cosine-squared window, and the solid line is for the Gaussian window.

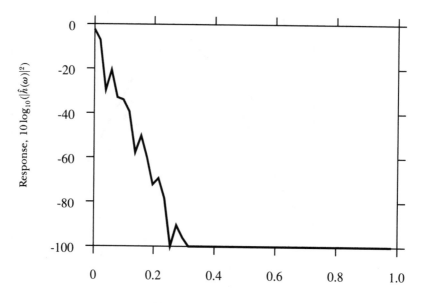

Figure 10.5   This is the magnitude transform of the 100-point super-Gaussian window.

The uncertainty products in each case are as follows:

type	length	Δt	$\Delta \omega$	$\Delta t \Delta \omega$
Gaussian	100	14.21	0.03496	0.497
Cosine-squared	100	14.21	0.03604	0.512
Super-Gaussian	100	14.21	0.04855	0.690

The truncated Gaussian is slightly better than the cosine-squared window in terms of the uncertainty product. The super-Gaussian window cannot be recommended on the basis of its uncertainty product. However, this is somewhat unfair for the super-Gaussian window. In Figure 10.1, all the windows have the same standard deviation in time. For the super-Gaussian, this means that quite a few points near the edges of the window are essentially zero. In practice, the standard deviation in time of the super-Gaussian window can be enlarged, in which case the corresponding standard deviation in frequency is lowered.

Notice that the uncertainty product for the truncated Gaussian is actually below the minimum uncertainty product attainable according to Theorem 8.11. There is no contradiction, because the theorem was based on functions defined on $\Re$ for all time, while here the windows are only 100 points long. Small differences like this must be expected. Major surprises, however, are not in the offing.

For some purposes, the deep nulls in the spectrum of the cosine-squared window may present a problem. For example, an echo reveals itself in the frequency domain by a series of nulls. If analysis of such echoes is important for

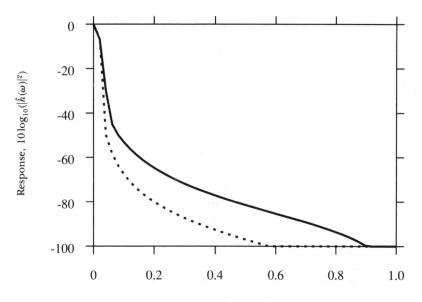

Figure 10.6   This figure compares the transforms of the cosine-squared and Gaussian windows of length 99, similar to the windows plotted in Figure 10.1 but one point shorter. The odd number of points eliminates the nulls. The solid line is for the Gaussian window, and the dotted line is for the cosine-squared window.

your work, this window may not be desirable. The truncated Gaussian window of the same length is much better in this respect. However, as shown in Figure 10.6, both of these windows look even better when 99 points are used instead of 100. The odd number of points in these windows eliminates the deep nulls apparent in the transforms of the windows of length 100. Using an odd number of points in the super-Gaussian window makes essentially no difference.

Where a series of overlapping windows is used to analyze a waveform in short pieces, the cosine-squared window is ideal. It is a partition of unity and has nearly the minimum uncertainty product. In other cases, there may be some preference for the truncated Gaussian or some similar window shape. However, in a practical sense, it is doubtful that these small differences would have any significant impact.

Whatever window you choose, make sure you understand its impact on your calculations. Any window function, rectangular or otherwise, changes the waveform you are trying to analyze.

10.4   PRACTICAL WINDOW COMPARISONS

What is the practical impact of these different windowing options? Why not just use the rectangular window? These questions are answered in this section by trying the various windows on two different waveforms: the sum of two sinusoids, and the impulse response of a system with two resonant frequencies (a four-pole filter).

10.4.1   Sum of Two Sines

First, Figure 10.7 is the sum of two equal-amplitude sinusoids; one with frequency 0.0933π radians per data point and the other with frequency 0.1333π radians per data point. The frequencies are chosen to be incommensurate with the window length and fairly close together, so we can test for the frequency resolution capabilities of the various windows.

Figure 10.8 shows the three different window functions used for this example. The cosine-squared and Gaussian windows are the same ones plotted in Figure 10.1, but the super-Gaussian now has the standard deviation of 38, instead of the standard deviation of 28.36 for the other two windows.

Using the right window can make a critical difference as shown by Figures 10.9 through 10.12. These figures all show the magnitude of the Fourier transform of the waveform in Figure 10.7, but with four different window functions. Figure 10.9 is for the rectangular window (no window function applied); Figure 10.10 is for the Gaussian window; Figure 10.11 is for the super-Gaussian window; and Figure 10.12 is for the cosine-squared window. All these transforms have been normalized to have unit energy (i.e. they sum to 1).

All four of these window choices are adequate to discriminate the two frequencies present. However, the differences are dramatic at "out-of-band"

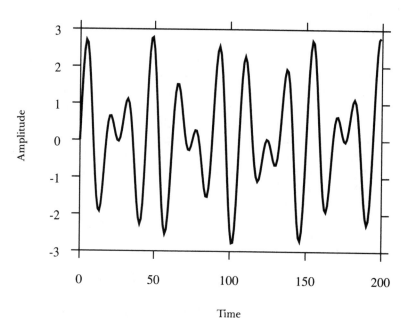

Figure 10.7   The sum of two sinusoids.

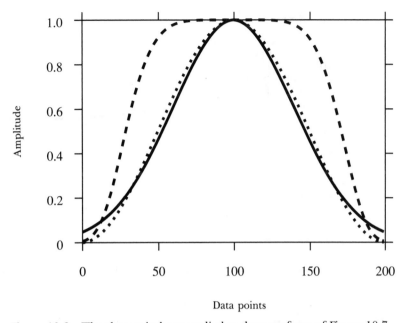

Figure 10.8 The three windows applied to the waveform of Figure 10.7. As in Figure 10.1, the solid line represents the Gaussian window, the dotted line the cosine-squared window, and the dashed line the super-Gaussian window.

frequencies. The rectangular window (Figure 10.9) is the worst, giving a very high response at frequencies that are simply not present in the original waveform. It shows a 0-frequency component of about −27 dB and a Nyquist component of about −45 dB. The Gaussian window (Figure 10.10) is much better in this respect, having a value of −53 dB at 0 and −65 dB at the Nyquist frequency. Notice, however, that the two frequencies are not quite as well separated. The super-Gaussian (Figure 10.11) does remarkably better than the Gaussian at both separating the individual frequencies and lowering the out-of-band response. In this case, the response is about −75 dB at 0 and about −90 dB at the Nyquist frequency. However, the "jaggies" in the central peak may be a problem in some cases. The cosine-squared window (Figure 10.12) is by far the best. It separates the two peaks nearly as well as the super-Gaussian and has a response of −70 dB at 0 and far below −100 dB at the Nyquist frequency.

10.4.2 Impulse Response

The second example is for the impulse response of the combination of two simple harmonic oscillators, the output of one serving as the input of the other. The location of the poles of this filter are $-0.01 \pm j\, 0.0933\pi$ and $-0.01 \pm j\, 0.1333\pi$. Thus, the resonant frequencies are the same as the frequencies of

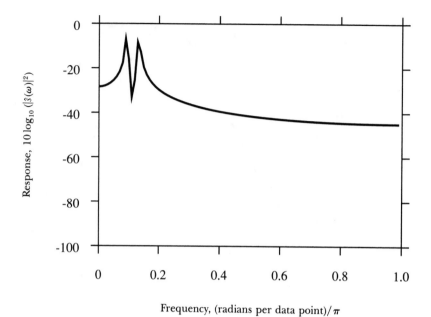

Figure 10.9   The Fourier transform magnitude of the sum of two sines using the rectangular window.

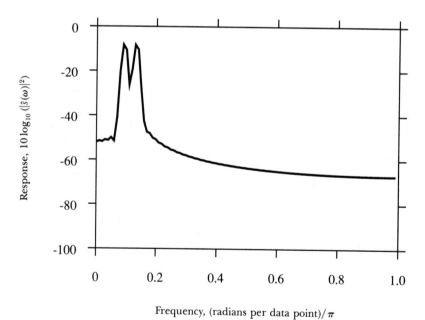

Figure 10.10   The Fourier transform magnitude of the sum of two sines using the Gaussian window.

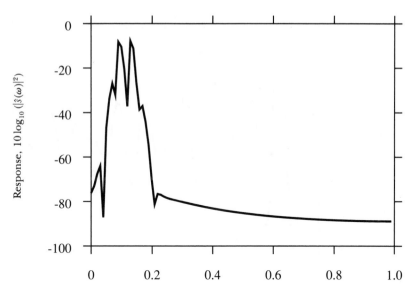

Figure 10.11   The Fourier transform magnitude of the sum of two sines using the super-Gaussian window.

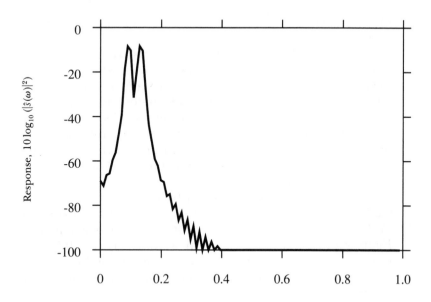

Figure 10.12   The Fourier transform magnitude of the sum of two sines using the cosine-squared window.

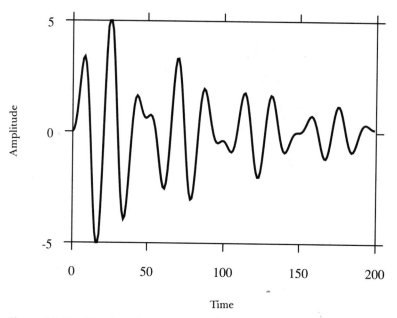

Figure 10.13   The impulse response of two cascaded simple harmonic oscillators (SHOs) provides the second test case for windowing.

the two sinusoids of Figure 10.7. Figure 10.13 is the impulse response of this system.

Figure 10.14 shows the three windows used in this case. They are half-windows, in the sense that if they were continued to negative time by reflecting them through time 0, they would be the same shape as the windows in Figure 10.8. It makes sense to use these half-windows for impulse responses, because the impulse response starts when the impulse hits and is zero before that. Thus, using these half-windows is the same as using a full window centered over the time of the impulse. The windows in Figure 10.14 are the cosine-squared and Gaussian windows, with standard deviation 56.64, and the super-Gaussian, with standard deviation 76.

Figure 10.15 is the theoretical frequency response for the pair of simple harmonic oscillators used in this example. Figures 10.16 through 10.19 compare the frequency responses calculated after applying one of four window functions. Figure 10.16 is for the rectangular window; Figure 10.17 is for the Gaussian window; Figure 10.18 is for the super-Gaussian window; and Figure 10.19 is for the cosine-squared window. As before, these transforms have been normalized to have length 1.

In this case, the differences among the four windows are not as dramatic as for the sum of two sines. The basic reason for this is that the impulse response is decaying away rather rapidly, being considerably smaller at the end of the time interval than at its peak. In fact, if enough of the waveform were used so

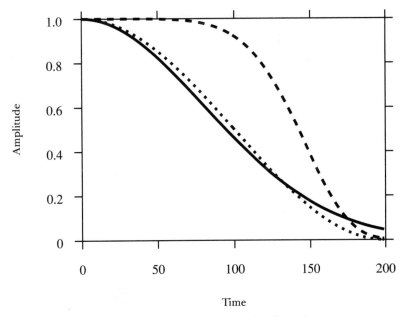

Figure 10.14   The windows used for analyzing impulse responses are half-windows. The cosine-squared (dotted line) and Gaussian (solid-line) windows both have standard deviation 56.64. The super-Gaussian (dashed line) has standard deviation 76.

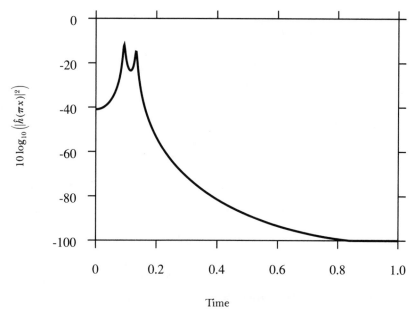

Figure 10.15   The theoretical frequency response of the cascaded simple harmonic oscillators clearly shows the two resonant frequencies.

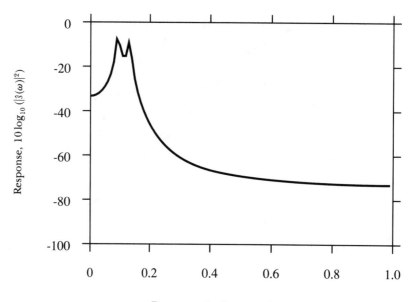

Figure 10.16 The Fourier transform magnitude of the sum of two SHOs using the rectangular window.

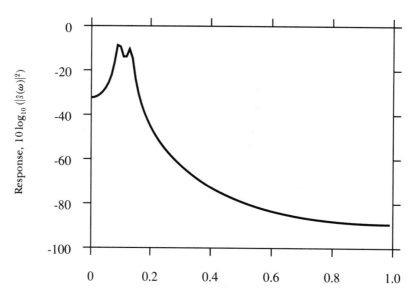

Figure 10.17 The Fourier transform magnitude of the sum of two SHOs using the Gaussian window.

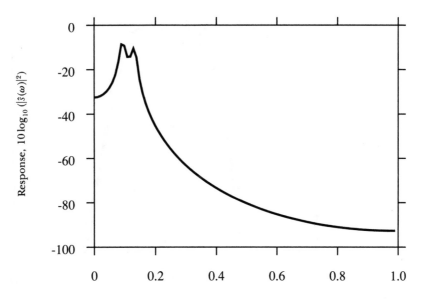

Figure 10.18   The Fourier transform magnitude of the sum of two SHOs using the super-Gaussian window.

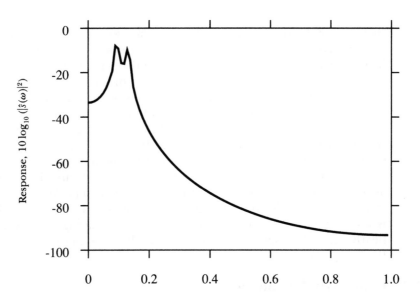

Figure 10.19   The Fourier transform magnitude of the sum of two SHOs using the cosine-squared window.

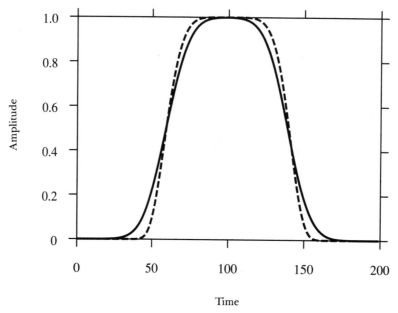

Figure 10.20   This figure compares a super-Gaussian window (dashed line) with a "Gaussian–pulse" window (solid line) of the same standard deviation.

that the amplitude near the end of the data window would be essentially zero, then the Fourier transform of the impulse response without any window would be essentially identical to Figure 10.15. In that case, none of the windows would make much difference. If a shorter segment of the impulse response were used, or if the impulse response decayed more slowly, then the differences among the results with these various windows would be more pronounced.

In this case, the rectangular window (Figure 10.16) is slightly better than the Gaussian window (Figure 10.17) at discriminating the two peaks, while the Gaussian window response at the Nyquist frequency is 20 dB lower than for the rectangular window. The super-Gaussian window (Figure 10.18) is just as good as the rectangular window at discriminating the two peaks and slightly better in terms of its out-of-band response. The cosine-squared window (Figure 10.19) is not as good as the super-Gaussian at discriminating the two peaks and has nearly identical response elsewhere. Overall, the super-Gaussian appears to be the best choice for this example.

10.4.3   Other Window Shapes

Many other window shapes have been used for signal processing. However, a casual look at the shape is not sufficient to choose a given window. The transform of the window must also be examined. For example, the convolution of a Gaussian with a rectangular pulse, pictured in Figure 8.2 on page 141 looks remarkably like the super-Gaussian window. Figure 10.20 compares the

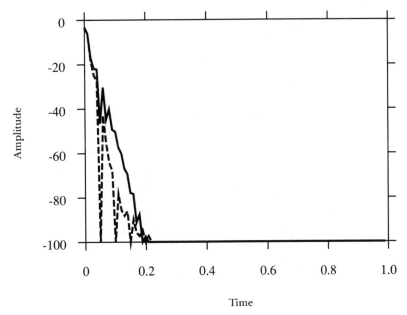

Figure 10.21   This figure shows the magnitude-only Fourier transform of both windows in Figure 10.2.

super-Gaussian window (dashed line) with a window generated by convolving a Gaussian with a square pulse (solid line), both with the same standard deviation, Δt.

Figure 10.21 plots the magnitude-only Fourier transform of the two windows in Figure 10.20. The Gaussian–pulse is significantly better than the super-Gaussian in terms of its uncertainty product, although it has deep nulls that may cause trouble in certain applications. In both cases, the standard deviation in time is 21.56. For the Gaussian–pulse, the standard deviation in frequency is 0.0266, giving an uncertainty product of 0.574. The super-Gaussian has a frequency uncertainty of 0.032, for an uncertainty product of 0.692.

There are many other windows that might be tried. However, the differences among them tend to be small. Don't strain at gnats when there are tigers in the jungle. Stick with the cosine-squared window, the Gaussian, and perhaps the super-Gaussian for special purposes. If the nulls of the cosine-squared window cause trouble for your particular application, consider using an odd number of points in the window. Other windows are needed only for special applications with unusual or extreme requirements.

10.5   IIR, FIR, AND DFT FILTERS

Digital signal processing provides two basic methods of filtering a waveform: *finite-impulse-response* (FIR) and *infinite-impulse-response* (IIR) filters. Filters implemented using the discrete Fourier transform (DFT) are by definition FIR filters—they have finite impulse responses. You may hear people claiming that FIR filters do not ring as badly or as long as IIR filters. On the surface, this sounds reasonable, just from the names of these filter classes. However, in a practical sense, there is no such thing as an infinite impulse response, because the amplitude of the impulse response falls (sooner or later) below the accuracy of the digital representation or (usually sooner) below other sources of noise. The fact is, the frequency response of a filter completely determines the impulse response and vice versa. If a filter with a particular frequency response is desired, it can be implemented as either an FIR or an IIR filter. The choice is a matter of convenience. Both implementations will have essentially the same impulse response if they have essentially the same frequency response.

DFT filters are implemented by applying the Fourier transform to a window of the waveform, applying the desired filter coefficients, then transforming back to the time domain. Where the original windows overlapped, the filtered waveforms are added to each other. If the original windows do not overlap, the filtered waveform is likely to have undesirable jumps where one window ends and the next begins. For this reason, overlapping windows are always used. These overlapping windows must be partitions of unity, since otherwise the process will introduce amplitude modulation on top of the time waveform.

CHAPTER 11

A *Unified View of Fourier Transforms*

Chapter 9 introduced the concept of the discrete Fourier transform and examined four cases generalizing the Fourier transform introduced in Chapter 8. This chapter is an introduction to *Abelian harmonic analysis,* the study of functions defined on a commutative group. By the end of this chapter, you will understand the underlying connections among all the manifestations of the Fourier transform presented individually in Chapters 8 and 9. All those Fourier transform theorems are special cases of Theorem 11.5 on page 199 in this chapter. All of the theory presented in this chapter is directed toward this one result.

Should you read this chapter, or should you skip ahead? That depends on your goals and your previous knowledge. This chapter introduces the concepts of a group and of analysis on commutative groups, a special case of harmonic analysis. These topics are certainly not mainstream engineering—at least they haven't been in the past. However, as digital signal processing, information theory, and coding theory intrude more and more into daily practice, the subjects of group theory and harmonic analysis become more important.

The concepts presented in this chapter are not difficult to master and will provide you with a firm foundation. The alternative to studying these beautiful (to the eye of a mathematician) subjects is to develop several ad hoc ways of explaining Fourier transforms, particularly the fast Fourier transform algorithm. These ad hoc techniques cannot provide insights into the underlying unity of the subject. If you decide to skip this chapter, you must also skip most of Chapter 12 on the fast Fourier transform and take the assertions of these chapters on faith. It is certainly possible to use the FFT routine provided in the Companion Library without understanding all the intricacies, and yes, the beauty, that lie behind it.

If you decide to skip ahead, first take a look at some of the central results in this chapter. Section 11.4 introduces the generalized concept of a convolution, stating the formal definition, Definition 11.23, on page 200. Theorem 11.6, in the same section, shows that the basic properties of convolutions known for the special cases explored in earlier chapters, hold in the general case. Section 11.5

gives the general Fourier transform theorem, Theorem 11.8, on page 204, and Theorem 11.9 lists some of the basic, frequently used properties.

11.1   GROUPS AND CHARACTERS

The Fourier transform is a special case of the theory of harmonic analysis, the study of the properties of functions defined on a group. As mentioned in Chapter 8, George Bachman's book, *Elements of Abstract Harmonic Analysis* [1] is an excellent introduction to this subject for interested readers who already understand group theory.

We do not need such a general theory for the cases required by digital signal processing. However, it is useful to approach the cases that are needed with a unified outlook, borrowing the special case of harmonic analysis that is required. This approach requires thinking about the concept of a group, although all that is needed is the familiar structures of the real line, the integers, and modular arithmetic.

The first and most important task in abstract Fourier analysis is to find a suitable set of orthogonal functions. Once this set of functions has been chosen, the Fourier transform is completely determined. For the continuous-time, infinite-duration case the functions had the form

$$\chi_\omega(t) = e^{j\omega t}$$

with one function for each real number ω. These functions are rather special functions, called *homomorphisms* from the group of real numbers (under addition) to the unit circle group in the complex plane (under multiplication).

11.1.1   Groups: Definition and Examples

So what is a group? And what is a homomorphism? The formal definitions are as follows:

Definition 11.1 Group: *A group, G, is a set S, together with a binary operation $\oplus$, $G = \{S, \oplus\}$ (read "the set S with the $\oplus$ operator" or "the set S under the $\oplus$ operation"), that satisfies the following conditions:*

Closure: For any two elements of the group $g, h \in G$, the group operator produces another element in the group:

$$g \oplus h \in G$$

Identity: There is a distinguished element $0_G \in G$ such that for every element $g \in G$,

$$0_G \oplus g = g \oplus 0_G = g$$

Inverses: For each element of the group $g \in G$, there is a unique element $-g \in G$ such that

$$g \oplus -g = -g \oplus g = 0_G$$

This definition is written using additive-style notation, because most of the groups used in this book are written additively. The following examples cover all the basic groups required for digital signal processing.

Example 1: The first example is the set of real numbers, $\Re$, with the + operator. This is a group, because

1. The sum of any two real numbers is again a real number, so closure is satisfied.
2. The real number 0 is the additive identity.
3. Every real number r has its additive inverse $-r$, which is also a real number.

Non-Example 2: The first non-example is the same set of real numbers, $\Re$, but with the multiplicative operator instead of the additive operator. In this case the operation is closed and an identity, 1, exists but there is one element, 0, without a multiplicative inverse, so this is not a group.

Example 3: The set of real numbers without 0, sometimes written as $\Re^*$, is a group under multiplication. In this case the inverse of an element $r \in \Re^*$ is written as r^{-1} or $1/r$.

Example 4: The set of all complex numbers, $\mathscr{C}$, is a group under addition, but not under multiplication.

Example 5: Like the real numbers, the set $\mathscr{C}^*$ of all complex numbers except 0 is a group under multiplication, but not under addition.

Example 6: The unit circle, S^1, in the complex plane is another example of a group, using the ordinary multiplication of complex numbers as the binary group operator. S^1 is equal to the set of all complex numbers of magnitude 1. For any two elements $z, q \in S^1$, the product is again on the unit circle, because $|zq| = |z| \times |q| = 1$, so closure is satisfied. The identity is the complex number 1. The inverse of any element $z \in S^1$ is its complex conjugate, $z^{-1} = \bar{z}$, which is also in S^1. This proves that S^1 is a group under multiplication.

Example 7: The set of all integers $\mathcal{Z} = \{\ldots, -2, -1, 0, 1, 2, \ldots\}$, under addition, is a group. The sum of any two integers is another integer; 0 is the group identity; the inverse of an integer k is its negative $-k$, which is again an integer.

Example 8: The set of all even integers, $2\mathcal{Z}$, under addition is also a group.

Example 9: The previous example can be generalized to the set of all multiples $N\mathbb{Z}$ of some fixed integer N. You can prove that this is a group under addition as an exercise.

Example 10: The group of integers modulo N for some fixed integer N, under addition, is written as $\mathbb{Z}/N\mathbb{Z}$. The notation is significant and will be explained in Section 11.1.2. This group can be written using the set $\{0, 1, 2, \ldots, N-1\}$. For example, if the group is $\mathbb{Z}/60\mathbb{Z}$, the integers run from 0 to 59. In this group, $59 + 1 = 0$. Equations like this can be quite confusing, so they are usually written as

$$59 + 1 \equiv 0 \pmod{60}$$

to remind the reader that the equation is only true modulo 60. This particular group is used to mark the minutes in an hour and the seconds in a minute. The hours in a day are marked using the group $\mathbb{Z}/24\mathbb{Z}$ for military time or $\mathbb{Z}/12\mathbb{Z}$ for the more familiar 12-hour clock. Binary computers use modular arithmetic to represent integers. For example, in a computer using a 16-bit unsigned integer, the equation $65535 + 1 = 0$ is true. This can cause a lot of confusion if the computer does not signal overflows.

Example 11: The set $\Re/\mathbb{Z}$ of real numbers modulo 1 is also a group under addition. In this case, the group elements can be taken as the interval, $[0, 1)$, including 0 but not 1; or as $(-1/2, 1/2]$, this time excluding the lower end point but including the upper one.

It turns out that, in some sense, all finite Abelian groups can be reduced to groups like $\mathbb{Z}/N\mathbb{Z}$. Infinite Abelian groups can be more complicated, like S^1 or $\Re/\mathbb{Z}$, but even these are easily grasped. The theory of Abelian groups reduces to the study of groups such as these—nothing more complicated. Sometimes the groups do not immediately appear to have one of these forms, but there is always a mapping (actually an *isomorphism*, see Section 11.1.5) that simply renames the group elements and reveals the underlying simplicity of the group.

Definition 11.2 *The order of a group G is the number of elements in the group. It is frequently written as $|G|$.*

The order of the groups $\mathbb{Z}$ and $2\mathbb{Z}$ are both infinite. The order of the groups $\Re$ and $\Re/\mathbb{Z}$ are also infinite, but it is a different kind of infinity. The integers are "countably infinite," while the reals are "uncountably infinite." The group $\mathbb{Z}/N\mathbb{Z}$ has N elements. For example, $\mathbb{Z}/2\mathbb{Z}$ contains only 2 elements; $\mathbb{Z}/60\mathbb{Z}$ contains 60.

There is one additional property shared by all groups required for digital signal processing. The operator is always *commutative* or *Abelian*.

Definition 11.3 *An Abelian group G is a group whose binary operator is commutative. That is, for any two group elements $g, h \in G$, we have*

$$g \oplus h = h \oplus g$$

It is a lucky thing that only Abelian groups are required, because the theory of non-Abelian harmonic analysis is much more complicated.

11.1.2 Subgroups, Cosets, and Factor Groups

Some of the example groups in Section 11.1.1 are subsets of others. For example, $2\mathbb{Z}$ is a subset of $\mathbb{Z}$. The group of nonzero real numbers, $\mathfrak{R}^*$, is a subset of the group of all real numbers, $\mathfrak{R}$. A *subgroup* of another group is a subset, but more is required by the definition:

Definition 11.4 *A subgroup H of any group G is a subset of G with a binary group operation inherited from G and with the same identity as G. The notation $H \leq G$ is used to specify that H is a subgroup of G. The notation $H < G$ means H is a subgroup not equal to G.*

The group $2\mathbb{Z}$ is a subgroup of $\mathbb{Z}$, because it is itself a group, its operation (addition) is inherited from the full group, and both groups have 0 for the identity.

What, exactly, does *inherited* mean as used here? It simply means that the sum of two even integers is the same, whether they are viewed as elements of $2\mathbb{Z}$ or as elements of $\mathbb{Z}$. The importance of this is illustrated by the second case mentioned above, $\mathfrak{R}^* \subset \mathfrak{R}$. In this case, the subset relation holds, but not the subgroup relation. In the group $\mathfrak{R}$, the operation is addition, so, for example, $1 + 2 = 3$ in this group. However, in the group $\mathfrak{R}^*$, the operation is multiplication, so the group operation on these same two elements in this case is $1 \times 2 = 2$, which is not equal to 3. Thus, the group operation of $\mathfrak{R}^*$ is not inherited from $\mathfrak{R}$, so $\mathfrak{R}^*$ is not a subgroup of $\mathfrak{R}$.

Similarly, the unit circle S^1 is a subset of $\mathfrak{C}$, but it is not a subgroup, because in S^1 the group operation is multiplication, while in $\mathfrak{C}$ it is addition.

For any fixed integer N, the group $N\mathbb{Z}$ is a subgroup of $\mathbb{Z}$. The group operation is inherited and the two groups have the same identity, 0.

The group $\mathbb{Z}/N\mathbb{Z}$ is not a subgroup of $\mathbb{Z}$ even if its elements are named $\{0, 1, 2, \cdots, N - 1\}$. The reason is that the group operation on $\mathbb{Z}/N\mathbb{Z}$ is not inherited from $\mathbb{Z}$. For example, in $\mathbb{Z}/60\mathbb{Z}$ the equation $59 + 1 = 0$ is true, which is *not* the case in $\mathbb{Z}$.

The integers $\mathbb{Z}$ form a subgroup of $\mathfrak{R}$ under addition.

The next concept defined, *cosets,* can be somewhat confusing. The notation overloads the group operator one more time, so that it appears to be operating on sets and elements at the same time. A couple of examples before the definition will help. The set of integers, $\mathbb{Z}$, has many subgroups, one of which is $2\mathcal{Z}$, all multiples of 2. The *cosets* of $2\mathcal{Z}$ in $\mathcal{Z}$ are $2\mathcal{Z}$ itself and $1 + 2\mathcal{Z}$, the set of all odd numbers. What is meant by this notation? The set $2\mathcal{Z}$ is all even numbers, any one of which can be written as $2k$ for some integer k. The set $1 + 2\mathcal{Z}$ is the set of all integers that can be written as $1 + 2k$ for some integer k, or, in other words, the set of all odd integers. This notion is generalized as follows:

Definition 11.5 Cosets: *Let G be a group with subgroup $H < G$. A coset of H in G is a subset of G of the form*

$$g \oplus H = \{g \oplus h \mid h \in H\}$$

where $g \in G$ is any element of G.

Now consider the subgroup $5\mathcal{Z}$ of $\mathcal{Z}$. In this case, there are five distinct cosets: $5\mathcal{Z}$, $1 + 5\mathcal{Z}$, $2 + 5\mathcal{Z}$, $3 + 5\mathcal{Z}$, $4 + 5\mathcal{Z}$. Respectively, these are the sets of integers divisible by 5; with remainder 1 modulo 5; with remainder 2 modulo 5; with remainder 3 modulo 5; and with remainder 4 modulo 5. Specifically, the coset $3 + 5\mathcal{Z}$ is the set of all integers that can be written as $3 + 5k$ for some integer k. Notice that this means $3 + 5\mathcal{Z} = 8 + 5\mathcal{Z}$, because any integer $3 + 5k$ can also be written as $8 + 5(k - 1)$ and vice versa. These are the same coset, just written slightly differently.

An example with a multiplicatively written group operation is $S^1 < \mathscr{C}^*$, the unit circle as a subgroup of all nonzero complex numbers. In this case, the cosets are gS^1, where g is any element $g \in \mathscr{C}^*$. Of course, many of these cosets are the same. For example, if $g \in S^1$, then $gS^1 = S^1$. In fact, every element $g \in \mathscr{C}^*$ can be written in "polar" notation as $g = r\omega$, where $\omega \in S^1$ and r is a strictly positive real number. Therefore, $gS^1 = r\omega S^1 = rS^1$. In other words, each coset is one of the circles of strictly positive radius. The set rS^1 is the circle of radius r.

There are three important things to notice in these examples:

1. The distinct cosets are all disjoint (they have empty intersections).
2. The union of all the cosets covers the full group.
3. The cosets form a group in a natural way.

The third point requires some clarification. The cosets of S^1 in $\mathscr{C}^*$ are the circles of positive radius. The group operation is multiplication of the radii, $rS^1 \times tS^1 = rtS^1$. The identity of this group is S^1 the unit circle. The inverse of rS^1 is $(1/r)S^1$. This group is written as $\mathscr{C}^*/S^1$. Evidently this group is in some sense the same as $\mathfrak{R}^{*+}$, the group of all strictly positive real numbers under multiplication.

The cosets of $5\mathcal{Z}$ in $\mathcal{Z}$ also form a group, this time using addition, since that is the operation of the groups used in this case. For any two cosets $a + 5\mathcal{Z}$ and $b + 5\mathcal{Z}$, the sum of the two cosets is defined to be

$$a + 5\mathcal{Z} \ + \ b + 5\mathcal{Z} = (a + b) + 5\mathcal{Z}$$

This may appear somewhat unnatural, but consider this: For any element $a + 5k$ of the first coset, and any element $b + 5\ell$ of the second, the sum of these two elements is a member of $(a + b) + 5\mathbb{Z}$, because

$$a + 5k + b + 5\ell = (a + b) + 5(k + \ell) \in (a + b) + 5\mathbb{Z}$$

Using the same group operator for the group formed by the cosets is another example of overloading. All these observations are summarized in the following theorem:

Theorem 11.1 *Let G be an Abelian group with subgroup $H < G$. Then*

1. *The intersection of any two distinct cosets of H in G is empty.*
2. *The union of all the cosets of H in G covers the whole group G.*
3. *The set of all cosets, denoted by G/H, with the inherited binary operation is also an Abelian group with identity H.*
4. *The order of the full group is equal to the number of cosets of H in G times the order of H:*

$$|G| = |G/H| \times |H|$$

Proof The proof of all these points in special cases, such as $G = \mathbb{Z}$ and $H = 5\mathbb{Z}$, reduces to elementary arithmetic. The proof in the general case is not very much more difficult. The four items will be proved in the order presented in the theorem.

Assume the two cosets $a \oplus H$ and $b \oplus H$ contain a common element, say $a \oplus h$ for some $h \in H$. Any element of $a \oplus H$ can be written as $a \oplus h'$ for some $h' \in H$. This arbitrary element of $a \oplus H$ can be rewritten as follows:

$$a \oplus h' = a \oplus h \oplus h' \oplus (-h)$$

which proves $a \oplus h' \in b \oplus H$ because $h' \oplus (-h) \in H$ and $a \oplus h \in b \oplus H$. This proves that $a \oplus H \subseteq b \oplus H$ whenever the two cosets have a common element. The argument is obviously symmetric, so in fact either $a \oplus H = b \oplus H$, or $(a \oplus H) \cap (b \oplus H) = \varnothing$.

For any $g \in G$, the coset $g \oplus H$ contains g, because $0 \in H$ (H is a group, so must contain the identity) so

$$g = g \oplus 0 \in g \oplus H$$

This proves that the union of all cosets covers the full group.

The set of all cosets, G/H, is an Abelian group, because for any two cosets $a \oplus H$ and $b \oplus H$ the sum of them is defined by

$$(a \oplus H) \oplus (b \oplus H) = (a \oplus b) \oplus H$$

This operation is clearly well defined, Abelian, and closed on the set of all cosets, G/H. The identity is H. The inverse of $a \oplus H$ is $-a \oplus H$, where $-a$ is the inverse of a in G.

The fourth item only makes sense if $|G|$ is finite. In that case, it is clear that all cosets have the same order, $|a \oplus H| = |H|$, by construction. There are $|G/H|$ of these sets, they are disjoint, and their union covers G. This proves the assertion.   ///

Now consider the example $G = \mathcal{Z}/20\mathcal{Z}$ and its subgroup $H = 5\mathcal{Z}/20\mathcal{Z}$. The elements of G have the form

$$20\mathcal{Z}, \quad 1 + 20\mathcal{Z}, \quad \ldots, \quad 19 + 20\mathcal{Z},$$

and the elements of H are

$$20\mathcal{Z}, \quad 5 + 20\mathcal{Z}, \quad 10 + 20\mathcal{Z}, \quad 15 + 20\mathcal{Z}.$$

What is the group G/H? The cosets of H in G are

$$H, \quad 1 + H, \quad 2 + H, \quad 3 + H, \quad 4 + H.$$

This is essentially the same group as $\mathcal{Z}/5\mathcal{Z}$. Notice also that G/H contains five elements and H contains four, the product of which is 20, the order of G.

11.1.3   Coset Representatives and Modular Arithmetic

It is cumbersome to write equations using expressions such as $3 + 5\mathcal{Z}$, so the *coset representatives* are frequently used instead:

Definition 11.6 *Let G be an Abelian group with a subgroup $H < G$. A set of coset representatives of H in G is a set S of elements of G such that every coset in G/H contains exactly one element of S.*

For example, the coset representatives of $5\mathcal{Z}$ in $\mathcal{Z}$ can be chosen as $0, 1, 2, 3, 4$; or $-2, -1, 0, 1, 2$; or even as $5, 11, 17, 23, 29$. In fact, there are infinitely many possible choices. The choice made in any circumstance depends on the convenience for the application at hand.

The coset representatives of $5\mathcal{Z}/20\mathcal{Z}$ in $\mathcal{Z}/20\mathcal{Z}$ can also be chosen in many ways; an example is $20\mathcal{Z}, 1 + 20\mathcal{Z}, 2 + 20\mathcal{Z}, 3 + 20\mathcal{Z}, 4 + 20\mathcal{Z}$. However, there are only finitely many choices, because $\mathcal{Z}/20\mathcal{Z}$ has only 20 elements. Although it is technically incorrect, these coset representatives are usually written as $0, 1, 2, 3, 4$, just because the notation is shorter.

When we use coset representatives instead of writing out the full coset notation itself, we need some reminder that the arithmetic is modular. This is done by using the following notation. If the group is $\mathcal{Z}/N\mathcal{Z}$, an equation like

$$(x + N\mathcal{Z}) + (1 + N\mathcal{Z}) = 0 + N\mathcal{Z}$$

is written instead as

$$x + 1 \equiv 0 \pmod{N\mathcal{Z}}$$

For example, the solution to the equation

$$x + 1 \equiv 0 \pmod{2^{16}}$$

is $x = 65,535$. This is only a notational convenience, but it makes writing the necessary formulas much easier.

11.1.4 Homomorphisms

Many different groups have been introduced, but so far we have no formal way of comparing one group with another. For example, the group $\mathcal{Z}$ of integers has a subgroup $2\mathcal{Z}$ of all even integers. Both groups have countably infinite order. Are they in some sense the same group? What about the groups $\mathfrak{R}/\mathcal{Z}$ and the unit circle group S^1? How do these groups compare?

The principal tools for comparing groups are called *homomorphisms*. There are special cases of homomorphisms, particularly the *isomorphisms* of Section 11.1.5 (page 187), that refine the comparisons between groups.

For any two groups G and K, there are many possible maps or functions from G to K. Homomorphisms are those that preserve the group structures:

Definition 11.7 Homomorphism: *A homomorphism f is a map from one group G to another group K,*

$$f : G \mapsto K$$

such that for any two group elements $g, h \in G$, the homomorphism preserves the group structures, meaning

$$f(g \oplus_G h) = f(g) \oplus_K f(h)$$

The subscripts are used as reminders that the group operation on the left is for the group G and that on the right is for the group K, which in general is different.

For example, the map $h : \mathcal{Z} \mapsto \mathcal{Z}/N\mathcal{Z}$ defined by $h(k) = k + N\mathcal{Z}$ is a homomorphism, as you can verify for an exercise. In this case, every element of $\mathcal{Z}/N\mathcal{Z}$ is an *image* of some element of $\mathcal{Z}$.

The map $m_2 : \mathcal{Z} \mapsto \mathcal{Z}$, which multiplies each integer by 2, $m_2(k) = 2k$, is also a homomorphism. However, this time the images of the homomorphism cover only the even integers, not all the integers.

A homomorphism that is particularly important for Fourier analysis is χ_ω, defined by

$$\chi_\omega(x) = e^{j\omega x}$$

for a fixed real number ω. This is a homomorphism from the group of real numbers $\Re$ to the unit circle S^1, because

$$\chi_\omega(x + y) = e^{j\omega(x+y)} = \chi_\omega(x)\chi_\omega(y)$$

for any two real numbers $x, y \in \Re$. Notice that on the left-hand side the $+$ operator is the group operation in $\Re$, while on the right-hand side the group operation in S^1 is multiplication of the complex numbers.

Thus, all the functions in the orthogonal set of functions used for the Fourier transform in Chapter 8 are homomorphisms from $\Re$ to S^1. This is also the case for all the "frequency component functions" used in every type of Fourier transform. In fact, this is a distinguishing feature in all of harmonic analysis. The Fourier transform expresses a function on a group G as a sum of homomorphisms from G to S^1.

11.1.5   Isomorphisms

There are three special classes of homomorphism, called *epimorphisms, monomorphisms,* and *isomorphisms.* The Greek prefixes almost define these variations. First, it is convenient to define the *kernel* of a homomorphism, as follows:

Definition 11.8 Kernel: *Let G and H be two groups, and let $f : G \mapsto H$ be a homomorphism. The kernel of f is the set of all elements $g \in G$ such that $f(g) = 0$, where 0 is the identity element of H. This set is sometimes written as*

$$Ker(f) = \{g \in G \mid f(g) = 0\}$$

Theorem 11.2 *Let f be a homomorphism from a group G to a group H. Then the kernel of f is a subgroup of G.*

Proof   Let $K = \mathrm{Ker}(f)$ be the kernel of f. Then, for any two elements $k, l \in K$, the sum $k + l$ is a member of K, because

$$f(k + l) = f(k) + f(l) = 0 + 0 = 0$$

Thus, K is closed under the group operation. The kernel contains 0, because, since f is a homomorphism,

$$f(g) = f(g + 0) = f(g) + f(0)$$

which implies $f(0) = 0$. Now we must prove that if $k \in K$, then its inverse $-k \in K$ is also in K. This is shown by the calculation

$$0 = f(0) = f(k - k) = f(k) + f(-k) = 0 + f(-k)$$

which proves $f(-k) = 0$.   ///

For example, the map $f : \mathcal{Z} \mapsto \mathcal{Z}/N\mathcal{Z}$ defined by $f(g) = g + N\mathcal{Z}$ is a homomorphism. Its kernel is $N\mathcal{Z}$, a subgroup of $\mathcal{Z}$.

The map $\chi_\omega : \mathfrak{R} \mapsto S^1$ is a homomorphism. Its kernel is $2\pi\mathcal{Z}$, all multiples of 2π. This is a subgroup of $\mathfrak{R}$.

Definition 11.9 Monomorphism: *Let f be a homomorphism from a group G to a group H. It is called a monomorphism if its kernel contains only one element (the identity element), $\mathrm{Ker}(f) = \{0\}$.*

The prefix *mono* means one. A monomorphism maps only one element of G onto each element of H that is in its image. In other words, if $f(g) = f(k)$, then $g = k$. This is obvious from its definition, because if $f(g) = f(k)$, then, because f is a homomorphism, this implies $f(g - k) = 0$, so $g - k \in \mathrm{Ker}(f)$ is an element of the kernel, which contains only 0 by definition. Therefore, $g = k$.

For example, the homomorphism $f : \mathcal{Z} \mapsto \mathcal{Z}/N\mathcal{Z}$ defined by $f(k) = k + N\mathcal{Z}$ is not a monomorphism, because its kernel is $\mathrm{Ker}(f) = N\mathcal{Z}$.

The map $m_2 : \mathcal{Z} \mapsto \mathcal{Z}$, which multiplies each integer by 2, is a monomorphism, because if $2k = 0$, then $k = 0$, proving that $\mathrm{Ker}(m_2) = \{0\}$.

Definition 11.10 Epimorphism: *Let f be a homomorphism from a group G to a group H. It is called an epimorphism if its image covers all of H. In other words, for every element $h \in H$, there is at least one $g \in G$ such that $f(g) = h$.*

The prefix *epi* means onto, or covering. For example, the homomorphism $f : \mathcal{Z} \mapsto \mathcal{Z}/N\mathcal{Z}$ is an epimorphism, even though it is not a monomorphism.

The map $m_2 : \mathcal{Z} \mapsto \mathcal{Z}$ is a monomorphism, but is not an epimorphism, because it misses all the odd numbers.

Definition 11.11 Isomorphism: *An isomorphism is a homomorphism that is both an epimorphism and a monomorphism.*

The epimorphism $f : \mathcal{Z} \mapsto \mathcal{Z}/N\mathcal{Z}$ is not an isomorphism, because its kernel is $N\mathcal{Z}$, not $\{0\}$. The monomorphism $m_2 : \mathcal{Z} \mapsto \mathcal{Z}$ is not an isomorphism, because it is not an epimorphism.

However, the homomorphism $m_2 : \mathfrak{R} \mapsto \mathfrak{R}$, which multiplies every real number by 2, is an isomorphism. So is the map $m_2 : \mathcal{Z} \mapsto 2\mathcal{Z}$, because now the target group is covered by its images. This may seem somewhat artificial, but it is essential.

Now for a less trivial example of an isomorphism. The exponential map

$$\chi_{2\pi} : \mathfrak{R}/\mathcal{Z} \mapsto S^1$$

defined by $\chi_{2\pi}(x + \mathcal{Z}) = e^{j2\pi x}$, is an isomorphism. It is well defined, because given any coset representative $x + k \in x + \mathcal{Z}$, we have

$$e^{j2\pi(x+k)} = e^{j2\pi x}$$

This homomorphism is clearly both a monomorphism and an epimorphism. In some sense, then, the two groups S^1 and $\Re/\mathcal{Z}$ are really the *same* group.

We say that two groups are *isomorphic* if there is an isomorphism from one to the other. Two groups that are isomorphic are, at least in an abstract sense, the same group. Their elements may have different names, and the operation may not even be written the same way, but a simple renaming, the isomorphism, reveals the underlying similarity of the two groups.

Another example of two isomorphic groups that is important for signal processing is $\mathcal{Z}/N\mathcal{Z}$ and the group S_N of all Nth roots of unity. In other words, S_N is defined by

$$S_N = \{1, z, z^2, \ldots, z^{N-1}\}, \quad z = e^{j2\pi/N}$$

The isomorphism between these two groups is again the exponential mapping

$$\chi_{2\pi/N} : \mathcal{Z}/N\mathcal{Z} \mapsto S_N$$

defined by

$$\chi_{2\pi/N}(k + N\mathcal{Z}) = e^{j2\pi k/N} = z^k$$

It does not matter which coset representative k is used, because given any element of the set $k + N\ell \in k + N\mathcal{Z}$, the image is the same:

$$e^{j2\pi(k+N\ell)/N} = e^{j2\pi k/N}$$

It is clear that this map covers S_N and that the kernel is 0. Proving that it is a homomorphism is the same as proving that the other exponential maps already examined are homomorphisms. Thus, in an abstract sense, the groups $\mathcal{Z}/N\mathcal{Z}$ and S_N are actually the same group. This isomorphism is used repeatedly in signal processing applications.

11.1.6 Cross Products

We have seen that smaller groups may be obtained from a group G by finding subgroups and by taking the coset group, sometimes also called the factor group. It is also possible to build larger groups out of two given groups, G and H, by using the *cross product*. This is a way of making a sort of two-dimensional group:

Definition 11.12 Cross Product: *Let S and T be any two sets. Then the cross product of these two sets is defined by*

$$S \times T = \{(s, t) \mid s \in S \text{ and } t \in T\}$$

Theorem 11.3   *Let G and H be any two Abelian groups. Then the cross product $G \times H$ is also an Abelian group with the group operation defined componentwise. In other words, for any two elements $(g, h), (g', h') \in G \times H$, the sum is defined by*

$$(g, h) \oplus (g', h') = (g \oplus g', h \oplus h')$$

The proof is left as an exercise for the reader.

For example, the group $Z/NZ \times Z/MZ$ contains the NM elements (a, b) for each $a \in Z/NZ$ and $b \in Z/MZ$. This is exactly the group that is needed for two-dimensional discrete Fourier transforms on an $N \times M$ array of points.

Now here is a good question. Since $Z/25Z$ and $Z/5Z \times Z/5Z$ both have 25 elements, are they isomorphic? Clearly, two finite groups must have the same number of elements if they are isomorphic, but is the converse true? In this case, the groups are not isomorphic. The following definitions will help explain why.

Definition 11.13   *Let G be a group with element $g \in G$, and let n be a positive integer. Then ng is defined recursively by the formulas*

$$1g = g$$
$$ng = (n - 1)g \oplus g$$

Definition 11.14 Cyclic Group: *A group G is called cyclic if there is a group element $g \in G$ such that every other group element has the form ng for some positive integer n. In that case, g is called a generator of G.*

The group Z is not cyclic, because $n1$ only covers the positive integers, $n(-1)$ only covers the negative integers, and $n0$ is 0 for all n.

For any integer N, the group Z/NZ is cyclic, because all group elements have the form $n1$ for some positive integer n. Other group elements might serve just as well, or they might not. For example, if $N = 10$, the group $Z/10Z$ is cyclic with generator $1 + 10Z$. The element $3 + 10Z$ is also a generator, because the multiples of 3 modulo 10 are

$$3, 6, 9, 2, 5, 8, 1, 4, 7, 0$$

covering the whole group. However, 2 is not a generator for this group, because its multiples are

$$2, 4, 6, 8, 0$$

only 5 elements.

Another example is the group $Z/9Z$. In this case, 1 is a generator, and so is 2. The multiples of 2 modulo 9 are

$$2, 4, 6, 8, 1, 3, 5, 7, 0$$

covering the full group. However, 3 is not a generator for this group, because the multiples of 3 modulo 9 are

$$3, 6, 0$$

only 3 elements.

It is an easy exercise to prove that if G is a cyclic group and f is an isomorphism from G to H, then H is also a cyclic group, and for every generator g of G, its image $f(g)$ is a generator of H.

The converse is also true. Given any two cyclic groups of the same order, G and H, choose a generator of each group $g \in G$ and $h \in H$. Then the map defined by $f(ng) = nh$, for all positive integers n, is an isomorphism from G to H. You might want to prove this as an exercise.

The group $G = \mathbb{Z}/5\mathbb{Z} \times \mathbb{Z}/5\mathbb{Z}$ is not cyclic, so it cannot be isomorphic to $\mathbb{Z}/25\mathbb{Z}$. To prove that G is not cyclic, choose any element $(a, b) \in G$ and prove that it cannot be a generator. The first step is to prove that neither component can be 0. The second step is to prove that $(a, 0)$ is not a multiple of (a, b). For the first part, if either of the components is 0, that same component is zero for all multiples $n(a, b) = (na, nb)$ of (a, b). Thus, if (a, b) is a generator, neither component can be zero. For the second step, suppose there is an integer n such that

$$n(a, b) = (a, 0)$$

Then, in particular, this means that

$$nb \equiv 0 \pmod 5$$

Since b is not zero, this forces $n = 5k$ for some integer k. But then

$$na = 5ka \equiv 0 \pmod 5$$

proving that

$$n(a, b) = (0, 0)$$

Since a was not zero, this proves that $(a, 0)$ is not a multiple of (a, b), so (a, b) cannot be a generator of the group. The group cannot be cyclic.

However, the group $G = \mathbb{Z}/3\mathbb{Z} \times \mathbb{Z}/5\mathbb{Z}$ is cyclic. It has many generators, one of which is $(1, 1)$. This can be shown by listing its multiples:

$$
\begin{array}{ccccc}
(1,1), & (2,2), & (0,3), & (1,4), & (2,0), \\
(0,1), & (1,2), & (2,3), & (0,4), & (1,0), \\
(2,1), & (0,2), & (1,3), & (2,4), & (0,0)
\end{array}
$$

and after that the cycle repeats.

We will not prove it here, because it is not needed in this book; however, the key difference between these last two examples is whether the orders of the two cyclic groups are relatively prime. If N and M are relatively prime, then $\mathcal{Z}/N\mathcal{Z} \times \mathcal{Z}/M\mathcal{Z}$ is a cyclic group; otherwise it is not.

11.2 INTEGRATION ON GROUPS

Fourier transforms require the existence of orthogonal functions for their definition. The definition of orthogonality depends on some notion of integration. In Chapter 8, the group was $\mathfrak{R}$, and two functions f and g were called orthogonal if

$$\langle f \mid g \rangle_{\mathfrak{R}} = 0$$

and the bracket was defined by

$$\langle f \mid g \rangle_{\mathfrak{R}} = \int_{-\infty}^{+\infty} \overline{f}(t)g(t)\,dt$$

$$= \int_{\mathfrak{R}} \overline{f}(t)g(t)\,dt$$

The subscript $\mathfrak{R}$ on the bracket reminds us that this is defined for functions that are defined on the group $\mathfrak{R}$. The subscript $\mathfrak{R}$ on the integral in the second line is supposed to mean that the integral is taken over all of $\mathfrak{R}$ from $-\infty$ to $+\infty$. The reason for this notation is to suggest the generalizations that are needed for other groups.

Harmonic analysis is based on extending this notion of integration of functions from $\mathfrak{R}$ to $\mathscr{C}$ to the more general setting of functions defined on a group G with values in $\mathscr{C}$. The proper extension of this idea is known as a *Haar measure* on the group.

Before we define the notion of a Haar measure, a little notation is required. One of the most important and useful properties of the measure normally used on the real line $\mathfrak{R}$ is that it is *invariant* with respect to the group operation. Stated this way, it sounds rather unfamiliar, but all it means is that the measure of an interval is the same even after it has been translated to another location. In other words, the measure of an interval $[a, b]$ is the same as the measure of $[a + t, b + t]$. It is this property that allows a change of variables in ordinary integration. For example, if f is a function defined on $\mathfrak{R}$, then

$$\int_{-\infty}^{+\infty} f(x)\,dx = \int_{-\infty}^{+\infty} f(x + a)\,dx.$$

Without this ability to change variables, ordinary calculus would be very difficult indeed.

Notice that the term *measure* is very natural at least in the case of $\mathfrak{R}$, because the usual measure of the interval $[a, b]$ is $b - a$, the length of the interval. This is the reason for the terminology. In a formal sense, a measure is actually a special mapping from some set of functions on the group to $\mathscr{C}$. However, it is more natural to think of the measure as somehow assigning a weight to the subsets of the group, just as the usual measure on $\mathfrak{R}$ defines the measures of intervals and other subsets of $\mathfrak{R}$. In fact, these viewpoints are equivalent. The following definition allows us to emphasize the second, more natural idea of a measure.

Definition 11.15 *Let G be an Abelian group, and $E \subseteq G$ be a subset of G. The characteristic function, ζ_E, is defined by*

$$\zeta_E(x) = \begin{cases} 1 & \text{if } x \in E \\ 0 & \text{otherwise} \end{cases}$$

A measure on a group is essentially a map from the subsets of the group to the positive real numbers. However, it must satisfy some restrictions to be called a measure. For example, if two subsets $E \subseteq F$ are two subsets of G, and E is contained in F, then the measure of E must be less than or equal to the measure of F. For example, in the real numbers with the usual measure, the open interval (a, b) is a subset of the closed interval $[a, b]$. The closed interval contains the end points, which are not part of the open interval. However, the measure of both is $b - a$. So it is possible for a strictly smaller subset of another set to have the same measure as the larger set. However, its measure cannot exceed the measure of the larger set.

Another complication is the fact that some subsets of $\mathfrak{R}$ are not measurable. In other words, there are some sets for which a length cannot be assigned. This is a fact that we will largely ignore in this book. However this restriction is acknowledged in the definitions by referring to *measurable sets*, meaning those sets for which a measure can be defined. With this understanding and the above definition, a measure can be defined as follows:

Definition 11.16 *A measure $\int_G$ on a group G is a function defined on the set of all characteristic functions ζ_E for measurable subsets E of G, with nonnegative real values on each of these characteristic functions; it must be countably additive, which means that for any countable set $\{E_k\}$ of disjoint measurable subsets $E_k \subset G$, the measure of the union $F = \bigcup_{k=0}^{\infty} E_k$ is equal to the sum of the measures of all the subsets:*

$$\int_G \zeta_F(g)\, dg = \sum_{k=0}^{\infty} \int_G \zeta_{E_k}(g)\, dg$$

Several comments are in order here. First, the dg is used only to make the measure appear similar to the usual integral notation on $\mathfrak{R}$. It serves as a reminder of which variable is being integrated over, but it is not actually required in the setting of this definition.

Second, *disjoint* subsets are subsets that have empty intersection. In this definition it means that the intersection of any two of these subsets, E_k and E_ℓ, for example, is empty, $E_k \cap E_\ell = \varnothing$, the empty set.

Third, the restriction to disjoint subsets is obviously necessary for a normal interpretation of a measure. Suppose, for example, the group is $\mathfrak{R}$. Without the restriction to mutually disjoint subsets in this definition, we could, for example, use $E_k = [0, 1]$ for all k. The union of all these sets is still only the interval $[0, 1]$, so the theorem would require

$$\int_\mathfrak{R} \zeta_{[0,1]}(t)\, dt = \sum_{k=0}^{\infty} \int_\mathfrak{R} \zeta_{[0,1]}(t)\, dt$$

which is only possible if the measure of $[0, 1]$ is zero. In other words, the only measure would be zero on all subsets — not a very interesting measure.

Fourth, countable additivity is essential to the usual notion of a measure. One consequence is that the measure of the empty set must be 0. This is true because $E_k = \varnothing$, for all k, is a set of disjoint subsets of G, so, just as in the previous paragraph, we can write

$$\int_G \zeta_\varnothing(g)\, dg = \sum_{k=0}^{\infty} \int_G \zeta_\varnothing(g)\, dg$$

which forces $\int_G \zeta_\varnothing(g)\, dg = 0$.

Fifth, it is essential to limit the notion of additivity to countably many sets. Without this restriction, for example, we could define the disjoint sets $E_x = \{x\}$ for every $x \in [0, 1]$. Then

$$[0, 1] = \bigcup_{x \in [0,1]} E_x$$

so the unconstrained additivity would imply

$$\int_\mathfrak{R} \zeta_{[0,1]}(t)\, dt = \sum_{x \in [0,1]} \int_G \zeta_{E_x}(t)\, dt$$

But, in the usual measure on $\mathfrak{R}$, the measure of any single point is 0, so this formula would imply that the measure of the unit interval must also be zero. This is clearly not desired.

Strictly speaking, we should now carefully consider how to extend this notion of a measure from just the characteristic functions on G to an arbitrary *measurable* function. Basically, the method is straightforward, but the details can be rather complicated. The idea is the same as the usual numerical approximation techniques for integrals. The actual function f is approximated by a sum of characteristic functions:

$$f(g) \approx \sum_{k=0}^{\infty} a_k \zeta_{E_k}(g)$$

using countably many disjoint sets E_k. The integral of f is then approximated as

$$\int_G f(g) \, dg \approx \sum_{k=0}^{\infty} a_k \int_G \zeta_{E_k}(g) \, dg$$

This approximation is then taken to a limit of smaller and smaller sets E_k, which under certain conditions will converge to the actual value of $\int_G f(g) \, dg$. For the purposes of this book, we skip the detailed development of these facts.

Now we can define the Haar measure on a group:

Definition 11.17   *For any group G, a measure $\int_G$ on the group is called a Haar measure if it is invariant under the group operation. That is, if for any measurable set $E \subset G$, the measure of E, $\int_G \zeta_E(g) \, dg$, is equal to the measure of the translated set $h + E$:*

$$\int_G \zeta_E(g) \, dg = \int_G \zeta_{h+E}(g) \, dg$$

for any $h \in G$.

In practice, this means that it is all right to do an ordinary change of variables. In other words, for any function f defined on the group G with a Haar measure, the integral equation

$$\int_G f(g) \, dg = \int_G f(g - h) \, dg$$

is valid.

The case of $\Re$ is the most difficult case needed for signal processing. Integration on $\mathbb{Z}/N\mathbb{Z}$, for example, reduces to finite sums; in fact, this is true for any finite group. It is also true for any group with countably many elements, such as $\mathbb{Z}$. This is easy to prove using the definition of a Haar measure. Let G be a group with only countably many elements (perhaps finitely many). Then every subset $E \subseteq G$ can be written as the countable union of disjoint subsets:

$$E = \bigcup_{e \in E} \{e\}$$

Since measures are countably additive, this means that the measure is completely determined by the measure of individual group elements. In particular, the identity $0 \in G$ must have a measure, say

$$\gamma = \int_G \zeta_{\{0\}}(g)\, dg$$

For any $h \in G$, the set $\{h\}$ is the *translate* of $\{0\}$ by h. Since the measure is a Haar measure, it is invariant under group translations. This means that

$$\gamma = \int_G \zeta_{\{h\}}(g)\, dg$$

for any group element h. The measure of every group element is the same. Thus, for countable groups, the Haar measure of a subset $E \subseteq G$ is some constant times the number of elements in the set. Usually this constant is chosen to be 1 as a matter of convenience. In that case, the measure of a set is equal to the number of elements in that set.

Thus, the Haar measure on all countable groups reduces to a simple summation. For $\mathbb{Z}/N\mathbb{Z}$, the integral of a function f defined on the group is, therefore,

$$\int_{\mathbb{Z}/N\mathbb{Z}} f(g)\, dg = \sum_{k=0}^{N-1} f(k)$$

The integral of a function f defined on $\mathbb{Z}$ is an infinite sum:

$$\int_{\mathbb{Z}} f(g)\, dg = \sum_{k=-\infty}^{+\infty} f(k)$$

What is the Haar measure on $G = \mathbb{Z}/N\mathbb{Z} \times \mathbb{Z}/M\mathbb{Z}$? This is a two-dimensional group, but it has only NM elements, so the measure of each element is a constant, usually chosen to be 1. The integration of a function on this group thus reduces to a double sum:

$$\int_G f(a, b)\, d(a, b) = \sum_{a=0}^{N-1} \sum_{b=0}^{M-1} f(a, b)$$

For groups with more than countably many elements, finding the Haar measure is more complicated. However, in all cases required for signal processing, the Haar measure is already familiar. If the group is $\Re$, the usual notion of integration is the right one. For the group $\Re/Z$, integration is defined by

$$\int_{\Re/Z} f(t)\, dt = \int_0^1 f(t)\, dt$$

This is easily shown to be a Haar measure.

Having defined integration on all these groups, we can also define the bracket using only one formula:

Definition 11.18 *For any group G with Haar measure $\int_G$, and for any two measurable functions f and g on the group with values in $\mathscr{C}$ (the complex numbers), the bracket of these two functions is defined by*

$$\langle f \mid g \rangle_G = \int_G \overline{f}(x) g(x)\, dx$$

For example, if the group is $G = Z/NZ$, the bracket of two functions is defined by

$$\langle f \mid g \rangle_{Z/NZ} = \sum_{k=0}^{N-1} \overline{f}(k) g(k)$$

For the group $G = Z$, the bracket is similar but with an infinite sum:

$$\langle f \mid g \rangle_Z = \sum_{k=-\infty}^{\infty} \overline{f}(k) g(k)$$

For a product group $G = Z/NZ \times Z/MZ$, the bracket involves the double sum

$$\langle f \mid g \rangle_{Z/NZ \times Z/MZ} = \sum_{k=0}^{N-1} \sum_{\ell=0}^{M-1} \overline{f}(k, \ell) g(k, \ell)$$

Definition 11.19 *Any two functions f and g defined on a group G will be called orthogonal if neither function is 0 on the whole group and*

$$\langle f \mid g \rangle_G = 0$$

Once integration is defined on a group, the notion of square integrable functions can also be defined, as is required for the theory of Fourier transforms.

Definition 11.20   *Let G be an Abelian group with a Haar measure. Then $\mathcal{L}_2(G)$ is the space of all square integrable functions from G to $\mathcal{C}$. This means that for any function $f \in \mathcal{L}_2(G)$, the integral*

$$\langle f \mid f \rangle_G = \int_G |f(g)|^2 \, dg$$

is defined and finite. Further, two functions that are the same almost everywhere relative to the Haar measure are identified.

In case $G = \mathfrak{R}$, we have $\mathcal{L}_2(\mathfrak{R}) = \mathcal{L}_2$, defined by Definition 8.3 (page 115).

In the case $G = \mathcal{Z}/N\mathcal{Z}$, every function is square integrable, because only a finite sum is required.

The final example is for $G = \mathcal{Z}$, in which case $\mathcal{L}_2(\mathcal{Z})$ is the set of all series that are square summable, that is, all series in which

$$\langle f \mid f \rangle_{\mathcal{Z}} = \sum_{k=-\infty}^{+\infty} |f(k)|^2$$

is well defined and finite.

11.3   THE GROUP OF CHARACTERS

This section is about a special class of homomorphisms called *characters*. The characters of an Abelian group are in fact the "frequency component" functions needed to define the abstract Fourier transform.

Definition 11.21   *For any Abelian group G, a character, χ, on the group is a homomorphism from G to the group S^1.*

Now there is a little twist. The set $\widehat{G}$ of all characters defined on an Abelian group G is another Abelian group, and a Haar measure can be defined on that group. For example, when $\mathfrak{R}$ was the group, the characters were the set of all functions

$$\chi_\omega(x) = e^{j\omega x}$$

for all real numbers $\omega \in \mathfrak{R}$. Each distinct real number ω gives a distinct character. Thus, the set of characters, $\widehat{\mathfrak{R}}$, corresponds one-to-one with the original group, $\mathfrak{R}$. But there is more. The set of characters naturally forms a group itself, and this group is isomorphic to $\mathfrak{R}$. The group operation for the set of characters is multiplication of the functions pointwise. The map from $\mathfrak{R}$ to $\hat{\mathfrak{R}}$ defined by

$$\omega \mapsto \chi_\omega$$

is an isomorphism. It is a homomorphism, because

$$\chi_\omega \chi_\sigma = \chi_{\omega + \sigma}$$

as you can easily verify. It is clearly also an epimorphism and a monomorphism.

It is not always true that the group of characters is isomorphic to the original group, but it is always an Abelian group with Haar measure that is obvious.

Theorem 11.4   *For any Abelian group G, the set of characters $\hat{G}$ also forms an Abelian group. The group operation on $\hat{G}$ is the pointwise multiplication of the functions.*

Proof   We must prove that the product of any two characters, $\chi, \rho \in \hat{G}$ is again a character, that there is an identity, and that every character has an inverse. The most difficult one is the first, closure. The product of the characters, $\chi\rho$, is the function defined by

$$(\chi\rho)(g) = \chi(g)\rho(g)$$

for any $g \in G$. This is easily proved to be a homomorphism by the following calculation. Let $g, h \in G$ be two group elements. Then

$$(\chi\rho)(g + h) = \chi(g + h)\rho(g + h)$$

$$= \chi(g)\chi(h)\rho(g)\rho(h)$$

$$= \chi(g)\rho(g)\chi(h)\rho(h)$$

$$= (\chi\rho)(g)(\chi\rho)(h)$$

which proves the product is a homomorphism. It is also a character, because all its values are on the unit circle, S^1. The identity for the group is the constant character, $I(g) = 1$, for any $g \in G$. The inverse of a character $\chi \in \hat{G}$ is its complex conjugate function, $\bar{\chi}$, which is also a character on G.   ///

What about the Haar measure on $\hat{G}$? This is more difficult and will be left out of the general theory. Fortunately, for the Abelian groups used in digital signal processing, the necessary measures are always the natural ones on the groups. For example, in Chapter 8, the group of characters naturally maps to the real line again, and the usual measure on the real line is the one that is required. The other cases work out just as easily or indeed easier.

Only one more concept is needed to complete the picture, and that one is surprising: going one step further brings you back to where you started. More precisely, the group of characters, $\widehat{G}$, of a group G, can itself be viewed as just another abstract group. Nesting the notation, we define $\widehat{\widehat{G}}$ to be the group of characters of $\widehat{G}$. The surprising fact is that $\widehat{\widehat{G}}$ is isomorphic to G. Some definitions are needed to prove this fact:

Definition 11.22 *Let G be an Abelian group, and $\widehat{G}$ be its group of characters. For any $g \in G$ the map σ_g from $\widehat{G}$ to S^1 defined by*

$$\sigma_g(\chi) = \chi(g)$$

is called the substitution mapping.

Theorem 11.5 *Let G be an Abelian group and $\widehat{G}$ its group of characters. Then the group of characters $\widehat{\widehat{G}}$ on $\widehat{G}$ is isomorphic to G. The isomorphism is defined by the mapping*

$$g \mapsto \sigma_g$$

from G to $\widehat{\widehat{G}}$.

Proof The easy part of the proof is that for every $g \in G$, the substitution mapping σ_g from $\widehat{G}$ to S^1 is a character. It is a homomorphism, because for any two characters $\chi, \rho \in \widehat{G}$,

$$\sigma_g(\chi\rho) = (\chi\rho)(g)$$

$$= \chi(g)\rho(g)$$

$$= \sigma_g(\chi)\sigma_g(\rho)$$

The homomorphism is a character, because all its values are in the unit circle, S^1.

The other part of the proof, that every element of $\widehat{\widehat{G}}$ has the form σ_g for some $g \in G$, is more difficult and is omitted.   ///

In fact, given an Abelian group G with a Haar measure, the Fourier transform $\hat{f}$ of a function f, from G to $\mathscr{C}$, is a function defined on $\widehat{G}$. Since $\widehat{G}$ is itself an Abelian group with a Haar measure, there is a notion of a Fourier transform for it also. If h is a function from $\widehat{G}$ to $\mathscr{C}$, its Fourier transform, $\hat{h}$ is a function defined from $\widehat{\widehat{G}}$ to $\mathscr{C}$. Since $\widehat{\widehat{G}}$ is isomorphic to G, the function $\hat{h}$ is usually thought of as a function from G to $\mathscr{C}$. This is why the inverse Fourier transform can be thought of as returning to the original domain. Without this isomorphism, there would be no notion of an inverse transform.

11.4 DISCRETE CONVOLUTIONS

The notion of a convolution is very handy for theoretical and applied purposes. In Chapter 8, the convolution of two functions was defined by

$$f * g(t) = \int_{-\infty}^{+\infty} f(t - z)g(z) \, dz$$

One reason that convolutions are useful in signal processing is the fact that the Fourier transform of a product of functions is equal to the convolution of the individual transform:

$$\sqrt{2\pi} \, \widehat{fg}(\omega) = \hat{f} * \hat{g}(\omega)$$

Conversely, the Fourier transform of the convolution of two functions is equal to the product of the two transforms:

$$\widehat{f * g}(\omega) = \sqrt{2\pi} \, \hat{f}(\omega)\hat{g}(\omega)$$

Fortunately, there is a notion of convolution on any Abelian group with a Haar measure, for which both of these properties hold. Furthermore, the definition of the convolution even looks the same in general, as it does for the specific case above:

Definition 11.23 Convolution: *Let G be an Abelian group with Haar measure $\int_G$, and let f and h be two measurable, complex-valued functions on the group. Then the convolution of these functions is defined by*

$$f * h(g) = \int_G f(g - z)h(z) \, dz$$

For example, if the group is $G = \mathbb{Z}/N\mathbb{Z}$, the convolution of two functions is just the sum

$$f * h(g) = \sum_{k=0}^{N-1} f(g - k)h(k)$$

where the function arguments are elements of $\mathbb{Z}/N\mathbb{Z}$, so the argument $g - k$ of f in this equation should be interpreted modulo N.

In the case $G = \Re/\mathcal{Z}$, the convolution is

$$f * h(g) = \int_0^1 f(g - z)h(z)\,dz$$

where once again the argument $g - z$ must be interpreted modulo 1.

For the two-dimensional case $G = \mathcal{Z}/N\mathcal{Z} \times \mathcal{Z}/M\mathcal{Z}$, the convolution is again just a sum:

$$f * h(m, n) = \sum_{k=0}^{N-1} \sum_{l=0}^{M-1} f(m - k, n - l)h(k, l)$$

where the first argument is modulo N and the second modulo M.

The delta function is also defined on any Abelian group with Haar measure:

Definition 11.24 Delta Function: *Let G be an Abelian group with Haar measure $\int_G$. Then the delta function, δ_G, is defined by requiring*

$$\int_G f(x)\delta_G(x)\,dx = f(0)$$

for any measurable function f on G.

For convenience, the delta function is usually written without the subscript. On a finite group like $\mathcal{Z}/N\mathcal{Z}$, the delta function is simply

$$\delta(x) = \begin{cases} 1 & \text{if } x = 0 \\ 0 & \text{otherwise} \end{cases}$$

This is also true for countably infinite groups like $\mathcal{Z}$, where the integration reduces to a summation. Only on groups like $\Re$ and $\Re/\mathcal{Z}$ does the delta function have the strange property of being 0 everywhere but one point, at which it is infinite.

We can now state the general version of Theorem 8.14 on page 139:

Theorem 11.6 *Let G be an Abelian group with Haar measure $\int_G$; let $f, h, w \in \mathcal{L}_2(G)$ be three square integrable functions on G, and a and b two complex constants. Then the following equations are true:*

The convolution operation is closed on $\mathcal{L}_2(G)$:

$$f * h \in \mathcal{L}_2(G) \tag{11.1}$$

Convolution is commutative:

$$f * h = h * f \tag{11.2}$$

Convolutions are linear and distributive over addition:

$$f * (ah + bw) = af * h + bf * w \tag{11.3}$$

The delta function on G relative to its Haar measure, δ_G, is the identity for convolutions:

$$f * \delta_G = f \tag{11.4}$$

The transform of the convolution is the product of the transforms:

$$\langle \chi_\omega \mid f * h \rangle_G = \langle \chi_\omega \mid f \rangle_G \langle \chi_\omega \mid h \rangle_G \tag{11.5}$$

where χ_ω is any of the characters on G.

The proof of this general form of Theorem 8.14 follows the proof of the earlier theorem closely. Both the Cauchy–Schwarz and the Minkowski inequalities are true for any Abelian group with Haar measure, so the proofs of the first four properties are essentially unchanged. The proof of Equation 11.5 also follows the earlier proof closely. The calculations require an interchange of the order of integration and a change of variables. The change of variables is valid because the measure being used is a Haar measure (invariant under translations) and the integration is over the whole group.

One point that has been rather breezed over is the convolution of two functions defined on the group of characters $\widehat{G}$, of an Abelian group G. In most cases the original group G is written using additive notation, whereas its group of characters is written multiplicatively. This changes the appearance, but not the theory, of convolutions. For any Abelian group $\widehat{G}$ with binary operator written multiplicatively, the definition of convolution becomes

$$f * h(\chi) = \int_{\widehat{G}} f\left(\chi\rho^{-1}\right) h(\rho)\, d\rho$$

because the multiplicative inverse, written ρ^{-1} for some group element ρ, takes the place of the additive inverse, written $-g$ for some group element g. This looks strange at first, but it is a simple translation from the additive notation to the multiplicative notation. Normally, all calculations can be done using additive notation, because, as we have seen, the group of characters $\widehat{G}$ for all Abelian groups we have examined can be recast in a natural way back into an additively written group. For example, the group $G = \Re$ has characters of the form

$$\chi_\omega(x) = e^{j\omega x}$$

and the binary operation of the characters is multiplicative. However, when two of them are multiplied together,

$$\chi_\omega \chi_\mu = \chi_{\omega+\mu}$$

the result is indexed by the sum of the individual indices. Normally, the equations are written using these indices instead of the characters themselves, using the natural identification of $\widehat{\mathfrak{R}}$ with $\mathfrak{R}$.

11.5   FOURIER TRANSFORM ON A GROUP

The central concept of a Fourier transform is to find the right set of "frequency component functions" that are mutually orthogonal and can be used to decompose every function of interest. In all cases these "frequency component functions" are exactly the set of all characters.

Theorem 11.7 *Let G be an Abelian group with Haar measure $\int_G$. Then, for any two characters χ and $\rho \in \widehat{G}$,*

$$\langle \chi \mid \rho \rangle_G = \kappa^2 \delta_{\widehat{G}}(\overline{\chi}\rho)$$

where κ is some constant that depends only on the group, not the characters chosen.

Notice that the delta function in this theorem is defined on the group of characters $\widehat{G}$, which is written multiplicatively. Thus, $\delta(\chi) = 0$ for all characters χ that are not the identity character. Since $\overline{\chi}$ is the inverse of χ, the right-hand side of the equation in this theorem is 0, unless $\chi = \rho$.

Proof   The theorem will be proved only for groups with finitely many elements. The detailed proof in the general case is quite involved. The proof in the finite case gets the central ideas across without getting bogged down in details.

First, consider the trivial case $\chi = \rho$. Then $\overline{\chi}(g)\rho(g) = 1$ for every $g \in G$. Therefore the sum reduces to

$$\langle \chi \mid \rho \rangle = \sum_{g \in G} \overline{\chi}(g)\rho(g)$$

$$= \sum_{g \in G} 1$$

$$= |G|.$$

Thus, for finite groups, $\kappa^2 = |G|$.

On the other hand, if $\chi \neq \rho$, there must be some group element $k \in G$ such that $\chi(k) \neq \rho(k)$. This group element is used to prove the theorem by a change of variables as follows:

$$\langle \chi \mid \rho \rangle = \int_G \bar{\chi}(g)\rho(g) \, dg$$

$$= \int_G \bar{\chi}(g - k + k)\rho(g - k + k) \, dg$$

and changing the variables with $u = g - k$ gives

$$= \int_G \bar{\chi}(u + k)\rho(u + k) \, du$$

$$= \int_G \bar{\chi}(u)\bar{\chi}(k)\rho(u)\rho(k) \, du$$

Because χ and ρ are homomorphisms,

$$= \bar{\chi}(k)\rho(k) \int_G \bar{\chi}(u)\rho(u) \, du$$

$$= \bar{\chi}(k)\rho(k)\langle \chi \mid \rho \rangle$$

But since $\chi(k) \neq \rho(k)$ by assumption, then $\bar{\chi}(k)\rho(k) \neq 1$. This forces $\langle \chi \mid \rho \rangle = 0$ and proves the theorem.   ///

If you have trouble with the change of variables in this proof, just think of $G = \Re$, in which case it is an ordinary integral, or $G = \mathcal{Z}$, in which case it is a summation, and the change of variable is only a shift of the index. Notice also that this theorem assumes that $\langle \chi \mid \rho \rangle$ is defined. As we saw in Chapter 8, this can be a tricky matter. If the group is finite, there is no problem, because the integration is just a finite summation, which is always defined if the functions are defined. Similarly, for the case $\Re / \mathcal{Z}$, the integral is only on the interval $[0, 1]$, so existence of the integral is not a problem. However, for the group $\mathcal{Z}$, the summation is infinite, which introduces the same sort of difficulties encountered with $\Re$.

Theorem 11.8 Fourier Transform on Abelian Groups: *Let G be an Abelian group with a Haar measure $\int_G$, $\widehat{G}$ the group of characters on G with its Haar measure $\int_{\widehat{G}}$, and $\kappa \in \Re$ a constant determined by the equation*

$$\langle \chi \mid \rho \rangle_G = \kappa^2 \delta(\bar{\chi}\rho)$$

where δ is the delta function on $\widehat{G}$. Then for any function $f \in \mathscr{L}_2(G)$, its Fourier transform,

$$\hat{f}(\chi) = \frac{1}{\kappa}\langle \chi \mid f \rangle_G = \frac{1}{\kappa}\int_G \overline{\chi}(g) f(g) \, dg$$

exists and belongs to $\mathscr{L}_2(\widehat{G})$.

For any function $\hat{f} \in \mathscr{L}_2(\widehat{G})$, the inverse Fourier transform,

$$h(g) = \frac{1}{\kappa}\langle \overline{\sigma}_g \mid \hat{f} \rangle_{\widehat{G}} = \frac{1}{\kappa}\int_{\widehat{G}} \hat{f}(\chi)\chi(g) \, d\chi$$

exists and belongs to $\mathscr{L}_2(G)$.

The inverse Fourier transform of the Fourier transform of a function on G is equal to the original function almost everywhere. In the notation of this theorem,

$$f(g) = h(g) \quad almost\ everywhere.$$

Notice that the Fourier transform of a function on G is actually a function on $\widehat{G}$. This means, for example, that in the case of $G = \Re$, we should have written the transform of a function as $\hat{f}(\chi_\omega)$. However, this is awkward and is shortened to $\hat{f}(\omega)$. It is similar in the other cases. In fact, in all cases the characters are exponential functions, and the group of characters is indexed in a similar way by some more familiar group on which the choice of Haar measure is obvious.

Already in Theorem 11.6, we have proved that the Fourier transform of the convolution of two functions is the product of their transforms. It is also true that the Fourier transform of the product of two functions is equal to the convolution of the transforms:

Theorem 11.9 *Let G be an Abelian group with Haar measure $\int_G$. Then, for any two functions $f, g \in \mathscr{L}_2(G)$, the following properties hold:*

The transform of the convolution is equal to the product of the transforms:

$$\widehat{f * g}(\chi) = \kappa \hat{f}(\chi)\hat{g}(\chi) \quad for\ any\ \chi \in \widehat{G} \tag{11.6}$$

The transform of the product is equal to the convolution of the transforms:

$$\kappa \widehat{fg}(\chi) = \hat{f} * \hat{g}(\chi) \quad for\ any\ \chi \in \widehat{G} \tag{11.7}$$

The energy of the waveform equals the energy of the transform:

$$\int_G |f(g)|^2 \, dg = \int_{\widehat{G}} |\hat{f}(\chi)|^2 \, d\chi \qquad (11.8)$$

Proof   Equation 11.6 is obtained from Theorem 11.6, Equation 11.5, simply by scaling with κ appropriately. Equation 11.7 can also be obtained from Equation 11.5 as follows. Beginning with the transforms of two functions $\hat{f}$ and $\hat{g}$ we have, according to Equation 11.5,

$$\langle \overline{\sigma}_g \mid \hat{f} * \hat{h} \rangle_{\widehat{G}} = \langle \overline{\sigma}_g \mid \hat{f} \rangle \langle \overline{\sigma}_g \mid \hat{h} \rangle$$

Then, according to Theorem 11.8, this equation becomes,

$$\langle \overline{\sigma}_g \mid \hat{f} * \hat{h} \rangle_{\widehat{G}} = \kappa^2 f(g) h(g)$$

The left-hand side of this equation is κ times the inverse Fourier transform of $\hat{f} * \hat{h}$. Therefore, by Theorem 11.8, we can take the forward transform on both sides, obtaining the equation

$$\kappa \hat{f} * \hat{h}(\chi) = \kappa^2 \widehat{f h}(\chi)$$

The final equation, Equation 11.8, is the equal power equation for the general case. As in the special case of Chapter 8, this equation can be obtained from a more general Parseval theorem, stated next. This formula is obtained from that theorem using $f = g$.   ///

Theorem 11.10 Parseval: *Let G be an Abelian group with Haar measure $\int_G$. Let $f, g \in \mathscr{L}_2(G)$. Then*

$$\langle f \mid g \rangle_G = \langle \hat{f} \mid \hat{g} \rangle_{\widehat{G}}$$

Proof   The proof of this theorem is a straightforward, if somewhat lengthy, calculation:

$$\langle \hat{f} \mid \hat{g} \rangle_{\widehat{G}} = \int_{\widehat{G}} \overline{\hat{f}(\chi)} \hat{g}(\chi) \, d\chi$$

which, by definition of the Fourier transform, is

$$= \frac{1}{\kappa^2} \int_{\widehat{G}} \overline{\langle \chi \mid f \rangle} \langle \chi \mid g \rangle \, d\chi$$

$$= \frac{1}{\kappa^2} \int_{\widehat{G}} \int_{G} \int_{G} \overline{\overline{\chi(t)}f(t)} \, \overline{\chi}(s)g(s) \, ds \, dt \, d\chi$$

Reversing the order of integration gives

$$= \int_{G} \int_{G} \overline{f(t)}g(s) \frac{1}{\kappa^2} \int_{\widehat{G}} \chi(t)\overline{\chi}(s) \, d\chi \, ds \, dt$$

$$= \int_{G} \int_{G} \overline{f(t)}g(s) \frac{1}{\kappa^2} \int_{\widehat{G}} \overline{\sigma_s(\chi)}\sigma_t(\chi) \, d\chi \, ds \, dt$$

where σ_s and σ_t are the substitution functions;

$$= \int_{G} \int_{G} \overline{f(t)}g(s) \frac{1}{\kappa^2} \langle \sigma_s \mid \sigma_t \rangle_{\widehat{G}} \, ds \, dt$$

which, by Theorem 11.7, is

$$= \int_{G} \int_{G} \overline{f(t)}g(s)\delta(t-s) \, ds \, dt$$

Integrating over s gives the result

$$= \int_{G} \overline{f(t)}g(t) \, dt$$

$$= \langle f \mid g \rangle_G$$

just as was claimed.   ///

11.6 SPECIAL CASES OF THE FOURIER TRANSFORM

All the special cases of the Fourier transform discussed in Chapters 8 and 9 are derived from the general Theorem 11.8. Two things are required for each special case. First, the characters on the group must be identified. Second, the value of κ in the general theorem must be calculated. This section examines each special case, calculating these items in each instance.

11.6.1   One Dimension, *N* points: $G = \mathbb{Z}/N\mathbb{Z}$

The simplest case is $G = \mathbb{Z}/N\mathbb{Z}$, where only N points are used, $0, 1, 2, \ldots, N-1$. What are the characters from G to $\mathscr{C}^*$? It turns out that every homomorphism from $\mathbb{Z}/N\mathbb{Z}$ to $\mathscr{C}^*$ is also a character. One theorem is required to help us find all the homomorphisms:

Theorem 11.11:   *Let G be an Abelian group and f a homomorphism from G to $\mathscr{C}^*$. Then, for any $g \in G$ and any integer $m \in \mathbb{Z}$,*

$$f(mg) = f(g)^m$$

where mg is g added to itself m times, according to Definition 11.13.

Proof   The proof of this theorem is by finite induction on m. Since f is a homomorphism, and $mg = (m-1)g + g$,

$$f(mg) = f((m-1)g + g) = f((m-1)g)f(g)$$

A repeated application of this formula proves the theorem:

$$f(mg) = f((m-1)g)f(g)$$
$$= f((m-2)g)f(g)^2$$
$$\vdots \quad \vdots$$
$$= f(g)f(g)^{m-1}$$
$$= f(g)^m \qquad \qquad ///$$

Since every element of $\mathbb{Z}/N\mathbb{Z}$ can be written in the form $m1$ (an integer multiple of 1), every homomorphism has the form

$$f(m) = f(1)^m = z^m \qquad \qquad (11.9)$$

for the complex number $z = f(1)$. In other words, they all look like exponentials—the basic waveforms explored in Chapter 1.

In fact, for any homomorphism f from $\mathbb{Z}/N\mathbb{Z}$ to $\mathscr{C}^*$, the complex number $z = f(1)$ must be an Nth root of unity. Why is this true? Since f is a homomorphism, it must map the identity of $\mathcal{Z}/N\mathcal{Z}$ to the identity of $\mathscr{C}^*$. In other words, $f(0) = 1$. But since f is a homomorphism, we can calculate as follows:

$$1 = f(0)$$
$$= f(N1)$$
$$= f(1)^N$$

proving that $f(1)$ is an Nth root of unity. In other words, the homomorphism can be written as

$$f(m) = e^{j2\pi ma/N}$$

for some integer a that depends on the homomorphism. Thus, every homomorphism is indeed a character, and there are only N of them, indexed by the integers $a = 0, 1, \ldots, N - 1$:

$$\chi_{2\pi a/N}(m) = e^{j2\pi ma/N}$$

This subscript is a bit complicated, so it is convenient to define the notation

$$\psi_x(t) = e^{j2\pi xt}$$

so that in what follows the 2π can be left out of the subscripts.

There are only N characters on $\mathcal{Z}/N\mathcal{Z}$, because any choice other than those listed above is equivalent to one of them. For example, if the integer $k = a + lN$ is tried for some choice of $0 \le a < N$ and l an integer, then the character $\psi_{k/N}$ is the same as the character $\psi_{a/N}$, because

$$\psi_{k/N}(g) = \psi_{(a+lN)/N}(g)$$
$$= e^{j2\pi g(a+lN)/N}$$
$$= e^{j2\pi ga/N} e^{j2\pi lg}$$
$$= \psi_{a/N}(g)$$

because gl is an integer, so $\exp(j2\pi lg) = 1$.

In the proof of Theorem 11.8, it was proved that for finite groups, $\kappa^2 = |G|$. Thus, the Fourier transform in this case is as stated in Theorem 9.1 on page 148.

11.6.2   One Dimension, Countably Many Points: $G = \mathcal{Z}$

In this case, the group $G = \mathcal{Z}$ is infinite, and questions about the convergence of infinite sums arise. We will mostly sidestep these questions, but it is important to realize that for this reason, the discrete delta function must give way to the Dirac delta function once more. This case is sort of a mix of the two cases $G = \Re$ and $G = \mathcal{Z}/N\mathcal{Z}$.

What are the homomorphisms from $\mathcal{Z}$ to $\mathscr{C}^*$? Theorem 11.11 provides the answer immediately, for if f is a homomorphism, then

$$f(k) = f(k1) = f(1)^k = z^k$$

for $z = f(1)$. Once again, the homomorphisms are the fundamental frequencies or waveforms introduced in Chapter 1. This time, however, there are many more of them, and there is no requirement that z be some Nth root of unity, because now the group is infinite. The characters are the homomorphisms with $f(1) = z$ on the unit circle. Notice that the homomorphism either is always on the unit circle (and therefore is a character) or never touches the unit circle. In this case, the characters can all be written in the form

$$\psi_a(k) = e^{j2\pi ak}$$

and these are unique for $-\frac{1}{2} < a \leq \frac{1}{2}$, $0 \leq a < 1$, or indeed any interval of length 1. Thus, the group of characters $\widehat{\mathcal{Z}}$, whether indexed by $-\frac{1}{2} < a \leq \frac{1}{2}$ or by $z = \exp(j2\pi a)$, is isomorphic to the unit circle:

$$\widehat{\mathcal{Z}} = S^1$$

Every element $z \in S^1$ defines a character:

$$k \mapsto z^k$$

It is generally more convenient to write $z = \exp(j2\pi a)$ and index the character with a as above.

It is surprising that the group of characters on $\mathcal{Z}$ is S^1. The original group is a discrete set of points, although there are infinitely many of them. The group of characters, though, has continuously many points, like the real line.

In order to state the Fourier transform theorem in this case, we must also know what the characters of the group S^1 are. Theorem 11.5 provides the answer immediately: They are the substitution functions when S^1 is viewed as the set of characters of $\mathcal{Z}$. In other words, all the characters have the form

$$\sigma_m(\psi_a) = \psi_a(m) = e^{j2\pi am}$$

for any choice of $m \in \mathcal{Z}$ and $-\frac{1}{2} < a \leq \frac{1}{2}$.

The only point that needs to be checked is the value of κ. In this case, it is not possible to calculate κ directly from the characters ψ_θ on Z, because a divergent infinite sum is involved:

$$\langle \psi_\theta \mid \psi_\theta \rangle_Z = \sum_{k=-\infty}^{+\infty} 1.$$

However, the inverse Fourier transform always requires the same value of κ as the forward transform. In this case, κ is easily calculated from the characters on S^1, as follows:

$$\kappa^2 = \langle \sigma_m \mid \sigma_m \rangle_{S^1}$$

$$= \int_{S^1} \bar{\sigma}_m(z) \sigma_m(z) \, dz$$

$$= \int_{S^1} z^{-m} z^m \, dx$$

$$= \int_{S^1} dz$$

$$= \int_{-1/2}^{+1/2} dz$$

$$= 1$$

This proves that $\kappa = 1$. The Fourier transform in this case is therefore as stated in Theorem 9.3 on page 151.

11.6.3 Finite Duration: $G = \mathfrak{R}/Z$

Here the group is a unit interval, for example $[0, 1)$ or $(-\frac{1}{2}, \frac{1}{2}]$, and the group operation is addition modulo 1. This group can be identified with the unit circle by mapping

$$x \mapsto e^{j2\pi x}$$

Because of this fact, the Fourier transform theorem in this case is almost identical to Theorem 9.3. The only difference is where the complex conjugates are required.

We already know that the characters on $\mathfrak{R}/Z$ are indexed by the integers:

$$\sigma_m(g) = mg \quad (\text{mod } 1)$$

which, in terms of S^1, is the mapping

$$z \mapsto z^m$$

The value of κ is 1, which is proved by the same calculation as for the previous case. The Fourier transform in this case is therefore as stated in Theorem 9.4 on page 152.

11.6.4 Two Dimensions, $N \times M$: $G = \mathbb{Z}/N\mathbb{Z} \times \mathbb{Z}/M\mathbb{Z}$

Two-dimensional Fourier transforms are commonly needed in picture processing. There is no essential difference between the two-dimensional case and the one-dimensional case. Theorem 11.8 covers not only one- and two-dimensional cases, but any number of dimensions required. The group $G = \mathbb{Z}/N\mathbb{Z} \times \mathbb{Z}/M\mathbb{Z}$ is exactly what is required for a two-dimensional transform with N points in one direction and M points in the other. The elements of this group are written as (g, h), where $g \in \mathbb{Z}/N\mathbb{Z}$ and $h \in \mathbb{Z}/M\mathbb{Z}$.

What are the characters of this group? This case is easily reduced to the one-dimensional case by calculating

$$f(g, h) = f((g, 0) + (0, h))$$

$$= f(g, 0)f(0, h)$$

$$= f(1, 0)^g f(0, 1)^h$$

$$= z^g w^h$$

and since $N(1, 0) = 0$, z is an Nth root of unity, and similarly w is an Mth root of unity. Therefore, every homomorphism is a character, and all the characters have the form

$$\phi_{(a,b)}(g, h) = e^{j 2 \pi a g / N} e^{j 2 \pi b h / M}$$

for some $(a, b) \in G$.

Since this is a finite group, the value of κ is as determined in the proof of Theorem 11.8, $\kappa = \sqrt{NM}$. The Fourier transform theorem in this case is therefore as stated in Theorem 9.5 on page 153.

The Fast Fourier Transform

The discrete Fourier transform (DFT) is a powerful tool for digital signal processing. The only problem is its large computational burden. Calculating a DFT on N points requires on the order of N^2 multiplications and additions. There is a technique called the fast Fourier transform (FFT) that reduces this to the order of $N \log(N)$ operations of each kind. The FFT was already used by C. F. Gauss in 1805! However, knowledge of Gauss's work was not widespread, and in 1965 the FFT was reinvented and became known for a time as the Cooley–Tukey DFT. (See [3] for a survey of numerical transforms including the FFT. The reference to Gauss himself is [5].)

12.1 THE BRUTE FORCE METHOD

The discrete Fourier transform is a linear map from the set of functions on a finite Abelian group G to the set of functions on the group of characters $\widehat{G}$. The set of complex-valued functions on a group G with N elements is an N-dimensional vector space with the vector elements indexed by the group elements. In other words, the Fourier transform is a linear map from one N-dimensional vector space to another. It is therefore expressible as an $N \times N$ matrix. If the group is $G = \mathcal{Z}/N\mathcal{Z}$, the Fourier transform matrix $\mathbf{F}$ can be written as

$$\mathbf{F} = \frac{1}{\sqrt{N}} \begin{pmatrix} 1 & 1 & 1 & 1 & \cdots & 1 \\ 1 & \overline{z} & \overline{z}^2 & \overline{z}^3 & \cdots & \overline{z}^{N-1} \\ 1 & \overline{z}^2 & \overline{z}^4 & \overline{z}^6 & \cdots & \overline{z}^{N-2} \\ 1 & \overline{z}^3 & \overline{z}^6 & \overline{z}^9 & \cdots & \overline{z}^{N-3} \\ \vdots & \vdots & \vdots & \vdots & \ddots & \vdots \\ 1 & z^{N-1} & z^{N-2} & z^{N-3} & \cdots & z \end{pmatrix}$$

213

where $z = \exp(j2\pi/N)$; repeated use has been made of the fact that $z^N = 1$. The inverse discrete Fourier transform uses the inverse of this matrix, $\mathbf{F}^{-1}$, which, according to Theorem 9.1, is the complex conjugate of $\mathbf{F}$. Therefore, each calculation of a transform or its inverse requires N^2 multiplications and a similar number of additions.

Any technique that reduces the burden of these calculations can increase the applicability of the Fourier transform in real-time systems, as well as reducing the execution time required for non-real-time applications. Often the time spent calculating the Fourier transforms dominates the execution time of the application.

12.2   THE FAST METHOD

The *fast Fourier transform* (FFT) technique reduces the number of multiplications required from N^2 to a number proportional to $N\log(N)$, which can lead to a dramatic decrease in execution time for large values of N. The FFT routine works for any finite Abelian group G. There are two principal cases of interest: $G = \mathcal{Z}/N\mathcal{Z}$ for one-dimensional signals and $G = \mathcal{Z}/L\mathcal{Z} \times \mathcal{Z}/M\mathcal{Z}$ for two-dimensional signals. Despite the differences between these groups, the FFT algorithms on these two groups are essentially the same in concept.

Notes on reading the rest of this chapter: Between here and section 12.3.4, the group theory developed in Chapter 11 is used to explain the basis of the fast Fourier transform. The goal is Theorem 12.4, which defines a generic FFT algorithm that applies to functions on any finite Abelian group. If you have not worked through Chapter 11, you should now skip ahead to Section 12.3.4, take a brief look at the code examples there, and then proceed to Section 12.4. The theory of fast Fourier transforms is an excellent example of a group theory application. The existence of the generic FFT algorithm can only be understood from a group-theoretic point of view. However, it is certainly possible to use the resulting algorithms without understanding the theory behind them.

The basic idea is to break the computation down into smaller pieces and then fit the pieces together to form the final result. The next theorem shows how this is done:

Theorem 12.1 *Let G be a finite Abelian group with subgroup H. Then the Fourier transform of a function f defined on G can be calculated by either of the two formulas:*

$$\hat{f}(\chi) = \frac{1}{\sqrt{|G|}} \sum_{g \in G} f(g)\overline{\chi}(g)$$

$$= \frac{1}{\sqrt{|G|}} \sum_{s \in S} \overline{\chi}(s) \sum_{h \in H} f(s + h)\overline{\chi}(h) \tag{12.1}$$

where S is a set of coset representatives for H in G, and $\chi \in \widehat{G}$.

Proof   The first formula is just the definition of the Fourier transform in this case, therefore serving as our starting point for deriving the second formula. This is easily done, as follows:

$$\frac{1}{\sqrt{|G|}} \sum_{g \in G} f(g)\chi(g) = \frac{1}{\sqrt{|G|}} \sum_{s \in S} \sum_{h \in H} f(s + h)\overline{\chi}(s + h)$$

which is true, because the sum still covers G exactly once,

$$= \frac{1}{\sqrt{|G|}} \sum_{s \in S} \overline{\chi}(s) \sum_{h \in H} f(s + h)\overline{\chi}(h)$$

because $\chi(s + h) = \chi(s)\chi(h)$.   ///

Many people first react to this formula with a "So what?" It is only a simple rearrangement of terms, hardly worthy of being called a theorem. This is true from a theoretical point of view, but as a practical matter it can make a big difference. This is not obvious, so watch closely. The inner sum in Equation 12.1 is

$$f_{s,H}(\chi) = \sum_{h \in H} f(s + h)\overline{\chi}(h) = \langle \chi \mid f_s \rangle_H$$

where the function f_s is defined by $f_s(h) = f(s + h)$. The character χ in this formula is evaluated only on the subgroup H. There are only $|H|$ distinct characters on H, so there are only $|H|$ choices of χ for which this formula must be computed, the others being repetitious. For each of these $|H|$ characters, the formula requires $|H|$ multiplications and additions to calculate. Thus, all possible values for $f_{s,H}$ can be calculated using only $|H|^2$ multiplications and additions. There are $|S|$ translates f_s for which this formula must be evaluated, so a total of $|S| \times |H|^2$ multiplications and additions are required to calculate all these values. Once these are calculated, they can be used in Equation 12.1 as follows to get the final result:

$$\hat{f}(\chi) = \sum_{s \in S} \chi(s) f_{s,H}(\chi)$$

This formula requires $|S|$ multiplications and additions for each of the $|G|$ possible values of χ, for a total of $|S| \times |G|$ multiplications and additions. The grand sum is therefore

$$|S| \times |G| + |S| \times |H|^2$$

multiplications and additions. Since $|G| = |S| \times |H|$, we have proved

Theorem 12.2 *Let G be a finite Abelian group with a subgroup H. Then, using Equation 12.1, the Fourier transform of a function on G can be calculated using only*

$$(|S| + |H|) \times |G|$$

multiplications and additions.

This can be a dramatic savings. For example, if $|G| = 10^4$ and $|H| = 10^2$, then a brute-force Fourier transform requires $10^4 \times 10^4 = 10^8$ multiplications and additions, while, using Equation 12.1, the same calculation requires only $(10^2 + 10^2) \times 10^4 = 2 \times 10^6$ of each operation, a factor of 50 fewer operations.

A concrete example should make this all easier to understand. For the group $G = \mathcal{Z}/15\mathcal{Z}$, we can choose $H = 3\mathcal{Z}/15\mathcal{Z}$. In this case, the coset representatives of $H = 3\mathcal{Z}/15\mathcal{Z}$ in G can be taken as $S = \{0, 1, 2\}$. Then Equation 12.1 becomes

$$\hat{f}(\chi) = \frac{1}{\sqrt{15}} \sum_{s=0}^{2} \chi(s) \sum_{h \in H} f(s + h)\chi(h)$$

where $H = 3\mathcal{Z}/15\mathcal{Z} = \{0, 3, 6, 9, 12\}$. Therefore, the inner sum can be written as

$$f_{s,H}(\chi) = \sum_{k=0}^{4} f(s + 3k)\chi(3k)$$

The character χ can be written as χ_g for some $g \in G = \mathcal{Z}/15\mathcal{Z}$, which is defined by

$$\chi_g(x) = e^{j2\pi gx/15}$$

The character in this sum is evaluated only on $H = 3\mathcal{Z}/15\mathcal{Z}$, which has elements of the form $h = 3k + 15\mathcal{Z}$. Thus, on H the character has the form

$$\chi_g(h) = \chi_g(3k) = e^{j2\pi g3k/15} = e^{j2\pi gk/5}$$

and so is distinguishable on H only for the values $g \in \{0, 1, 2, 3, 4\}$. Therefore, only 25 multiplications and additions are required to calculate these values for each of the 3 choices of $s \in S$, for a total of $3 \times 25 = 75$ multiplications and additions. Putting these values back into Equation 12.1 to calculate the final result requires 3 of each operation for each of the 15 values of χ, thus requiring another 45 of each operation. Thus, the total is $45 + 75 = 120$ multiplications and additions instead of the $15^2 = 225$ required by the direct calculation.

12.3   THE FAST FOURIER TRANSFORM

Since Equation 12.1 reduces the calculations required for a DFT, it is natural to wonder about squeezing as much as possible from the technique. This section develops a general fast Fourier transform (FFT) algorithm that can be used on any finite Abelian group.

12.3.1   Composition Series

The transform of the various translates of the original function f must be calculated on the subgroup H, so naturally, Equation 12.1 can be used iteratively to reduce the calculations required to obtain the DFTs on this subgroup. In the case $G = \mathbb{Z}/15\mathbb{Z}$, the subgroup $H = 3\mathbb{Z}/15\mathbb{Z}$ has no proper subgroups (that is, subgroups other than $\{0\}$ and H). Moreover, the only subgroups of G that contain H are H and G, the full group.

However, if the group is $G = \mathbb{Z}/75\mathbb{Z}$, then there is a sequence of subgroups

$$G = \mathbb{Z}/75\mathbb{Z} > 3\mathbb{Z}/75\mathbb{Z} > 9\mathbb{Z}/75\mathbb{Z} > \{0\}$$

so there are two intermediate subgroups that can be used to reduce the calculations required. First, Equation 12.1 can be used to calculate the transforms on $9\mathbb{Z}/75\mathbb{Z}$; then these results can be used to calculate the transforms on the group $3\mathbb{Z}/75\mathbb{Z}$. This technique can be extended to any sequence of subgroups. The maximum benefit is obtained when the sequence of subgroups leaves no intermediate gaps. Such a chain of subgroups is called a *composition series*.

Definition 12.1 Composition series: *Let G be an Abelian group. A chain of subgroups*

$$G = G_n > G_{n-1} > G_{n-2} > \cdots > G_1 > G_0 = \{0\}$$

is called a composition series for G if every subgroup in the chain is a proper subgroup of the one before it (in other words, $G_j \neq G_{j+1}$) and if there are no intermediate subgroups between any two in the chain. More precisely, if H is a subgroup of G such that $G_{j+1} \geq H \geq G_j$ for some choice of j, then either $H = G_j$ or $H = G_{j+1}$.

12.3.2   Storage Considerations

Calculating the DFT iteratively using Equation 12.1 requires that all the intermediate results be stored somehow. This storage requirement could easily get out of hand without some careful planning. Moreover, the storage technique should be easy to implement in a computer program.

A function defined on any finite group G is stored as a vector of $|G|$ elements. If the group is $G = \mathbb{Z}/L\mathbb{Z} \times \mathbb{Z}/M\mathbb{Z}$, the function might be expressed as an $L \times M$ matrix or as a vector of $N = LM$ points. Either way, the function can be thought of as a vector indexed by the group elements. Group theory provides just the packing of intermediate results that is required to keep the storage requirements to a minimum.

At each stage of the calculation, exactly $|G|$ numbers must be stored. This can be explained as follows. At the kth stage of the iteration, the group G_k is playing the part of the subgroup $H < G$ of Equation 12.1. At this stage, the Fourier transforms of each of the translates f_σ of f on the group H must be stored. Each of these transforms requires $|H|$ storage positions, and there are $|G/H|$ coset representatives σ. Thus, a total of

$$|G/H| \times |H| = |G|$$

storage positions are required at each stage.

In theory, any arrangement of the $|G|$ elements required at each stage will do the job. However, a computer algorithm demands a definite and efficient arrangement. Group theory provides the required storage order that works for all cases.

If G is any finite Abelian group, the group of characters $\widehat{G}$ is isomorphic to G. Choose an isomorphism:

$$\Gamma_G : \widehat{G} \mapsto G$$

Any subgroup $H < G$ is also isomorphic to its group of characters. However, any character $\chi \in \widehat{G}$ is also a character on H by restriction of its domain. What we really require is a homomorphism

$$\Gamma_H : \widehat{G} \mapsto H$$

which can be obtained by first restricting a character χ to the subgroup H to obtain a character on H, then applying an isomorphism from $\widehat{H}$ to H.

This allows packing all the required information into one vector of length $|G|$, as follows:

$$\mathbf{v}\,(\sigma + \Gamma_H(\chi)) = \langle \chi \mid f_\sigma \rangle_H$$

for every coset representative σ of H in G and every character $\chi \in \widehat{H}$. The index of $\mathbf{v}$ runs over G exactly once, because the union of all the cosets of H in G covers G without any overlap, as explained in Theorem 11.1 on page 183.

An example will help make this clear. Let the group be $G = \bar{Z}/15\bar{Z}$ with subgroup $H = 5\bar{Z}/15\bar{Z}$. Every character of G can be written as

$$\chi_g(x) = e^{j2\pi gx/15}$$

for some $g \in G$, as explained before. We can choose the isomorphism Γ_G to be

$$\Gamma_G (\chi_g) = g$$

The group H is isomorphic to $\mathcal{Z}/3\mathcal{Z}$, and so is its group of characters. The character $\chi_g \in \widehat{G}$ is also a character on H by restriction. Any element $h \in H$ can be written as $h = 5k + 15\mathcal{Z}$ for some integer k. Then the character χ_g operating on this element is

$$\chi_g(5k + 15\mathcal{Z}) = e^{j2\pi 5kg/15} = e^{j2\pi kg/3}$$

from which it is obvious that only the value of g modulo 3 is significant. Therefore we can define the homomorphism

$$\Gamma_H : \widehat{G} \mapsto H$$

by

$$\Gamma_H(\chi_g) = 5g + 15\mathcal{Z}$$

which is an element of H. The kernel of this homomorphism is another subgroup of G:

$$\mathrm{Ker}\,(\Gamma_H) = 3\mathcal{Z}/15\mathcal{Z}$$

The set of coset representatives for H in G can be taken as $\{0, 1, 2, 3, 4\}$. In that case the intermediate vector $\mathbf{v}$ is defined by

$$\mathbf{v}(\sigma + 5g) = \langle \chi_g \mid f_\sigma \rangle_H$$

for each $g \in \{0, 1, 2\}$.

We are almost ready to state and prove the generic FFT algorithm, but first a technical result is needed on a special way to construct coset representatives that are particularly useful for calculations. This theorem looks complicated, but, as the examples following it show, it is actually quite natural:

Theorem 12.3 *Let G be an Abelian group with subgroups $G > H > K$. Let T be a set of coset representatives for H in G, and let U be a set of coset representatives for K in H. Then the set defined by*

$$T + U = \{t + u \mid \text{for all } t \in T, \, u \in U\}$$

is a set of coset representatives for K in G.

Proof   Two questions must be answered. First, are all the elements of $T + U$ distinct coset representatives? Second, are there enough of them? The first question is answered by assuming that $t + u$ and $t' + u'$ both represent the same coset of K in G. In other words, there is an element $k \in K$ such that

$$t + u = t' + u' + k \qquad (12.2)$$

But since u, u' and $k \in H$ are all elements of H, this implies that t and t' both represent the same coset of H in G. Since t and t' both came from T, a set of coset representatives for H in G, this implies that $t = t'$. Using this fact in Equation 12.2 reduces it to the equation

$$u = u' + k$$

with $k \in K$. In other words u and u' both represent the same coset of K in H. Again, since they both belong to U and U is a set of coset representatives of K in H, this implies that $u = u'$. Therefore, every element $t + u$ represents a different coset of K in G.

How many of these coset representatives are there? The answer is exactly the required number:

$$|T| \times |U| = |G/H| \times |H/K| = |G/K|$$

This proves the theorem.   ///

This may seem a rather strange theorem at first, but consider the example $G = \mathbb{Z}/27\mathbb{Z}$, $H = 3\mathbb{Z}/27\mathbb{Z}$, and $K = 9\mathbb{Z}/27\mathbb{Z}$. Then $T = \{0, 1, 2\}$ is a set of coset representatives for H in G, and $U = \{0, 3, 6\}$ is a set of coset representatives for K in H. The sum of these two sets

$$T + U = \{0, 1, 2, 3, 4, 5, 6, 7, 8\}$$

is a set of coset representatives for K in G. Thus, although the theorem looks rather foreboding and technical, in practice it reduces to a very natural set of coset representatives. It works out this way in all cases.

Now we can state and prove the algorithm for the general fast Fourier transform:

Theorem 12.4   *Let G be any finite Abelian group, let f be a complex-valued function on G, let*

$$G = G_n > G_{n-1} > \cdots > G_1 > G_0 = \{0\}$$

be a composition series for G, and let P_k be a set of coset representatives of G_k in G_{k+1} for each $k = 0, 1, \ldots, n - 1$. Let $S_n = \{0\}$, and define S_k inductively by the formula

$$S_k = S_{k+1} + P_k$$

so that, by Theorem 12.3, S_k is a set of coset representatives for G_k in G. Finally, let Γ_k be a homomorphism from $\widehat{G}$ to G_k.

The Fourier transform $\hat{f}$ of f on G may be calculated using the iteration:

1. *Set the loop control variable $k = 0$ and define $f^0 = f$.*
2. *Calculate the formula*

$$f^{k+1}(\sigma + \Gamma_{k+1}(\chi)) = \sum_{s \in P_k} \overline{\chi}(s) f^k(\sigma + s + \Gamma_k(\chi))$$

   for every $\sigma \in S_{k+1}$ and $\chi \in G_{k+1}$.
3. *Increment k.*
4. *If $k < n$, go to step 2.*
5. *Normalize by the factor $\dfrac{1}{\sqrt{|G|}}$.*

When the iteration is finished, $\hat{f} = f^n$.

Proof   The proof is by induction. The induction assumption is that

$$f^k(\sigma + \Gamma_k(\chi)) = \langle \chi \mid f_\sigma \rangle_{G_k} \tag{12.3}$$

for all $\sigma \in S_k$ and all $\chi \in \widehat{G_k}$. To get the induction started, we prove that this is true for $k = 1$. In that case, step 2 reduces to

$$f^1(\sigma + \Gamma_1(\chi)) = \sum_{s \in G_1} \overline{\chi}(s) f(\sigma + s) = \langle \chi \mid f_\sigma \rangle_{G_1}$$

because $P_0 = G_1$, and $G_0 = \{0\}$, so, necessarily, the homomorphism Γ_0 is the constant 0. This proves the induction assumption for $k = 1$ by the definition of the bracket.

Now assume that Equation 12.3 is true for k. The following calculation proves that, with this assumption, it is also true for $k + 1$. The calculation is

$$\langle \chi \mid f_\sigma \rangle_{G_{k+1}} = \sum_{q \in G_{k+1}} \overline{\chi}(q) f(\sigma + q)$$

$$= \sum_{s \in P_k} \sum_{h \in G_k} \overline{\chi}(s + h) f(\sigma + s + h)$$

$$= \sum_{s \in P_k} \overline{\chi}(s) \sum_{h \in G_k} \overline{\chi}(h) f(\sigma + s + h)$$

and the inner sum can be expressed using the bracket notation as

$$= \sum_{s \in P_k} \overline{\chi}(s) \langle \chi \mid f_{\sigma+s} \rangle_{G_k}$$

Now the induction assumption can be used to express the bracket as

$$= \sum_{s \in P_k} \overline{\chi}(s) f^k \left(\sigma + s + \Gamma_k(\chi) \right)$$

which, by step 2 of the iteration, is exactly

$$= f^{k+1} \left(\sigma + \Gamma_{k+1}(\chi) \right) \qquad\qquad ///$$

12.3.3 Counting the Advantage

How many arithmetic operations are required to compute the FFT using this theorem? The formula is easily obtained from the explicit iteration given above:

Theorem 12.5 *Let G be an Abelian group with composition series and coset representatives as in Theorem 12.4. Then the number of multiplications and additions required to calculate the FFT is*

$$|G| \sum_{k=0}^{n-1} |P_k|$$

Proof Each iteration of step 2 requires $|P_k|$ multiplications and additions for each choice of $\sigma + \Gamma_k(\chi)$, a total of $|G|$ possibilities, for a total of $|G| \times |P_k|$ of each operation. The sum of all these terms is as claimed in the theorem.   ///

For example, if the group is $G = \mathcal{Z} / p^n \mathcal{Z}$, where p is a prime and n is a positive integer, then each P_k will contain exactly p elements, and the formula reduces to

$$|G| \sum_{k=0}^{n-1} |P_k| = p^n n p = n p^{n+1}$$

If, on the other hand, the group is $G = \mathcal{Z} / N \mathcal{Z}$ and $N = p^n q^m$ contains two primes p and q, then there will be n terms with $p = |P_k|$ and another m terms with $q = |P_k|$. In this case, the formula becomes

$$|G| \sum_{k=0}^{n-1} |P_k| = p^n q^m (np + mq)$$

Taking a specific numerical example illustrates the advantage obtained. Suppose

$$N = 2000 = 2^4 5^3$$

Then calculating the DFT by brute force requires

$$2000 \times 2000 = 4,000,000$$

multiplications and additions. Using the FFT requires only

$$2000(4 \times 2 + 3 \times 5) = 46,000$$

of each operation. The advantage grows rapidly as the powers of the primes increase. For example, one project I'm aware of used 2^{20}-point FFTs. In that case the ratio advantage of using the FFT was

$$20 \times 2^{21}/2^{40} = 5 \times 2^{-17} = 3.8 \times 10^{-5}$$

12.3.4 One Dimension: $G = \mathbb{Z}/N\mathbb{Z}$

This section shows how to transform Theorem 12.4 into a practical program to calculate each of the iterations. The first step is to choose the composition series

$$G = G_n > G_{n-1} > \cdots > G_0 = \{0\}$$

that will be used, each of the sets P_k of coset representatives, and the coset representatives of G_k in G_{k+1} for each k. There are many choices for the composition series, but they are all equivalent in terms of the number of calculations required to solve the problem. Finding a composition series is as simple as factoring N and constructing a sequence of integers,

$$1 = m_n < m_{n-1} < \cdots < m_1 < m_0 = N$$

such that each one divides the next evenly, and $m_{k-1}/m_k = p_k$ is a prime. Then

$$G = \mathbb{Z}/N\mathbb{Z} = m_n\mathbb{Z}/N\mathbb{Z} > m_{n-1}\mathbb{Z}/N\mathbb{Z} > \cdots > m_1\mathbb{Z}/N\mathbb{Z} > \{0\}$$

is a composition series for G. For convenience, these groups will be labeled $G_k = m_k\mathbb{Z}/N\mathbb{Z}$. There is a natural set of coset representatives P_k for G_k in G_{k+1}. They are

$$P_k = \{0, m_{k+1}, 2m_{k+1}, \ldots, (p_{k+1} - 1)m_{k+1}\}$$

because the next one in this sequence is $p_{k+1}m_{k+1} = m_k$. With this choice for the coset representatives, the set S_k of coset representatives of G_k in G is

$$S_k = \{0, 1, 2, \ldots, m_k - 1\}$$

This is the set of coset representatives guaranteed by Theorem 12.3 and discussed in the example following that theorem.

The heart of the required FFT routine calculates step 2 of Theorem 12.4. The following function, `iterate_fft`, accomplishes this iteration step. The symbols in Theorem 12.4 correspond to the program variables as follows:

Symbol	Variable
m_{k+1}	`m`
p_{k+1}	`p`
$G_k = m_{k+1}p_{k+1}\mathcal{Z}/N\mathcal{Z}$	`mpZ/NZ`
$G_{k+1} = m_{k+1}\mathcal{Z}/N\mathcal{Z}$	`mZ/NZ`
P_k	`{ 0, m, 2m, ..., m(p-1)}`
f^k	`f0`
f^{k+1}	`f1`
σ	`r`
$\chi = \chi_g$	`g`
$\Gamma_{k+1}(\chi_g)$	`gm = g*m`
$\Gamma_k(\chi_g)$	`gmp = g*m*p`
$\exp(j2\pi k/N)$	`roots[k]`

```
#include <numeric.inc>


/* Function f0 is assumed to contain the DFTs of all the
 * translates of the original function f on the group
 * mpZ/NZ.  This function returns the function f1
 * containing the DFTs of all the translates of the
 * original function f on the group mZ/NZ.
 */
void iterate_fft(int N, int m, int p, Complex *roots,
VectorComplex *f0, VectorComplex *f1)
{
    /* These declarations increase the efficiency of
     * handling the vector interface. */
    Complex
        *f1b = f1->buffer + f1->first,
        *f0b = f0->buffer + f0->first;
    int
        spacing_0 = f0->spacing,
        spacing_1 = f1->spacing;
    /* This product is needed several times */

    int mp = m*p;


    /* The first loop iterates through the elements of
     * the group mZ/NZ using the loop variables g, gm,
     * and gmp.  Both g and gmp are initialized negative,
```

```
    * but the first value used in both cases is 0 */
int
    g = -1,
    g_limit = N/m,
    gm = 0,
    gmp = -mp;
for(; ++g < g_limit; gm += m)
{
    /* The second loop iterates through all the coset
     * representatives of mZ/NZ in Z/NZ using r */
    int r = m;

    /* gmp is g*m*p modulo N */
    gmp += mp;
    if(gmp >= N) gmp -= N;

    while(r--)
    {
        /* Next is the summation loop.  It sums
         * over the coset representatives of
         * mpZ/NZ in mZ/NZ using s */
        Complex sum = {0, 0};
        int s = 0, gs = 0;
        for(; s < mp; s += m)
        {
            Complex
                w = roots[gs],
                f = f0b[spacing_0*(r + s + gmp)];
                /* Multiply by the complex conjugate
                 * of W */
                sum.x += w.x * f.x + w.y * f.y;
                sum.y += w.x * f.y - w.y * f.x;

            /* gs = g*s modulo N */
            gs += gm;
            if(gs >= N) gs -= N;
        }
        flb[spacing_1*(r + gm)] = sum;
    }
}
}
```

This routine was designed for readability and close adherence to the statement of Theorem 12.4. It may be possible to program it more efficiently, and you are welcome to try. However, don't congratulate yourself on success until you actually time your new version against this one, using Borland's profiler or some other timing technique.

Notice that the variables $gs = g*s \pmod{N}$ and $gmp = g*m*p \pmod{N}$ are calculated as sums with a conditional check on the magnitude, instead of simply writing $gs = g*s \% N$ and $gmp = gm*p \% N$. The approach used may or may not be faster than using the $\%$ operator, but there is a more important reason than speed. The products $g*s$ and $gm*p$ may both exceed N, so they might overflow the integer storage space on the computer being used. The approach used, while more cumbersome, is much less likely to lead to overflow problems. Using the addition approach, overflow is only possible if $2*N$ overflows the integer. For the multiplication approach, overflow might occur any time N^2 overflows the integer. For a 16-bit signed integer representation, overflow using the multiplication approach is possible for any $N > 2^{7.5} \approx 181$. The addition approach, on the other hand, can overflow only for $N > 2^{15}/2 = 2^{14} = 16,384$. On most computers, this limit cannot be reached, because the address word is usually equal to the length of an integer, and a floating-point number usually occupies at least 4 bytes of storage. Thus, the limited address space usually sets the ceiling, instead of the integer overflows within the routine.

12.3.5 Pre-Computing for FFT

The FFT routine requires the factorization of N and the calculation of all the Nth roots of unity. In many applications, the FFT is calculated many times for one or only a few choices of N. It is therefore beneficial to precalculate the factors of N and the roots of unity that are needed. The necessary working space can also be preallocated. However, if memory is scarce, it will be better to allocate memory only when it is required. That is the approach used here, since it adds very little overhead anyway.

The header file containing the required structures and function prototypes for calculating FFTs is `numeric.inc`. The relevant portion of that file is

```
#ifndef NUMERIC_INC
#define NUMERIC_INC

#include <vector.inc>

/* The PrimePower structure stores a prime and its power
 * in the factorization of N.
 */

typedef struct { int prime, power; } PrimePower;
/* The PrimeFactorization structure stores the prime
```

```
 * factorization of N.  There are number_of_primes
 * elements in the array pp.  pp[k] stores the k'th prime
 * and its power in the factorization.
 */
typedef struct {
    int N, number_of_primes;
    PrimePower *pp;
} PrimeFactorization;


PrimeFactorization factor(int N);


/* The FFT structure stores all the information
 * required by each FFT calculation for one particular
 * vector length N.
 */
typedef struct {
    PrimeFactorization factors;
    double scale;
    Complex *roots;
} FFT;


/* Allocates and initializes a control structure
 */
FFT *new_fft(int N);


/* Calculates the FFT of f, putting the result in dft
 */
int fft(
    FFT *control, VectorComplex *f, VectorComplex *dft);


/* Calculates the FFT of two real vectors
 */
int fft_pair(
    FFT *control, VectorDouble *f1, VectorDouble *f2,
    VectorComplex *dft1, VectorComplex *dft2);


#endif
```

The `fft` routine uses the prime factorization information as follows:

```
int fft(FFT *control,
VectorComplex *f, VectorComplex *dft)
{
```

```
      if(control->factors.N != f->length)
      {
         error_message("fft---The control structure and"
             the "vector length do not agree");
         return 0;
      }
      if(f->length != dft->length)
      {
         error_message("fft---The two vectors must be the"
         " same length");
         return 0;
      }
      /* Now the iteration loop.  Two vectors of length N
       * are needed.  One is the output vector dft, the
       * other is allocated here.  These two vectors are
       * used alternately as the input and output vectors
       * for the iteration step.  Pointers to these vectors
       * are stored in the array t[2].  The variable flop
       * chooses which one of them is the input, and which
       * is the output.
       */
      {
         int prime_count =
             control->factors.number_of_primes,
             flop = 0, N = control->factors.N, m = N;
         VectorComplex *t[2];
         t[0] = new_VectorComplex(N);
         if(!t[0])
         {
             error_message("fft---Could not allocate the"
             " temporary vector");
             return 0;
         }
         t[1] = dft;
         copy_vector_complex(f, t[0]);
         while(prime_count--)
         {
             int p = control->factors.pp[prime_count].prime,
                 k = control->factors.pp[prime_count].power;

             for(; k--; flop ^= 1)
             {
                 m /= p;
                 iterate_fft(N, m, p, control->roots,
```

```
                  t[flop], t[flop^1]);
            }
        }
        if(!flop) copy_vector_complex(t[0], dft);
        old_VectorComplex(t[0]);
        scale_vector_complex(control->scale, dft);
    }
    return 1;
}
```

The `new_fft` routine must factor the integer **N** and fill in the array of roots of unity. The factorization routine works as follows. First, all the factors of 2 are removed by dividing by 2 until the result is odd. This odd value is stored in the same storage location **N**. Next, an iteration is started that checks to see if **N** is divisible by any of the odd numbers, starting with 3. When an odd divisor **p** is found, **N** is reduced by this factor repeatedly until it is no longer divisible by **p**. This divisor must be a prime, for if it is not, then $p = rq$ is a product of two numbers, both of which are odd and less than **p** but larger than 2. But all these smaller odd factors have already been removed from **N**, so this is a contradiction. The factorization function is as follows:

```
PrimeFactorization factor(int N)
{
    PrimeFactorization pf;
    /* There cannot be more primes in the factorization
     * of an integer than there are bits in an integer.
     * The extra space will be released before exiting
     * this routine.
     */
    int P = sizeof(PrimePower)*CHAR_BIT*sizeof(int);
    pf.N = N;
    pf.number_of_primes = 0;
    pf.pp = malloc(P);
    if(!pf.pp)
    {
        error_message("factor---Could not allocate"
            " space");
        return pf;
    }
    memset(pf.pp, 0, P);
    if(N <= 1) return pf;

    /* Check for powers of 2 */
    if((N & 1) == 0)
```

```
        {
            pf.number_of_primes = 1;
            pf.pp[0].prime = 2;
            while((N & 1) == 0)
            {
                N /= 2;
                pf.pp[0].power++;
            }
        }

        /* Now start with the odd primes.  The loop actually
         * checks each odd number from 3 on up until N is
         * reduced to 1. If one of these odd numbers divides
         * N it is a prime because all lower primes have
         * already been factored out.
         */
        for(P = 3; N > 1; P += 2)
        {
            int power = 0;
            while(N % P == 0)
            {
                power++;
                N /= P;
            }
            if(power)
            {
                pf.pp[pf.number_of_primes].prime = P;
                pf.pp[pf.number_of_primes].power = power;
                pf.number_of_primes++;
            }
        }
        pf.pp = realloc(
            pf.pp, sizeof(PrimePower)*pf.number_of_primes);
        return pf;
    }
```

The **new_fft** function uses the factorization routine, then computes all the **N**th roots of unity as follows:

```
FFT *new_fft(int N)
{
    FFT *s = malloc(sizeof(FFT) + sizeof(Complex)*N);
    if(!s)
    {
```

```
        error_message("new_fft---Could not allocate "
            "space");
        return NULL;
    }
    s->factors = factor(N);
    if(s->factors.number_of_primes == 0)
    {
        error_message("new_fft---Could not factor N");
        free(s);
        return NULL;
    }
    s->scale = 1.0/sqrt(N);
    /* Now calculate all the roots of unity required */
    s->roots = (Complex *)(s + 1);
    s->roots[0].x = 1;
    s->roots[0].y = 0;
    {
        int k = N/2;
        long double x = 2*M_PI/N;
        if((N & 1) == 0)
        {
            s->roots[k].x = -1;
            s->roots[k].y = 0;
            k--;
        }
        for(; k; k--)
        {
            long double w = k*x;
            s->roots[k].x = s->roots[N-k].x = cos(w);
            s->roots[N-k].y = -(s->roots[k].y = sin(w));
        }
    }
    return s;
}
```

12.4 THE FFT OF TWO REAL VECTORS

The Fourier transform inherently takes a complex vector as its input and delivers a complex vector as its output. However, in many signal processing applications, the input vectors are real. Two of these real vectors could be used to compose one complex vector of the same length, whose Fourier transform can then be calculated. Can the Fourier transform of each real input vector be extracted from the result? The answer is yes. The advantage is that two Fourier transforms are then calculated for essentially the same amount of computation previously required for just one.

The key to unraveling the Fourier transforms of each real input function is the observation that

$$\overline{\hat{g}}(\omega) = \hat{g}(-\omega) \tag{12.4}$$

for any real-valued function $g(t)$. This equation is proved by the calculation

$$\overline{\hat{g}}(\omega) = \frac{1}{\kappa}\overline{\langle \chi_\omega \mid g \rangle}$$

$$= \frac{1}{\kappa}\langle \overline{\chi}_\omega \mid \overline{g} \rangle$$

and, since g is real-valued and $\overline{\chi}_\omega = \chi_{-\omega}$,

$$= \frac{1}{\kappa}\langle \chi_{-\omega} \mid g \rangle$$
$$= \hat{g}(-\omega)$$

by the definition of the Fourier transform.

Given two real-valued functions g and h, a complex-valued function is formed by

$$f(t) = g(t) + jh(t)$$

Since the bracket is complex-linear in its ket component, this means that

$$\hat{f}(\omega) = \hat{g}(\omega) + j\hat{h}(\omega)$$

Using this and Equation 12.4 on both g and h gives

$$\overline{\hat{f}}(-\omega) = \hat{g}(\omega) - j\hat{h}(\omega)$$

These two equations can be solved for $\hat{g}$ and $\hat{h}$ as follows:

$$\hat{g}(\omega) = \frac{\hat{f}(\omega) + \overline{\hat{f}}(-\omega)}{2}$$

$$\hat{h}(\omega) = \frac{\hat{f}(\omega) - \overline{\hat{f}}(-\omega)}{2j}$$

These equations are used in the routine **fft_pair** as follows:

```
#include <numeric.inc>
#include <generic.inc>

int fft_pair(FFT *control,
VectorDouble *f1, VectorComplex *df1,
VectorDouble *f2, VectorComplex *df2)
{
    if(f1->length != control->factors.N
    !! f2->length != f1->length
    !! df1->length != f1->length
    !! df2->length != f1->length)
    {
        error_message(
        "fft_pair---All vectors must be of length N");
        return 0;
    }
    /* Make one complex vector out of the two real
     * vectors */
    {
        Complex *c = df1->buffer + df1->first;
        double
            *real = f1->buffer + f1->first,
            *imag = f2->buffer + f2->first;
        int
            sc = df1->spacing,
            sr = f1->spacing,
            si = f2->spacing,
            k = f1->length;

        for(; k--; c += sc, real += sr, imag += si)
        {
            c->x = *real;
            c->y = *imag;
        }
    }
    /* Now take the fft */
    error_option++;
    if(!fft(control, df1, df1))
    {
        if(--error_option) return 0;
        else exit(-1);
    }
```

```
        error_option--;
        /* And finally unwrap the FFT to obtain the two
         * individual ones */
        {
            int s1 = df1->spacing,
                s2 = df2->spacing,
                k = f1->length;
            Complex
                *up1 = df1->buffer + df1->first,
                *dn1 = up1 + s1*(k - 1),
                *up2 = df2->buffer + df2->first,
                *dn2 = up2 + s2*(k - 1);

            up2->x = up1->y;
            up2->y = 0;
            up2 += s2;
            up1->y = 0;
            up1 += s1;
            for(k = (k - 1)/2; k--;
            up1 += s1, up2 += s2, dn1 -= s1, dn2 -= s2)
            {
                Complex u = *up1, d = *dn1;
                dn2->x = up2->x = (u.y + d.y)*0.5;
                dn2->y = -(up2->y = (d.x - u.x)*0.5);
                dn1->x = up1->x = (u.x + d.x)*0.5;
                dn1->y = -(up1->y = (u.y - d.y)*0.5);
            }
            if((f1->length & 1) == 0)
            {
                Complex u = *up1;
                up2->x = u.y;
                up2->y = 0;
                up1->x = u.x;
                up1->y = 0;
            }
        }
        return 1;
    }
```

PART III

Waveforms and Filters

This part contains the second project: the analysis of a glockenspiel and a piano waveform. The goal is to find a way, using digital signal processing, to recreate the sounds of these instruments. This is not easily accomplished, and the final results are not perfect replicas of the original sounds. In particular, the "attack" of an instrument is very important to its perceived tonal quality, but only the "sustain" is addressed here.

Chapter 13 introduces the project by giving a deceptively simple statement of the problem in Equation 13.1. This leads to a consideration of impulse responses and FIR and IIR filtering as well as spectral analysis of the waveforms.

Chapter 14 explains the basics of DSP filters and derives all the formulas required to implement them and to calculate their gain as a function of frequency. Chapter 15 completes these considerations by showing how to implement these filters in C routines.

Chapter 16 introduces the (generalized) LP (linear predictive) method of filter estimation. The LP method is tested on waveforms generated by known digital filters, then applied to segments of the glockenspiel and piano waveforms.

Finally, the reader is challenged to carry this process further by analyzing the French horn and trumpet waveforms and using the results to create a multiple-voice music synthesizer.

CHAPTER *13*

From Waveforms to Filters

13.1 INTRODUCTION

Part I of this book was primarily concerned with waveform synthesis using simple harmonic oscillators. We now turn to the task of waveform analysis: obtaining information from a waveform. A receiver, for example, must separate the desired signal from the noise. In other cases, the desired signal is not known a priori as it is for receiver designs, and the goal is to learn something about the physics of the object producing the waveform. There is always noise mixed with the desired signal, and the noise must somehow be rejected even when the signal is not well specified.

For example, a pulsed radar sends discrete pulses of microwave radiation toward a target and waits for a return. The radiated signal is known, but the environment scatters the signal; moving targets cause doppler shifts; birds, buildings, and the ground bounce part of the energy back to the receiver; and some targets do their best to hide from or jam the radar. In the midst of all that clutter, the radar receiver is supposed to extract useful information about the significant targets.

In this part of the book, we will analyze waveforms from various musical instruments and attempt to construct digital filters that could have produced these waveforms when properly driven. The equation to be solved in this process is deceptively simple. Every linear filter can, as discussed below, be expressed as a convolution. If y is the filter output, x is the filter input, and $\mathcal{F}$ is the impulse response of the filter, then these quantities are related by

$$y = \mathcal{F} * x \tag{13.1}$$

where the $*$ represents convolution, as defined in Section 8.14 (page 139) for continuous-time functions and in Section 11.4 (page 200) for the general case. In this equation, the only known quantity is y, the filter output, and it is corrupted with noise. The driving waveform x is known in some cases or can be guessed. For example, percussive instruments, such as the glockenspiel analyzed later, are driven by isolated hammer blows, which can be adequately modeled as impulses. However, the precise timing of the impulse is not known, and this uncertainty must be dealt with.

What about a trumpet or French horn? These instruments are not percussive. For brass instruments in general, it is the repetitive opening and closing of the player's lips and the resulting impulse-like bursts of air into the horn that drive the sound. What is the driving waveform in that case? The choice of the driving force x will make a difference in the filter estimate $\mathcal{F}$. The best choice is not at all obvious.

Real musical instruments are much more complicated than the simple harmonic oscillators used in Part I for the bell choir. The *Scientific American* article [6] on the acoustics of the harpsichord, for example, explains the many intricacies of that instrument. The vibrating string serves mainly as the energy source, driving a very complicated resonator composed of the wooden sound board, the instrument case, and the enclosed air space. The sound waves are radiated by the resonators, not directly by the string.

Another *Scientific American* article [2], analyzes the physics of brass instruments, explaining their acoustics by using partial differential equations similar to those of quantum mechanics. The changes of impedance, as the bells of these instruments flare, reflect a portion of the energy back into the instrument, thus creating a standing wave that leaks out of the bell.

The physics of musical instruments is fascinating, but we will not deal with it in this book. We focus instead on finding a filter $\mathcal{F}$ and driving force x combination that is capable of producing the observed waveform using Equation 13.1. We can only succeed to the extent that the chosen instruments can be modeled as linear filters. Any nonlinearities will necessarily be lost.

13.2   THE IMPULSE RESPONSE TELLS ALL

The impulse response of any linear, time-invariant system completely describes that system. This fact is explained in this section. First, take a look at the waveforms plotted in Figures 13.1 and 13.2. Figure 13.1 is the first 50 ms of a piano's

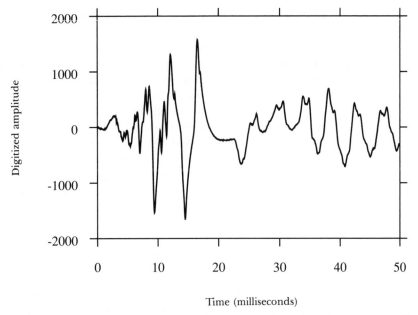

Figure 13.1   This figure plots the first 50 ms of the impulse response of a piano. The initial response in the first 25 ms is quickly replaced by the sustained note of the piano.

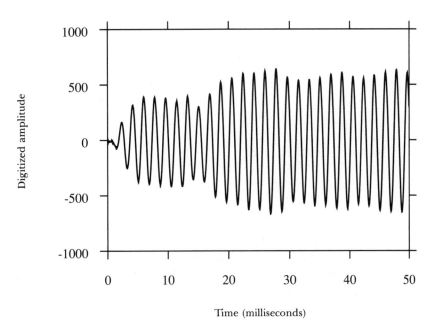

Figure 13.2   The impulse response of a glockenspiel, as plotted here, is much cleaner looking than that of the piano in Figure 13.1.

waveform following a hammer blow. Figure 13.2 is the same, but for a glockenspiel. Although the blow of a hammer is not a perfect impulse, we assume here that these waveforms are adequate representations of the impulse response of the respective instruments. Compare these with the impulse response of the simple harmonic oscillator in Figure 2.2 on page 25. Even the glockenspiel is considerably more complicated than the simple harmonic oscillator. The tones produced by both the piano and the glockenspiel decay slowly, lasting for several seconds each, if not stopped prematurely by the player.

These impulse responses could be used directly to reproduce the piano or glockenspiel sounds. In fact, that is precisely the way many commercial music synthesizers work. They store recorded waveforms for each instrument and play them back when the key is pressed. For percussive instruments, it is important to have an accurate record of the impulse response, or the synthesized sound will not be realistic.

13.2.1   Reconstruction with Impulse Response Only

The impulse response of a linear, time-invariant system can be used to construct the response of that system to an arbitrary input. In fact, that is precisely what is meant by a "finite-impulse-response" (FIR) filter. This is the way it works. Let Γ be a linear, time-invariant system. Its impulse response, $\gamma(t)$, is calculated by hitting the system with an ideal impulse:

$$\gamma(t) = \Gamma(\delta(t))$$

where δ is the Dirac delta function. Then we can also determine the system response to two isolated impulses at different times:

$$\Gamma(a\delta(t) + b\delta(t - \tau)) = a\Gamma(\delta(t)) + b\Gamma(\delta(t - \tau))$$

because Γ is linear, and

$$= a\gamma(t) + b\gamma(t - \tau)$$

because it is time-invariant. In other words, the two impulse responses are just superimposed with their respective amplitudes and with the appropriate time shifts. For digital signal processing, this is almost the end of the story. Any driving function x can be thought of as a sequence of impulses at each discrete time point, so the system response can be calculated by

$$\Gamma(x)(t) = \Gamma\left(\sum_{k=-\infty}^{+\infty} x(k)\delta(t - k\Delta t) \right)$$

$$= \sum_{k=-\infty}^{+\infty} x(k)\Gamma(\delta(t - k\Delta t))$$

$$= \sum_{k=-\infty}^{+\infty} x(k)\gamma(t - k\Delta t)$$

which, according the definition of convolution in Section 11.4, is

$$= (\gamma * x)(t)$$

This is precisely what was stated in Equation 13.1. Only a little more work is required to obtain the same result for continuous-time systems. The sum must be replaced by an integral:

$$x(t) = \int_{-\infty}^{+\infty} x(u)\delta(u - t)\, du$$

and used as follows:

$$\Gamma(x)(t) = \Gamma\left(\int_{-\infty}^{+\infty} x(u)\delta(u - t)\, du\right)$$

$$= \int_{-\infty}^{+\infty} x(u)\Gamma(\delta(u - t))\, du$$

because Γ is linear, and

$$= \int_{-\infty}^{+\infty} x(u)\gamma(u - t)\, du$$

because it is time-invariant. Finally,

$$= (x * \gamma)(t)$$

according to the definition of convolution in Section 8.14.

13.2.2 The FIR Technique

So, it is possible to use the system impulse response directly to reconstruct the system response to any input. This is precisely what the FIR (finite-impulse-response) filtering technique does. Of course, the impulse response used must be finite, or the computation will never deliver even the first point. To see how this works, let $\mathcal{G}$ be a finite impulse response that is nonzero only for integer arguments from 0 to $N - 1$. Then Equation 13.1 can be used directly to compute the system response as follows:

$$\mathcal{G} * x(\ell) = \sum_{k=-\infty}^{+\infty} \mathcal{G}(\ell - k)x(k)$$

But, since $\mathcal{G}$ is nonzero only from 0 to $N - 1$, this reduces to

$$\mathcal{G} * x(\ell) = \sum_{k=\ell-N+1}^{\ell} \mathcal{G}(\ell - k)x(k) \tag{13.2}$$

In other words, only the values of the driving force at the current point and the $N - 1$ previous points are required to determine the system output at the current point.

The FIR filter technique, Equation 13.2, is important in digital signal processing. However, it is used only if the impulse response is short or if the forcing function x is nonzero in only a few places within any stretch of N points. In general, each output point obtained with this technique requires N multiplications and $N - 1$ additions. The piano and glockenspiel impulse responses each persist for several seconds. The waveforms were digitized with 40,000 samples per second, so the impulse response in each case is well over 100,000 points long. For such long impulse responses and general forcing functions the FIR technique is clearly impractical.

13.2.3 The IIR Technique

In contrast, the filter used in Section 4.2 to generate a bell tone of arbitrarily long impulse response required the storage of the two constants, `c1` and `c2` in the program, and only two multiplications and one addition per point computed, creating, for example, the waveform in Figure 4.1 on page 48. This same filter was used in Section 4.3 with random noise as the driving force to generate the organ-like waveform pictured in Figure 4.2 on page 50.

Filters such as those used in Chapter 4 are called infinite-impulse-response (IIR) filters, because they have (theoretically) an infinitely long response to an impulse. They are also called "recursive" filters, because they depend not only on the driving force, but on their own previous outputs. It is the recursive nature of the filters that makes it possible to have such long impulse responses.

However, such simple filters are not usually what is required. For example, the organ-like waveforms generated in Section 4.3 sound more like cheap whistles than any organ. A more realistic organ requires much more complicated filters. Sometimes an FIR filter is just what is required. Frequently a combination of both techniques is required.

13.3   FREQUENCY ANALYSIS OF WAVEFORMS

So, starting with waveforms such as those in Figures 13.1 and 13.2, how can we find a filter that might have produced these waveforms via Equation 13.1? Spectral estimation is an essential tool for this process, and the discrete Fourier transform is the principal spectral analysis tool available. The most obvious thing to try is taking the Fourier transform on both sides of Equation 13.1, which, according to Equation 8.25 on page 139, becomes

$$\hat{y}(\omega) \;=\; \sqrt{2\pi}\,\widehat{\mathcal{F}}(\omega)\hat{x}(\omega) \tag{13.3}$$

This equation can be immediately solved for $\widehat{\mathcal{F}}$, but, alas, this does not solve the problem. The procedure does indeed lead to a filtering technique, DFT filtering, previously mentioned in Section 10.5. It is an important technique. The procedure is to transform the input signal, multiply by the filter coefficients $\widehat{\mathcal{F}}(\omega)$, and then take the inverse transform to obtain the filtered waveform. This is usually done in overlapping segments rather than all at once.

The DFT filter approach is an FIR filter technique. The impulse response of a DFT filter is finite by definition, because the transforms can only be taken in finite windows. The DFT filter approach, therefore, suffers from the same problems as the FIR filter technique if the impulse response of the desired filter is long.

Even though Equation 13.3 does not directly reveal the required filter design, it does prove that the Fourier transform of the waveform can be used to estimate the frequency response of the desired filter. The impulse responses of both the piano and the glockenspiel are both far too long to be used all at once, so the waveforms are broken into shorter windows, each of which can be analyzed separately. The importance of the window shape was explored in Section 10.1 starting on page 155. If you have not read that section yet, do so now before continuing.

13.3.1   The Steady-State Portion

Before attempting to analyze the impulse responses plotted in Figures 13.1 and 13.2, let's tackle the easier job of analyzing the waveform after the initial transient has died away. Figure 13.3 shows 20 ms of the same piano waveform as plotted in Figure 13.1, but starting several hundred ms after the hammer blow. By this time, the waveform is highly repetitive. The irregularity of the waveform in each period indicates that the note is not a simple single tone but must contain many strong harmonics. In this case, the note is the A below middle C, 220 Hz.

A longer stretch of the piano waveform, plotted in Figure 13.4, is used to analyze its frequency content. The longer the segment used, the more frequency information can be obtained. This is a result of the uncertainty principle stated

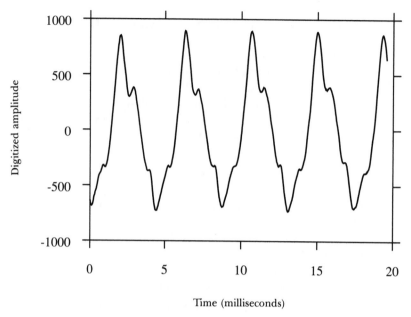

Figure 13.3   This is 20 ms of the same waveform as plotted in Figure 13.1, but after the initial transient has died out.

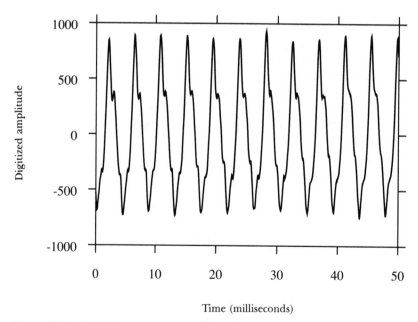

Figure 13.4   This longer segment of the piano waveform is used to analyze its frequency content, because it provides more detailed information.

in Theorem 8.11 on page 129. In this case, 2000 points of the waveform are used, spanning 50 ms.

All the waveforms used in Part III were digitized using a 12-bit A/D converter, taking 40,000 samples per second. As explained in Section 1.3, this means that the highest frequency that can be represented in this data, the Nyquist frequency, is 20 kHz. As explained in Section 1.4, higher frequencies present in the original waveform masquerade as lower frequencies, below 20 kHz. It is therefore important to exclude these higher frequencies. This was done by filtering the waveforms with an "anti-aliasing" filter before digitizing them. The "anti-aliasing" filter used is a low-pass filter with no attenuation out to 12 kHz. The attenuation then rapidly increases until it is more than 80 dB for frequencies above 20 kHz. In other words, any frequencies present above 20 kHz in the original signal are suppressed by at least 80 dB before the waveform was digitized. It is not possible to provide infinite attenuation; 80 dB is sufficient for almost any purpose.

At 40,000 samples per second, the sampling period is $25\mu s$. Thus, the 50 ms waveform of Figure 13.4 contains 2000 points. The DFT of a 2000-point waveform provides 2000 complex frequency components. However, as discussed in Section 12.4, nearly half of this information is redundant, because the waveform is real, not complex. If f is the waveform and $\hat{f}$ is its Fourier transform, then

$$\hat{f}(\omega) = \overline{\hat{f}(-\omega)} \tag{13.4}$$

assuming only that f is real. In this case, the Fourier transform used is the one stated in Theorem 9.1 on page 148 with $N = 2000$ points. The result is $\hat{f}$, also defined on 2000 points. These 2000 points in the frequency domain are arranged equally spaced around the unit circle in the complex plane, as explained in Chapter 1. The points from $\hat{f}(0)$ through $\hat{f}(1000)$ cover the top half of the circle, including both points on the real axis, 1 and -1. The points from $\hat{f}(1001)$ through $\hat{f}(1999)$ continue around the bottom half of the circle.

Because the frequencies are on the unit circle, the point $\hat{f}(2000)$ is precisely the same as $\hat{f}(0)$. In terms of Theorem 9.1, this is because the argument of f actually belongs to $\mathcal{Z}/N\mathcal{Z}$, the integers modulo N, which in this case is 2000. Thus the points on the bottom half of the circle could just as well be labeled as $\hat{f}(-1)$ through $\hat{f}(-999)$. These are the points that, according to Equation 13.4, are redundant. For example,

$$\hat{f}(-1) = \hat{f}(1999) = \overline{\hat{f}(1)}$$

For this reason, when plotting spectra of real functions obtained with DFTs, usually only the first half of the points are plotted, in this case 1001 points. In general, for N points, the number is $[(N + 2)/2]$, where the brackets indicate that the ratio should be truncated to an integer.

Thus, $\hat{f}(0)$ is the 0 Hz, or DC, component of the waveform. The Nyquist frequency component is $\hat{f}(1000)$. In this case the Nyquist frequency is 20 kHz, so each frequency bin of the DFT is 20 Hz wide. As shown in Section 10.1, it is important to shape the window carefully to obtain the maximum amount of usable frequency discrimination. (In fact, the "noise bandwidth" of each frequency bin is 20 Hz, no matter what window shape is used. However, different window shapes will distribute that same 20 Hz bandwidth differently.) The piano waveform in Figure 13.4 provides a good illustration of the importance of windowing in what follows.

Figure 13.5 shows the waveform after multiplying by a cosine-squared window, as illustrated in Figure 10.1 on page 159. Figure 13.6 is the magnitude of the Fourier transform of Figure 13.5 There is very little or no musical energy above 4 kHz. The relatively strong spectral lines above 12 kHz are evidently caused by the computer controlling the digitizer. They cannot have come from the recording environment, the piano, or the tape recorder, because of the anti-aliasing filter used just before the A/D converter. They were probably generated by the CRT display or some other repetitive instrument, such as a switching power supply. In any case, these lines are of no interest for this project.

Figure 13.7 shows the first 4 kHz of the frequency axis. Now the spectral lines are clearly visible. The fundamental frequency is 220 Hz, the A below middle C. All the other spectral lines are multiples of this fundamental. The spectrum of any repetitive waveform has similarly sharp line features—that is the only way to get a repetitive waveform. The repetition period determines the fundamental frequency. All other strong frequencies in the waveform must be multiples of the fundamental; otherwise, the periodic structure of the waveform cannot be maintained.

Now compare the windowed DFT in Figure 13.7 with the unwindowed DFT in Figure 13.8. Clearly, the windowing process dramatically improves the resolution of the fundamental frequency and all its harmonics. In fact, the higher harmonics in the unwindowed version are entirely missed. It may seem paradoxical that applying a window function, which is, after all, throwing away part of the energy, should actually improve the analysis. Section 10.2 explains this apparent paradox. Just remember that using the proper window is essential.

13.3.2 Processing Gain

The dynamic range in Figure 13.6 is 80 dB, but the A/D converter used provides only 12 bits, a range of 4096, from -2048 to $+2047$. This is a dynamic range of only

$$20 \log_{10}\left(2^{12}\right) = 12 \times 20 \log_{10}(2) \approx 72 \text{ dB}$$

Is something wrong? No, there is *processing gain* associated with calculating the Fourier transform with 2000 points. It works as follows. Consider what happens to a sine wave of amplitude a when the DFT is calculated. Let $\omega_k = 2\pi k/N$,

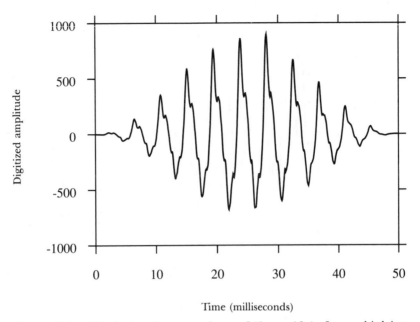

Figure 13.5 This is the piano waveform of Figure 13.4 after multiplying by a cosine-squared window function.

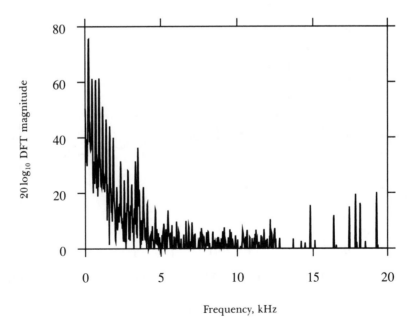

Figure 13.6 This is the magnitude-only Fourier transform of the windowed piano waveform. There is very little or no musical energy past 4 kHz.

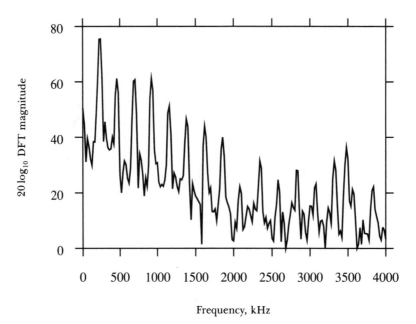

Figure 13.7   This is the portion of the DFT of the windowed piano waveform from 0 to 4 kHz.

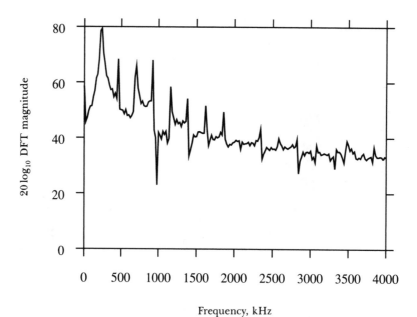

Figure 13.8   This is the portion of the DFT of the unwindowed piano waveform from 0 to 4 kHz. The spectral lines are no longer as obvious. In fact the weaker ones at higher frequencies are lost entirely.

where k is an integer and N is the number of data points used. When the DFT of the function $a \sin(\omega_k \tau)$ is calculated, the only frequencies that are nonzero are ω_k and $-\omega_k$, because all the other frequencies are orthogonal. The DFT can be calculated easily using the bracket notation by writing

$$\sin \omega_k \tau = \frac{1}{2} [\psi_{k/N}(\tau) - \psi_{-k/N}(\tau)]$$

and using Theorem 9.1 on page 148, as follows:

$$\frac{1}{\sqrt{N}} \langle \psi_{k/N} \mid a \sin(2\pi k \tau/N) \rangle = \frac{a}{2\sqrt{N}} \langle \psi_{k/N} \mid \psi_{k/N} - \psi_{-k/N} \rangle$$

$$= \frac{a}{2\sqrt{N}} \langle \psi_{k/N} \mid \psi_{k/N} \rangle$$

$$= \frac{a}{2\sqrt{N}} N$$

$$= \frac{a\sqrt{N}}{2}$$

This result is translated into decibels by taking $20 \log_{10}$ of the magnitude, which is

$$20 \log_{10}(a\sqrt{N}/2) = 20 \log_{10} a + 10 \log_{10}(N/4).$$

In this particular case, $N = 2000$, so the calculation becomes

$$= 20 \log_{10} a + 27.$$

For example, a sine wave with amplitude equal to one-half least significant bit registers as $+21$ dB on this scale. The top of the range is a sine wave of amplitude 2048, which is 93 dB, accounting for the 72 dB range delivered by the A/D converter. Yet, in Figure 13.7 and all the other spectral plots, many features below 21 dB are visible.

It may seem paradoxical, but small-amplitude sine waves can be detected using the Fourier transform if they are carried on top of other signals or noise. There is a processing gain built into the DFT process. Consider a signal that consists of white noise W plus a single sinusoid $S(t) = a \sin(\omega_k t)$. If $|\widehat{W}(\nu)| = b$, then the RMS voltage of the noise is $\sqrt{N} b$. In contrast, the RMS voltage of the sinusoid is $a/\sqrt{2}$, and, as we have just calculated, its Fourier transform magnitude is

$$|\widehat{S}(\ell)| = \begin{cases} a\sqrt{N}/2 & \text{if } \ell = \pm k \\ 0 & \text{otherwise} \end{cases}$$

Thus, we have some hope of detecting the presence of the sinusoid in the signal plus noise, $W + S$, as long as

$$b \le a \sqrt{N}/2 \qquad (13.5)$$

It is enlightening to put this in terms of the RMS voltages of the noise and the signal. The RMS voltage of the sinusoid is $v = a/\sqrt{2}$, so multiplying Equation 13.5 on both sides by $\sqrt{N}$ and replacing a with v gives

$$\sqrt{N}b \le vN/\sqrt{2}$$

In other words, it may be possible to detect a sinusoid that is $N/\sqrt{2}$ times weaker than the noise in which it is embedded, in terms of their respective RMS voltages. In our case, with $N = 2000$, this is a factor of 1414. However, things are not really this simple. Random noise also produces random-looking magnitude spectra. The sinusoid must produce a spectral peak that is significantly greater than most, if not all, of the peaks created by the noise. Figure 13.9, for example, is the spectrum of white Gaussian noise with RMS voltage of 1, plus a sinusoid at frequency 0.25π radians per data point and amplitude 0.45. This spectrum was calculated using floating-point numbers for the waveform. Figure 13.10 is the spectrum of the same waveform obtained after truncating all the floating-point numbers to integers. The energy in most frequency bins is lower than in Figure 13.9, because of the integer truncation. However, the peak due to the sinusoidal signal is still 13 dB higher than the other peaks. This experiment can be repeated with a sine wave of half the amplitude used here, 0.225, and the peak due to the sine wave will still be 7 dB above the background, enough to be detected. However, this is far from the theoretical factor of 1414 discussed above. To actually achieve any such processing gain, many spectra must be averaged together so that the random frequency spikes caused by the Gaussian noise average out to a much lower level.

13.3.3 The Glockenspiel

It is interesting to contrast the waveform and spectrum of the piano, analyzed before, with that of the glockenspiel, a much simpler instrument. Figure 13.11 is the waveform of the glockenspiel, some time after the initial transient of Figure 13.2 has disappeared. This waveform looks almost like a pure sine wave. Its spectrum, plotted in Figure 13.12, shows that this is almost, but not quite, true. The fundamental frequency, 554 Hz, the C# an octave above middle C, has significantly greater width than a pure sine wave. Its first overtone (second harmonic), at 1108 Hz, is quite weak, almost not noticeable. Its third harmonic, at 1662 Hz, is somewhat stronger, but still much weaker than the fundamental. Further harmonics, while perhaps present, are barely distinguishable from the background noise.

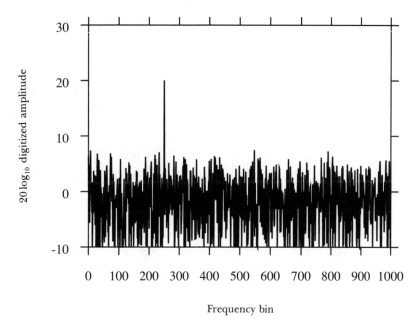

Figure 13.9   The spectrum of Gaussian noise plus a weak sine wave.

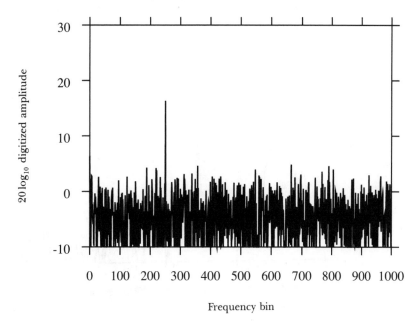

Figure 13.10   The spectrum of the same waveform as used in Figure 13.9, but after truncating the waveform to integer values. The sine wave is still detectable, even though it would not even toggle the least significant bit in the absence of the noise.

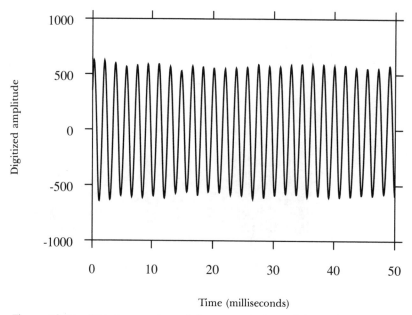

Figure 13.11   This is a portion of the same glockenspiel waveform plotted in Figure 13.2, but after the initial start-up transient has died away.

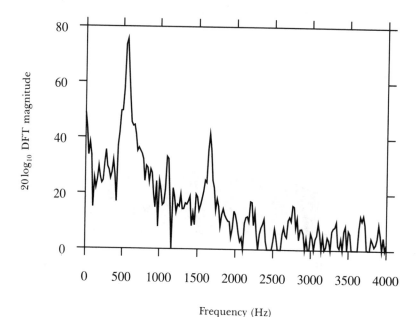

Figure 13.12   By comparison with the spectrum of the piano waveform, this spectrum of the glockenspiel looks particularly simple. The second harmonic is very weak. The third harmonic is somewhat stronger, but still weak. Higher harmonics are basically absent.

13.4 SPECTRA OF THE INITIAL TRANSIENTS

The initial transients of the piano and glockenspiel, shown in Figures 13.1 and 13.2 respectively, are important for the perception of music. Cheap music synthesizers ignore the initial transients and just play back the middle portion of the waveform. Higher-quality synthesizers must somehow model the "attack" of each instrument to make it as natural as possible.

The spectra of these initial transients can sometimes be quite different from the spectra of the rest of the waveforms. The piano is a case in point. As was discussed in Section 10.2, the proper window to use for these initial transients is half of a cosine-squared or other window. In this case, half of a cosine-squared window is used, 2000 points long. Figure 13.13 is the product of the piano impulse in Figure 13.1, multiplied by the half cosine-squared window. Figure 13.14 is the Fourier transform of this windowed waveform.

Compare the spectra in Figure 13.14 with that in Figure 13.6. The spectrum of the initial impulse response has only a poorly defined fundamental frequency at 220 Hz, and none of its overtones can be discerned. Evidently, the start-up transient is not very "tuneful." However, it is an important part of the piano's sound.

Now let's do the same analysis for the glockenspiel. Figure 13.15 is the windowed version of the start-up transient of the glockenspiel, plotted in Fig-

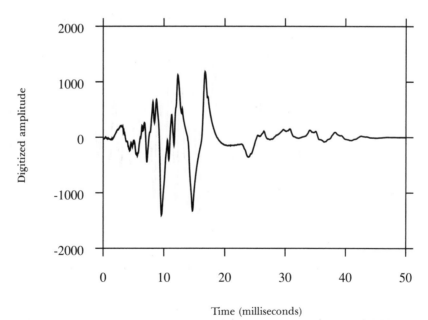

Time (milliseconds)

Figure 13.13   This is a windowed version of the initial piano impulse response plotted in Figure 13.1.

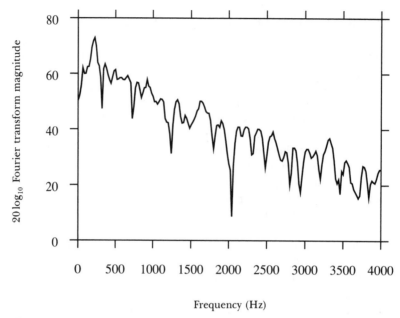

Figure 13.14   The Fourier transform of the initial piano impulse response contains very little frequency information. The fundamental is evident, but none of its harmonics are apparent.

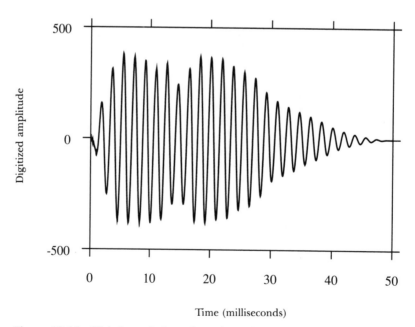

Figure 13.15   This is a windowed version of the initial glockenspiel impulse response plotted in Figure 13.2.

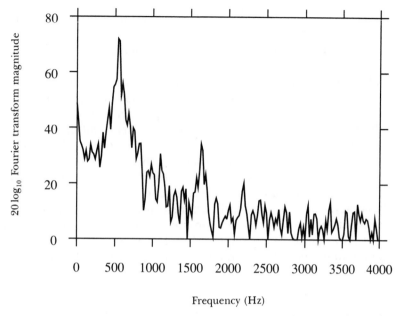

Figure 13.16   The Fourier transform of the initial glockenspiel impulse response is very similar to the spectrum of the later portions of its waveform, as plotted in Figure 13.12.

ure 13.2. Figure 13.16 is the Fourier transform of this windowed waveform. In contrast to the case of the piano, the spectrum of the initial transient of the glockenspiel is very similar to the spectrum of later portions of the waveform, such as in Figure 13.12. There are some significant differences, however. The fundamental and the third harmonic are both somewhat sharper and better defined in the later portions of the waveform. The glockenspiel is a much simpler instrument than the piano.

13.5   SPECIFYING THE FILTER

The goal is to obtain a filter which, when struck with a single impulse, will provide a waveform similar to the piano or glockenspiel. In many cases, and particularly for music, it is enough to find a filter with the same (magnitude) spectral response as the instrument being studied. In any case, finding a filter with a spectral response similar to the system being modeled is an important part of the process. If, for some reason, phase-related information is also important, more work will be required.

There are three central questions that must be addressed before we are finished:

1.   What are the various filtering options?

2. How can the spectral response of these filters be matched to the system being modeled?
3. How should the filters be implemented?

These are the subjects for the remainder of this book.

As for item 1, we have already seen how to implement a simple harmonic oscillator in Chapter 3, and in this chapter the notion of an FIR filter was introduced. These represent the two components of all digital filters. As explained in Chapter 14, all digital filters are a combination of these two basic types.

Item 2 is the most complicated of these three questions. There are several techniques that could be used, including simply trying various filter combinations by hand until the desired frequency response is achieved to some desired accuracy. Such an approach is time-consuming at best and may not deliver a satisfactory result even after considerable effort. Chapter 16 explores this topic.

After answering questions 1 and 2, question 3 is a matter of the best programming method. This question is addressed in Chapter 15.

Filtering and Z-Transforms

INTRODUCTION

This chapter introduces the concepts of *poles* and *zeros* as the components of linear filters. Every linear, time-invariant differential equation may be characterized in terms of the poles and zeros of its frequency response function. The same notion carries over into discrete-time systems. Discrete-time versions of the continuous-time poles and zeros are used to build arbitrary discrete-time filters (assuming linearity and time invariance).

This chapter begins by analyzing the continuous-time case, starting from the general differential equation and continues by developing the discrete-time solutions, computing the gains of these discrete-time systems, and comparing them to the continuous-time systems.

POLES AND ZEROS FROM DIFFERENTIAL EQUATIONS

14.2.1 The All-Pole Equations

Every linear differential equation can be translated into the language of linear filters and vice versa; they are equivalent concepts. Usually, physical systems are initially modeled with linear differential equations, from which the filter can be calculated. In this text we are concerned only with time-invariant systems. The general form of an nth-order, time-independent, linear differential equation is

$$y^{(n)} + a_{n-1} y^{(n-1)} + \cdots + a_1 y' + a_0 y = u(t)$$

In terms of the differential operator D, the derivative with respect to time, this can be written as

$$q(D)y = u \qquad (14.1)$$

257

where q is the polynomial

$$q(X) = X^n + a_{n-1}X^{n-1} + \cdots + a_1 X + a_0$$

The method of solving this equation is to factor the polynomial, just as we did for the second-order equation in Section 2.4.3, into linear terms:

$$q(X) = \prod_{\ell=1}^{n}(X - v_\ell)$$

where v_ℓ are the complex roots of the polynomial. Equation 14.1 can be transformed into an algebraic equation by taking the Fourier transform on both sides. Equation 8.15 on page 124 shows that the Fourier transform of the term Dy becomes $j\omega\hat{y}(\omega)$. This equation can be iterated for higher-order terms, showing that $D^k y$ transforms into $(j\omega)^k\hat{y}(\omega)$. Applying this to all the terms of the polynomial on the left-hand side of Equation 14.1 transforms it into

$$q(j\omega)\hat{y}(\omega) = \hat{u}(\omega)$$

This equation is easily solved for $\hat{y}$:

$$\hat{y}(\omega) = \frac{\hat{u}(\omega)}{q(j\omega)}$$

$$= \frac{\hat{u}(\omega)}{\prod_{\ell=1}^{n}(j\omega - v_\ell)}$$

From this equation it is evident that the Fourier transform of y, $\hat{y}$, has a *pole* at each point $j\omega = v_\ell$, for each root of the polynomial q. Such points are called poles because, as $j\omega$ approaches v_ℓ, the magnitude of $\hat{y}(\omega)$ grows without bound. A plot of the magnitude of $\hat{y}(\omega)$ would appear, more or less, like a tent, with a tall pole holding up the fabric of the tent at $j\omega = v_\ell$.

14.2.2   All Poles Lie in the Negative Half-Plane

Of course, we are normally only interested in real values of ω, so the denominator of the equation never becomes zero unless one of the roots v_ℓ has zero real part. For any physical system, this is never the case. The location of all poles must be such that the system response is always finite when its input u is finite. This is the case only if all the roots of the polynomial have a nonzero real part. In other words, it must be a complex frequency with a nonzero damping term. In fact, the damping term of each root must be negative, or the system response will grow without limit as time increases. This is obvious from the solutions to the corresponding homogeneous equation:

$$q(D)y_h = 0$$

which have the general form

$$y_h(t) = \sum_{\ell=1}^{n} \gamma_\ell e^{v_\ell t}$$

If any of the roots has a positive real part, then that component of the homogeneous solution grows indefinitely. If any of the roots is pure imaginary, then that part of the homogeneous solution remains at a constant amplitude, never decaying away. A positive real part for one of the roots v_ℓ would violate conservation of energy. A zero real part would imply perpetual motion. The real part of every root must therefore be negative. In other words, all the poles for an equation representing a real-world system must be in the left half of the complex plane, with real part strictly negative.

14.2.3 Zeros from Differential Equations

Poles are not the only important component of discrete-time or continuous-time filters. Equation 14.1 can be generalized one step more by writing

$$q(D)y = p(D)x \tag{14.2}$$

where $p(D)$ is another general polynomial. Now, from the point of view of solving general differential equations, a derivative on the right-hand side, such as this, is trivial. The forcing function x can just be differentiated, as implied by the polynomial, and that differentiated version used to drive the simpler differential equation, Equation 14.1. However, if the action of $p(D)$ should naturally be considered part of the apparatus being modeled rather than part of the driving force, then Equation 14.2 is the right way to look at things.

Equation 14.2 can be transformed into an algebraic equation just as Equation 14.1 was: by taking the Fourier transforms on both sides. This gives

$$\hat{y}(\omega) = \frac{p(j\omega)}{q(j\omega)}\hat{x}(\omega)$$

Factoring both polynomials as before gives

$$= \frac{\prod_{k=1}^{m}(j\omega - z_k)}{\prod_{\ell=1}^{n}(j\omega - v_\ell)}\hat{x}(\omega) \tag{14.3}$$

Thus, the roots of the polynomial $p(u)$ are the zeros in the frequency response of this system, z_k.

Equation 14.3 is the most general version of the solution to linear, time-invariant differential equations. Every linear time-invariant filter is specified by a list of poles and zeros in the complex frequency plane.

14.3 DISCRETE-TIME POLES AND ZEROS

The continuous-time solution to Equation 14.2 can be obtained from the factored polynomials or written in terms of its Fourier transform, as in Equation 14.3. Now the problem is to find the discrete-time version of the solution to this equation.

14.3.1 Emulating the Continuous-Time Solutions

Actually, the essence of discrete-time poles and zeros has already been explored in Chapter 3. Changing the notation to match the current situation, Equation 3.5 on page 29 shows that the discrete-time version of the solution to the equation

$$(D - v_k)y = u$$

is given by the recursion formula

$$y_{n+1} = e^{v_k \Delta t} y_n + (T_{v_k} u)[(n + 1)\Delta t] \tag{14.4}$$

where the transformation $T_{v_k \Delta t}$ represents a sort of average of the driving force

$$(T_{v_k} u)(t) = e^{v_k t} \int_{t-\Delta t}^{t} e^{-v_k \tau} u(\tau) \, d\tau \tag{14.5}$$

This transformation is required to make the response of the discrete-time equation match that of the continuous-time equation it was derived from. As we saw in Chapter 3, the best approximation that can be obtained for this transformation is Equation 3.7. However, our purpose here is somewhat different. The general discrete-time filter consists of a set of poles and zeros, and we will be looking for the particular filter that best approximates the observed waveform. The linear combination

$$\alpha u_n + \beta u_{n+1}$$

is itself a zero at the Nyquist frequency (see Equation 14.12 on page 262). We therefore use the approximation

$$(T_{v_k} u)_{n+1} \approx u_{n+1} \frac{e^{v_k \Delta t} - 1}{v_k}$$

If any zeros are needed, they will be added later.

14.3.2   Discrete-Time Poles

Before continuing, it is convenient to introduce some new notation to make writing the equations easier. The constants γ_ℓ and κ_ℓ are introduced as follows to make the equation easier to write:

$$\gamma_\ell = e^{v_\ell \Delta t} \tag{14.6}$$

$$\kappa_\ell = \frac{e^{v_\ell \Delta t} - 1}{v_\ell} \tag{14.7}$$

$$y_{t+1} = \gamma_\ell y_t + \kappa_\ell u_{t+1} \tag{14.8}$$

This equation is the recursive, discrete-time version of the solution to the first-order differential equation:

$$(D - v_\ell)y = u$$

The constants γ_ℓ and κ_ℓ are computed once, then used repeatedly in the recursion formula, Equation 14.8.

The solution to the full Equation 14.1 is obtained by successive applications of the equation for each pole in the frequency response. Section 3.3 showed how this is done for a special case: the simple harmonic oscillator. The general case is similar. The nth-order differential equation Equation 14.1 can be reduced to n first-order differential equations by introducing the auxiliary functions

$$f^{\{k\}} = \prod_{\ell=k+1}^{n} (D - v_\ell)y$$

for $0 \le k \le n - 1$ and

$$f^{\{n\}} = y$$

Using these definitions, Equation 14.1 reduces to a sequence of first-order equations

$$(D - v_n)y = f^{\{n-1\}}$$

$$(D - v_{n-1})f^{\{n-1\}} = f^{\{n-2\}}$$

$$\vdots$$

$$(D - v_2)f^{\{2\}} = f^{\{1\}}$$

$$(D - v_1)f^{\{1\}} = u$$

These equations are solved by first solving the last equation for $f^{\{1\}}$ (u is the forcing function), then using this solution as the forcing function for the previous equation, thus solving for $f^{\{2\}}$, and so forth all the way up the line until finally y is obtained by solving the first of these equations.

We already have the discrete-time solutions for each of these first-order equations given by Equation 14.8. The solution to the whole system is obtained by applying the solution to each one in turn as follows:

$$y_{t+1} = \gamma_n y_t + \kappa_n f_{t+1}^{\{n-1\}}$$
$$f_{t+1}^{\{n-1\}} = \gamma_{n-1} f_t^{\{n-1\}} + \kappa_n f_{t+1}^{\{n-2\}}$$
$$\vdots \tag{14.9}$$
$$f_{t+1}^{\{2\}} = \gamma_2 f_t^{\{2\}} + \kappa_2 f_{t+1}^{\{1\}}$$
$$f_{t+1}^{\{1\}} = \gamma_1 f_t^{\{1\}} + \kappa_1 u_{t+1}$$

Just as for the continuous-time system of equations, this system is solved by first obtaining $f^{\{1\}}$ from the last equation. Then this solution is used in the previous equation to solve for $f^{\{2\}}$, and so forth, until the first equation can be solved for y by using $f^{\{n-1\}}$ as the forcing function.

14.3.3 Discrete-Time Zeros

Now that the poles are taken care of, what about the zeros? We have seen how to obtain the discrete-time solution to Equation 14.1 in the previous section. To complete the picture, we must do the same for the other half of Equation 14.2, which can be stated as

$$u = p(D)x$$

But this is really no different from Equation 14.1; the only thing that has changed is which function is the solution and which is the input. That means that Equations 14.6, 14.7, and 14.8 can be modified to give the discrete-time solution for zeros, as well as poles, in the differential equation. For the zero

$$u = (D - z_k)x$$

the discrete-time solution can be written as

$$\zeta_k = e^{z_k \Delta t} \tag{14.10}$$

$$\alpha_k = \frac{e^{z_k \Delta t} - 1}{z_k} \tag{14.11}$$

$$u_{t+1} = \frac{1}{\alpha_k}(x_{t+1} - \zeta_k x_t) \tag{14.12}$$

where ζ_k and α_k are constants that depend only on the location of the zero, z_k, and are only calculated once. The last equation is obtained by solving the equivalent of Equation 14.8:

$$x_{t+1} = \zeta_k y_t + \alpha_k u_{t+1}$$

for u_{t+1}.

Also, just as for multiple poles, multiple zeros can be implemented one at a time by defining the sequence of functions

$$g^{\{k\}} = \prod_{\ell=k+1}^{m} (D - z_\ell)\, x$$

for $1 \le k \le m - 1$, and

$$g^{\{m\}} = x$$

This leads to the sequence of equations

$$g^{\{m-1\}} = (D - z_m)\, x$$

$$g^{\{m-2\}} = (D - z_{m-1})\, g^{\{m-1\}}$$

$$\vdots$$

$$g^{\{1\}} = (D - z_2)\, g^{\{2\}}$$

$$u = (D - z_1)\, g^{\{1\}}$$

This sequence of first-order equations translates to the discrete-time solutions:

$$g_{t+1}^{\{m-1\}} = \frac{1}{\alpha_m} (x_{t+1} - \zeta_m x_t)$$

$$g_{t+1}^{\{m-2\}} = \frac{1}{\alpha_{m-1}} \left(g_{t+1}^{\{m-1\}} - \zeta_{m-1} g_t^{\{m-1\}} \right)$$

$$\vdots \tag{14.13}$$

$$g_{t+1}^{\{1\}} = \frac{1}{\alpha_2} \left(g_{t+1}^{\{2\}} - \zeta_2 g_t^{\{2\}} \right)$$

$$u_{t+1} = \frac{1}{\alpha_1} \left(g_{t+1}^{\{1\}} - \zeta_1 g_t^{\{1\}} \right)$$

This system of equations is used just like Equations 14.9, only in forward order. The first equation is used to calculate $g^{\{m-1\}}$, this is used in the second to calculate $g^{\{m-2\}}$, and so forth; until, in the last equation, $g^{\{1\}}$ is used to solve for u.

14.4 THE GENERAL DISCRETE-TIME FILTER

The system of equations Equation 14.9 shows how to implement a series of poles in discrete-time, and the system in Equation 14.13 shows how to implement a series of zeros. Combining these two systems provides the most general form of a discrete-time filter. The system of zeros, Equation 14.13 can be used to calculate u_t from the input function x_t, and then u_t can be used as the input to the system of poles, Equation 14.9, which then delivers the final result, y_t.

Notice that, within each of these systems of equations, the ordering of the poles and zeros does not matter. That is because we started with linear, time-independent differential equations. The factors of each of the polynomials, $q(D)$ and $p(D)$, can be rearranged in any order without changing the differential equation. Perhaps a little less obviously, it does not matter whether the poles are calculated using the output of the zeros as its input, or the zeros are calculated using the output of the poles as input. In fact, the poles and zeros can be combined in any order with the same (theoretically anyway) result at the end. This fact is at least hinted at by Equation 14.3, the equation for the frequency response of the continuous-time equation. It clearly makes no difference whether the denominator or the numerator is evaluated first—the quotient will be the same.

However, it can make a great deal of practical difference which order the equations are used. Maintaining numerical accuracy can be difficult for filters with sharp skirts in the frequency domain or other extreme features. This is very similar to the problem of realizing a demanding filter design in hardware. If the filter has sharply defined passbands and stopbands, then the components (the resistors, capacitors, and inductors) of the filter must be precise. Of course, for digital filters it is not the value of the components that matter, but rather numerical inaccuracies and compounding effects of multiple roundoff errors. A filter with a sharp edge between the passband and stopband will have very high-Q poles. Some designs also contain zeros very close to these poles. In such cases, the order of evaluation can matter very much indeed. In general, the zeros can be thought of as subtracting energy from the waveform and do not present problems for numerical analysis. The poles, on the other hand, produce sharp spikes in the spectral output and can be very difficult to handle. In general, the sharpest poles should be computed last.

To see that the order of the poles and zeros does not matter, consider the particular example,

$$(D - v_1)y = (D - z_1)x$$

According to Equation 14.12, the zero can be implemented by calculating the recursion formula:

$$u_{t+1} = \frac{1}{\alpha_1}(x_{t+1} - \zeta_1 x_t)$$

The pole is implemented using Equation 14.8:

$$y_{t+1} = \gamma_1 y_t + \kappa_1 u_{t+1}$$

Combining these two equations into one gives

$$y_{t+1} = \gamma_1 y_t + \frac{\kappa_1}{\alpha_1}(x_{t+1} - \zeta_1 x_t)$$

which can be rearranged to the equation

$$\alpha_1 y_{t+1} - \alpha_1 \gamma_1 y_t = \kappa_1 x_{t+1} - \kappa_1 \zeta_1 x_t \tag{14.14}$$

which is not a useful way to write it for computations, but does serve the purpose here, revealing the symmetry between the various coefficients.

To show the same result is obtained by reversing the order of the pole and zero, start with the equation for a pole:

$$u_{t+1} = \gamma_1 u_t + \kappa_1 x_{t+1} \tag{14.15}$$

apply the zero to its output:

$$y_{t+1} = \frac{1}{\alpha_1}(u_{t+1} - \zeta_1 u_t) \tag{14.16}$$

Using Equation 14.16 twice on the left-hand side of Equation 14.14 gives

$$\alpha_1 y_{t+1} - \alpha_1 \gamma_1 y_t = (u_{t+1} - \zeta_1 u_t) - \gamma_1(u_t - \zeta_1 u_{t-1})$$
$$= u_{t+1} - (\gamma_1 + \zeta_1)u_t + \gamma_1 \zeta_1 u_{t-1}$$

Doing the same for the right-hand side of Equation 14.14, using Equation 14.15 twice, gives

$$\kappa_1 x_{t+1} - \kappa_1 \zeta_1 x_t = (u_{t+1} - \gamma_1 u_t) - \zeta_1(u_t - \gamma_1 u_{t-1})$$
$$= u_{t+1} - (\gamma_1 + \zeta_1)u_t + \gamma_1 \zeta_1 u_{t-1}$$

which is the same as for the right-hand side. Therefore, it does not matter whether the pole is computed first, or the zero first.

14.5   COMPUTING THE ZEROS ALL AT ONCE

The order of the zeros does not matter, and, in fact, it is possible to compute them all at once instead of one at a time as implied by Equation 14.13. This works as follows. The last computation to be made is

$$u_{t+1} = \frac{1}{\alpha_1} \left(g_{t+1}^{\{1\}} - \zeta_1 g_t^{\{1\}} \right)$$

The next-to-last equation can be substituted for $g^{\{1\}}$, giving

$$= \frac{1}{\alpha_1} \left(\frac{1}{\alpha_2} \left(g_{t+1}^{\{2\}} - \zeta_2 g_t^{\{2\}} \right) - \zeta_1 \frac{1}{\alpha_2} \left(g_t^{\{2\}} - \zeta_2 g_{t-1}^{\{2\}} \right) \right)$$

which reduces to

$$= \frac{1}{\alpha_1 \alpha_2} \left[g_{t+1}^{\{2\}} - (\zeta_1 + \zeta_2) g_t^{\{2\}} + \zeta_1 \zeta_2 g_{t-1}^{\{2\}} \right]$$

This equation is very similar to the product of two monomials:

$$a(X) = (X - \zeta_1)(X - \zeta_2) = X^2 - (\zeta_1 + \zeta_2)X^1 + \zeta_1 \zeta_2 X^0$$

This is no accident. In fact, as we shall see later, in some cases the computation actually is a polynomial evaluation. For now, it is enough to notice that a formal substitution works. For a driving force r, putting r_{t-1+i} in the polynomial, where i is the power of X for that term, results in

$$a(r) = r_{t-1+2} - (\zeta_1 + \zeta_2)r_{t-1+1} + \zeta_1 \zeta_2 r_{t-1+0}$$

which is precisely the equation derived above, with $r = g^{\{2\}}$. Actually proving that this pattern works for all the terms of the system of Equations 14.13 would require a proof by induction. We will not prove that fact here, because the proof is not particularly illuminating. The general rule is as follows. Combining all the Equation 14.13, as was done for the last two, results in the "all-at-once" version given by the polynomial

$$P(X) = \prod_{k=1}^{m} \frac{1}{\alpha_k} (X - \zeta_k) \tag{14.17}$$

$$= \frac{1}{\prod_{k=1}^{m} \alpha_k} \left(X^m + b_1 X^{m-1} + b_2 X^{m-2} + \cdots + b_m X^0 \right)$$

where the b_k are the polynomial coefficients computed by multiplying out all the monomials in Equation 14.17. This polynomial is used by formal substitution as follows:

$$u_{t+1} = \frac{1}{\prod_{k=1}^{m} \alpha_k} \left(x_{t+1} + b_1 x_t + b_2 x_{t-1} + \cdots + b_m x_{t+1-m} \right) \qquad (14.18)$$

Notice that these coefficients are all real. In general, any single zero requires complex coefficients, but because they appear in complex conjugate pairs for most filters, the complex arithmetic can be avoided by doing all the zeros at once, or at least doing them in pairs.

14.6 THE GAIN OF A SYSTEM OF ZEROS

The formal polynomial of Equation 14.17 can also be used to calculate the gain of this system of discrete-time zeros as a function of frequency. In fact, the process is very easy. As discussed in Chapter 1, a discrete-time frequency is a complex number z that generates the waveform

$$1, z, z^2, z^3, \ldots, z^k, \ldots$$

the generalized form of a sinusoid. The gain of the system of zeros at frequency z is calculated by substituting this basic waveform for x_t:

$$x_t = z^t$$

and calculating the response of the system. Putting $x_t = z^t$ into Equation 14.18 gives

$$\begin{aligned} u_t &= \frac{1}{\prod_{k=1}^{m} \alpha_k} \left(z^t + b_1 z^{t-1} + b_2 z^{t-2} + \cdots + b_m z^{t-m} \right) \\ &= z^{t-m} \frac{1}{\prod_{k=1}^{m} \alpha_k} \left(z^m + b_1 z^{m-1} + b_2 z^{m-2} + \cdots + b_m \right) \\ &= z^t \frac{z^{-m}}{\prod_{k=1}^{m} \alpha_k} P(z) \end{aligned} \qquad (14.19)$$

Notice carefully the correspondence between this polynomial and $p(j\omega)$ in the numerator of Equation 14.3. The differences are that the discrete-time frequency $z = e^{j\omega\Delta t}$ has replaced the continuous-time frequency $j\omega$; the discrete-time zero location $\zeta_k = e^{jz_k\Delta t}$ has replaced the continuous-time zero location z_k; and a scale factor α_k is required for each zero. With these substitutions and scalings, the polynomial $P(z)$ is obtained from the original polynomial $p(j\omega)$, which in turn came from the original differential operator $p(D)$ from Equation 14.2.

14.7   COMPUTING THE POLES ALL AT ONCE

The same computation works for the system of equations, Equation 14.9, for the sequence of poles in the filter. In fact, there is almost nothing left to do, except writing down the equations, copying from the case for the zeros. The procedure is to rearrange the system of Equations 14.9 so that it has the same form as Equation 14.13, then to compute the polynomial as before, obtaining

$$Q(X) = \prod_{\ell=1}^{n} \frac{1}{\kappa_\ell} (X - \gamma_k) \tag{14.20}$$

$$= \frac{1}{\prod_{\ell=1}^{n} \kappa_\ell} \left(X^n + c_1 X^{n-1} + c_2 X^{n-2} + \cdots + c_n X^0 \right)$$

which is used by formal substitution:

$$u_{t+1} = P(y)$$

$$= \frac{1}{\prod_{\ell=1}^{n} \kappa_\ell} \left(y_{t+1} + c_1 y_t + c_2 y_{t-1} + \cdots + c_n y_{t+1-n} \right) \tag{14.21}$$

However, in this case the equation must be solved for y_{t+1}, which gives

$$y_{t+1} = \left(\prod_{\ell=1}^{n} \kappa_\ell \right) u_{t+1} - \left(c_1 y_t + c_2 y_{t-1} + \cdots + c_n y_{t+1-n} \right) \tag{14.22}$$

14.8   GAIN OF THE POLES AND RINGING

What about the gain of this set of poles? It works just the same as the gain of the set of zeros, but it is harder to see why. We could make very quick work of it by arguing from the symmetry of the equations, obtaining the result by running time backward. However, it is more enlightening to look at what happens to a single pole as time progresses. In other words, what happens to Equation 14.8 for the input function $u_t = z^t$ for some discrete-time frequency z? The answer is easily calculated as follows, assuming $y_0 = 0$:

$$y_1 = \kappa_\ell z$$

$$y_2 = \gamma_\ell y_1 + \kappa_\ell z^2$$

$$= \kappa_\ell z (\gamma_\ell + z)$$

$$y_3 = \gamma_\ell y_2 + \kappa_\ell z^3$$

$$= \gamma_\ell \kappa_\ell z (\gamma_\ell + z) + \kappa_\ell z^3$$

$$= \kappa_\ell z \left(\gamma_\ell^2 + \gamma_\ell z + z^2 \right)$$

$$y_4 = \gamma_\ell y_3 + \kappa_\ell z^4$$

$$= \gamma_\ell \kappa_\ell z \left(\gamma_\ell^2 + \gamma_\ell z + z^2 \right) + \kappa_\ell z^4$$

$$= \kappa_\ell z \left(\gamma_\ell^3 + \gamma_\ell^2 z + \gamma_\ell z^2 + z^3 \right)$$

and by now the general pattern should be plain:

$$y_t = \kappa_\ell z \sum_{\ell=0}^{t-1} \gamma_\ell^{t-1-\ell} z^\ell$$

which can be computed using the geometric series:

$$= \kappa_\ell z \frac{z^t - \gamma_\ell^t}{z - \gamma_\ell}$$

The γ_ℓ^t part of the numerator is the transient response of the filter, because for any real system, as discussed in Section 14.2.2, the real part of v_ℓ is strictly negative, which implies that

$$|\gamma_\ell| = |e^{v_\ell \Delta t}| < 1$$

Notice here that the transient response will die out quickly if the real part of v_ℓ is a large negative number, but may last a very long time if the real part is very close to zero so that $|\gamma_\ell|$ is very close to 1. In other words, poles with very little damping ring for a very long time. Notice also that regardless of the input frequency z, the pole rings at its own characteristic frequency γ_ℓ.

Regardless of its length, the transient response is not included in the gain calculation, so only the steady-state portion is used:

$$y_t = \kappa_\ell z \frac{z^t}{z - \gamma_\ell}$$

Thus, the steady-state system response at frequency z is

$$y_t = z^t \prod_{\ell=1}^{n} \kappa_\ell \frac{z}{z - \gamma_\ell}$$

$$= z^{n+t} \prod_{\ell=1}^{n} \frac{\kappa_\ell}{z - \gamma_\ell}$$

$$= z^{n+t} \frac{\prod_{\ell=1}^{n} \kappa_\ell}{Q(z)} \qquad (14.23)$$

14.9 THE GAIN OF DISCRETE-TIME FILTERS

Now we can put the whole thing together and calculate the steady-state system response to an input function $x_t = z^t$. According to Equation 14.19, the response of the zeros can be written as

$$u_t = z^{t-m} P(z) / \prod_{k=1}^{m} \alpha_k$$

which is just a gain constant times z^t again. Equation 14.23 provides the steady-state contribution from the poles, so the overall system response is

$$y_t = z^{t-m+n} \frac{\prod_{\ell=1}^{n} \kappa_\ell}{\prod_{k=1}^{m} \alpha_k} \frac{P(z)}{Q(z)} \tag{14.24}$$

In most expositions, the gain of the zeros and poles is written slightly differently. I prefer the form of Equation 14.24, because it seems more intuitive. However, changing to the equations found in other texts is trivial. The only difference is the way the polynomials are written. The polynomial for the gain of the zeros, for example, is

$$z^{-m} P(z) = z^{-m} \left(z^m + b_1 z^{m-1} + \cdots + b_m \right)$$

which in most expositions is written instead as

$$= 1 + b_1 z^{-1} + \cdots + b_m z^{-m}$$

Use whichever version you are more comfortable with.

Once again, notice that the polynomials P and Q in Equation 14.24 are closely related to the polynomials p and q of the original differential equation

$$q(D)y = p(D)x$$

These are the same polynomials that appear in Equation 14.3, which gives the frequency response of the continuous-time system. All the same comments made above about the relationship between p and P also apply to q and Q.

In fact, to first order in Δt, the continuous-time polynomials are equal to the discrete-time polynomials when the effect of the constants α_k and κ_ℓ are taken into account. This is easily seen by using the first-order expansion of the exponentials,

$$e^X \approx 1 + X$$

for values of X close to zero. For example, the gain of a discrete-time zero is given by

$$\frac{z - \zeta_k}{\alpha_k}$$

where

$$\zeta_k = e^{z_k \Delta t}$$

which, using the linear approximation for the exponential, is

$$\approx 1 + z_k \Delta t$$

Similarly,

$$\alpha_k = \frac{e^{z_k \Delta t} - 1}{z_k}$$

$$\approx \frac{1 + z_k \Delta t - 1}{z_k}$$

$$\approx \Delta t$$

The gain of this discrete-time zero at $z = e^{j\omega \Delta t}$, to first order in Δt, is

$$\frac{1 + j\omega \Delta t - (1 + z_k \Delta t)}{\Delta t} = j\omega - z_k$$

which is the same as for the continuous-time version. Once again, this shows that "sufficient accuracy" may be obtained by choosing a small Δt. The Nyquist criterion specifies a maximum size for Δt, which is usually too large by a factor of 10 or more when the goal is to model an existing analog system.

Programming the Filters

Writing a program to implement an arbitrary combination of poles and zeros, as described in Chapter 14, is now a straightforward endeavor. Equation 14.18 on page 267 shows how to implement all the zeros simultaneously, and Equation 14.21 on page 268 shows how to implement all the poles simultaneously.

Actually calculating the filter coefficients and implementing the filter require several capabilities. First, the filter coefficients are nothing but the coefficients of polynomials with a given set of roots. We therefore need a routine that can multiply polynomials together. We also need two structures: one to define the poles and zeros required and one, to be used by the filtering routine itself, that defines the filter. Finally, of course, we must write the filter routine.

Perhaps it is not obvious, but the filter routine requires some sort of buffer to contain a list of previous inputs and filter outputs. A filter with m zeros requires knowledge of the m previous inputs. A filter with n poles requires knowledge of the n previous outputs. Efficient handling of these buffers is important to the execution speed of the filtering routines.

15.1 NUMERICAL ERRORS

Despite the innocuous appearance of the equations for the poles and zeros, difficulties caused by roundoff errors or even overflow can occur, especially if the poles are particularly sharp (with very small damping terms). In such cases, the order of the poles and zeros can be important, not for theoretical reasons but purely for computational reasons.

In general, the zeros should be applied to the input data, then the poles to the output of the zeros. Heuristically, this is because the zeros are subtracting energy from the waveform, while the poles are adding energy, perhaps in a very narrowly defined range of frequencies. However, these questions will not be explored further in this book. The issues are not peculiar to signal processing. Any good book on numerical analysis addresses these issues in a more comprehensive way than is possible here. However, in practice it may be necessary to do the filtering in stages—first some of the zeros, then some of the poles, then more zeros, and so forth.

15.2 CIRCULAR BUFFERS

Implementing the digital filters requires remembering a list of the N most recent filter inputs or outputs. In other words, at time t we need to have access to the data for time $t, t - 1, t - 2, \ldots, t - N$. But at the next iteration the time is $t + 1$, so we can forget the value at time $t - N$ but must insert the new value into the buffer for use on the next iteration.

A *circular buffer* is just the structure required to implement this requirement efficiently. A circular buffer is a region of memory that is conceptually considered to be arranged in a circle. Of course, all memory in current computers is linear. However, addressing overflows can make them appear to be circular. For example, in the Intel 8086 chip, the address is 16 bits long. The chip does not signal an overflow when an address computation overflows the address word. Thus, the next address after $2^{16} - 1$ is 0.

The idea of a circular buffer is to obtain this same sort of behavior from a shorter stretch of memory, and without relying on overflows of the address word. A circular buffer of length N has, conceptually, N data locations with addresses 0 through $N - 1$. Further, the next address above $N - 1$ is 0, and the first address below 0 is $N - 1$. In other words, the address is computed modulo N.

Computing the address modulo N, in general, requires logic something like the following:

```
index += 1;
if(index >= N) index -= N;
```

assuming that **index** started inside the correct range. Such comparisons and subtractions take considerable time and a jump in the program counter every time the comparison fails. Furthermore, this logic only works if the addressing increment is positive and less than N.

If, however, N is a power of 2, $N = 2^k$, and the computer uses two's complement arithmetic, then the computation can be done without any additions, subtractions, or comparisons. The code can be simplified to

```
int mask = N - 1;
    •
    •
    •

index = (index + 1) & mask;
    •
    •
    •
```

Furthermore, this masking operation is valid no matter what the value of **index** is to begin with. Masking with $2^k - 1$ always gives the original integer modulo 2^k, even if it was originally a negative number. This fact is most easily understood by considering the binary representation of $2^k - 1$: a string of k 1's. The masking operation is very fast on most computers, and always faster than the logic required if N is not a power of 2.

If you ever run across a computer that uses, say, base 5 arithmetic instead of base 2, the same argument works, but N will have to be a power of 5.

The structure I use for circular buffers (of length a power of 2) is

```
typedef struct {
    double *h;
    int mask, index;
} CircularBufferDouble;
```

where **h** is a pointer to the allocated memory for the buffer, **mask** is $N - 1$ (the mask that will be used); and **index** is the index into the buffer where the next data value should be inserted. The routines that allocate and deallocate a circular buffer are

```
#include <filter.inc>
#include <stdlib.h>
#include <generic.inc>
#include <mem.h>

CircularBufferDouble *new_CircularBufferDouble(int length)
{
    CircularBufferDouble *cb
        = malloc(sizeof(CircularBufferDouble));
    if(!cb)
    {
        error_message(
        "new_CircularBufferDouble---Out of memory");
        return NULL;
    }
    memset(cb, 0, sizeof(CircularBufferDouble));
    /* Find the required length---a power of 2 */
    {
        int k = 1;
        while(k < length) k *= 2;
        cb->h = malloc(sizeof(double)*k);
        if(!cb->h)
        {
            error_message(
            "new_CircularBufferDouble---Out of memory");
```

```
                old_CircularBufferDouble(cb);
                return NULL;
            }
            memset(cb->h, 0, k*sizeof(double));
            cb->mask = k - 1;
        }
        return cb;
}

void old_CircularBufferDouble(CircularBufferDouble *cb)
{
    if(cb)
    {
        if(cb->h) free(cb->h);
        free(cb);
    }
}

void clear_buffer_d(CircularBufferDouble *cb)
{
    if(cb)
    {
        cb->index = 0;
        if(cb->h)
        memset(cb->h, 0, sizeof(double)*(cb->mask + 1));
    }
}
```

The last routine clears the buffer to its original state with all entries equal to 0.

Once the circular buffer is allocated, its use is simply a matter of remembering to use the mask when updating the index. For examples of its use, see Section 15.5, where circular buffers are used in the filtering routine.

15.3 REPRESENTING THE POLES AND ZEROS

We must devise some way of representing the poles and zeros required for a given filter. There are many ways this might be done. For example, should the pole and zero locations be given in Hertz? Such an approach, while appealing in some ways, implies knowledge of the sampling frequency that is to be used.

Another question that must be settled is whether the location of the singularities should be expressed in terms of the continuous-time frequencies or the discrete-time frequencies. Using discrete-time frequencies (exponentials of the continuous-time frequencies) would be the most direct method. However, most people are used to thinking in terms of the continuous-time notions of damping and frequency:

$$z = -d + j\omega$$

This is the form used in the library.

The sample interval is always assumed to be one time unit. In other words, assume $\Delta t = 1$ in Equations 14.6 and 14.10. Any translation to other terms that might be of interest to the user of the program must be left as a function of the user interface, not of the basic structures of the DSP software.

With this in mind, the structure that defines a singularity is quite simple:

```
typedef enum {
    SinglePole, PolePair, SingleZero, ZeroPair
} SingularityType;

typedef struct {
    Complex z;                /* The singularity location */
    SingularityType type;
    int count;
} FilterSingularity;
```

A list of these singularities can be as simple as an array of these structures or perhaps a linked list. In what follows, we assume it is just an array.

If **s** is a **FilterSingularity** structure, then its components are interpreted as follows:

s.z is the complex frequency where the singularity resides: **s.z.x** is the damping per data point (negative), **s.z.y** is the radian frequency per data point.

s.type is the type of the singularity.

s.count is the number of these singularities in the filter.

Note that if the filter is to have real coefficients, then any single pole or single zero must be at radian frequency 0 or π. In other words, the singleton root of the polynomial $\exp(\mathbf{s.z})$ must be real.

15.4 COMPUTING THE COEFFICIENTS

Computing the coefficients, for both poles and zeros, is merely a matter of computing a polynomial with roots in the required locations. Since the polynomial we seek has all real coefficients, any complex roots must occur in complex-conjugate pairs. The polynomial with these two roots is a real-coefficient, second-order equation:

$$(X - z)(X - \bar{z}) = X^2 - (z + \bar{z})X + |z|^2$$

By thus combining all the complex roots, we can solve the problem with only real-coefficient polynomials.

The basic routine for this process is one that multiplies two polynomials together. Once written, that routine can be used inductively to obtain the required polynomial. The following **polynomial_multiply_d** routine does the job. It takes as arguments two vectors that are interpreted as polynomials. Vector component 0 is the constant term of the polynomial. The kth vector component is the coefficient of X^k. The routine creates a new vector of the proper length, calculates the polynomial product, and returns a pointer to the new vector.

For two polynomials a and b, the product is computed as follows:

$$\left(a_0 + a_1 X + \cdots + a_n X^n\right)\left(b_0 + b_1 X + \cdots + b_m X^m\right)$$

$$
\begin{aligned}
= \quad a_0 b_0 \quad &+ a_0 b_1 X \quad &+ \cdots \quad &+ a_0 b_m X^m \\
&+ a_1 b_0 X \quad &+ \cdots \quad &+ a_1 b_{m-1} X^m \quad + a_1 b_m X^{m+1} \\
&\ddots \\
&+ a_n b_0 X^n \quad &+ \cdots \quad &+ \cdots \quad + \cdots \quad a_n b_m X^{n+m}
\end{aligned}
$$

The routine accomplishes this computation one row at a time. The b polynomial is multiplied by each a coefficient and added to the product vector with the appropriate shift as indicated.

```
#include <generic.inc>
#include <numeric.inc>

VectorDouble *polynomial_multiply_d(
const VectorDouble *a, const VectorDouble *b)
{
    int length = a->length + b->length - 1;
    VectorDouble *ab = new_VectorDouble(length);
    if(!ab)
    {
        error_message("polynomial_multiply---"
            "Out of memory"); return ab;
    }
    /* Now multiply the polynomials */
    {
        int i = a->length,
        as = a->spacing,
        bs = b->spacing;
```

```
        while(i--)
        {
            double *abp = ab->buffer + i,
                   *bp = b->buffer + b->first,
                   x = a->buffer[a->first + i*as];
            int j = b->length;
            for(; j--; bp += bs, abp++) *abp += *bp * x;
        }
    }
    return ab;
}
```

With this routine written, it is a simple matter to compute the coefficients for any desired filter. However, a structure is needed to hold the results along with the circular buffers needed to actually implement the filter. The structure I use is

```
typedef struct {
    VectorDouble *poles, *zeros;
    CircularBufferDouble *x, *y;
} FilterDouble;
```

where **poles** is the vector of coefficients for the poles given by Equation 14.21 and **zeros** is the vector of coefficients for the zeros given by Equation 14.18. The circular buffer **x** is for previous filter inputs, and **y** is for previous filter outputs. The following routine allocates all these structures and calculates the coefficients, given an array of poles and zeros, **fs**, with **count** entries:

```
#include <filter.inc>
#include <stdlib.h>
#include <generic.inc>
#include <mem.h>
#include <math.h>

FilterDouble *new_FilterDouble(
    FilterSingularity *fs, int count)
{
    FilterDouble *fd = malloc(sizeof(FilterDouble));
    /* term is used for the new factor of the polynomial
     * determined by the root(s) being added.  It is
     * either linear or quadratic
     */
    VectorDouble *term = new_VectorDouble(3);

    if(!fd || !term)
```

```
    {
        error_message("new_FilterDouble---Out of memory");
        if(fd) free(fd);
        if(term) old_VectorDouble(term);
        return NULL;
    }
    memset(fd, 0, sizeof(FilterDouble));
    /* The two polynomials are initially of order 0,
     * with constant value equal to 1. */
    fd->poles = new_VectorDouble(1);
    fd->zeros = new_VectorDouble(1);
    if(!fd->poles || !fd->zeros)
    {
        error_message("new_FilterDouble---Out of memory");
        old_FilterDouble(fd);
        old_VectorDouble(term);
        return NULL;
    }
    fd->poles->buffer[0] = 1;
    fd->zeros->buffer[0] = 1;
    /* Now run through all the singularities */
    {
        int i = count;
        FilterSingularity *s = fs;
        for(; i--; s++)
        {
            int k = s->count;
            VectorDouble **p = NULL;
            if(k)
            {
                double e = exp(s->z.x);
                int ok = 0;
                switch(s->type)
                {
                    case SinglePole:
                        p = &(fd->poles);
                        ok = 1;
                    case SingleZero:
                        if(!ok) p = &(fd->zeros);
                        /* Linear factor, must be a real
                         * root.  Force it to be real */
                        term->length = 2;
                        term->buffer[0] = 1;
                        if(s->z.y < M_PI/2)
                            term->buffer[1] = -e;
```

```
                    else term->buffer[1] = e;
                    break;
                case PolePair:
                    p = &(fd->poles);
                    ok = 1;
                case ZeroPair:
                    if(!ok) p = &(fd->zeros);
                    /* Quadratic factor. */
                    term->length = 3;
                    term->buffer[0] = 1;
                    term->buffer[1] = -2*e*cos(s->z.y);
                    term->buffer[2] = e*e;
                    break;
                }

                /* Multiply the polynomial by term
                 * once for each time it is supposed
                 * to be in the filter */
                while(k--)
                {
                    VectorDouble *t = *p;
                    *p = polynomial_multiply_d(term, *p);
                    if(!*p)
                    {
                        error_message(
                            "new_FilterDouble---"
                            "Out of memory");
                        old_FilterDouble(fd);
                        return NULL;
                    }
                    old_VectorDouble(t);
                }
            }
        }
    }
    if(fd->zeros->length > 1)
    {
        fd->x = new_CircularBufferDouble(
            fd->zeros->length);
        if(!fd->x)
        {
            error_message("new_FilterDouble---"
                "Out of memory");
            old_FilterDouble(fd);
            return NULL;
```

```
        }
    }
    else
    {
        old_VectorDouble(fd->zeros);
        fd->zeros = NULL;
    }
    if(fd->poles->length > 1)
    {
        fd->y = new_CircularBufferDouble(
            fd->poles->length);
        if(!fd->y)
        {
            error_message("new_FilterDouble---"
                "Out of memory");
            old_FilterDouble(fd);
            return NULL;
        }
    }
    else
    {
        old_VectorDouble(fd->poles);
        fd->poles = NULL;
    }
    return fd;
}
void old_FilterDouble(FilterDouble *fd)
{
    if(fd)
    {
        if(fd->zeros) old_VectorDouble(fd->zeros);
        if(fd->poles) old_VectorDouble(fd->poles);
        if(fd->x) old_CircularBufferDouble(fd->x);
        if(fd->y) old_CircularBufferDouble(fd->y);
        free(fd);
    }
}
void clear_FilterDouble(FilterDouble *fd)
{
    if(fd)
    {
        if(fd->x) clear_buffer_d(fd->x);
        if(fd->y) clear_buffer_d(fd->y);
    }
}
```

15.5 THE FILTERING ROUTINE

The filter routine itself is fairly simple and certainly efficient. In many signal processing applications, the waveform to be filtered either will not fit into one vector or (in a real-time application) is not known ahead of time. It is therefore essential that the filtering routine be capable of filtering successive sections of the waveform on successive calls to the routine. This is accomplished in this case by keeping all the required data in the allocated **FilterDouble** structure. This structure contains all the coefficients and all the previous inputs and outputs required for each computation.

The circular buffers in the **FilterDouble** structure are copied into local storage for more efficient access during the computations. It is essential to remember to copy them back to their previous locations before exiting the procedure. Here is the routine:

```
void filter_d(FilterDouble *fd, VectorDouble *v)
{
    /* If the x-buffer is defined, calculate the zeros */
    if(fd->x)
    {
        int i = v->length, vs = v->spacing;
        CircularBufferDouble xh = *(fd->x);
        double *vp = v->buffer + v->first;

        for(; i--; vp += vs)
        {
            double sum = 0;
            int k = fd->zeros->length, l = xh.index;
            double *b = fd->zeros->buffer;
            /* First put the new input into the history */
            xh.h[xh.index] = *vp;
            xh.index = (xh.index + 1) & xh.mask;
            /* Now apply the zero-coefficients */
            for(; k--; b++)
            {
                l = (l - 1) & xh.mask;
                sum += *b * xh.h[l];
            }
            *vp = sum;
        }
        *(fd->x) = xh;
    }
    /* If the y-buffer is defined, calculate the poles */
    if(fd->y)
    {
```

```c
    int i = v->length, vs = v->spacing;
    CircularBufferDouble yh = *(fd->y);
    double *vp = v->buffer + v->first;

    for(; i--; vp += vs)
    {
        double sum = *vp;
        int k = fd->poles->length - 1, l = yh.index;
        double *c = fd->poles->buffer + 1;
        for(; k--; c++)
        {
            l = (l - 1) & yh.mask;
            sum -= *c * yh.h[l];
        }
        /* Last, put the new output in the history */
        yh.h[yh.index] = sum;
        yh.index = (yh.index + 1) & yh.mask;
        *vp = sum;
    }
    *(fd->y) = yh;
    }
}
```

Extracting the Filter from a Waveform

Chapter 14 showed how all linear digital filters can be implemented as a combination of poles and zeros or, equivalently, as polynomials, in Equations 14.18 and 14.21. But we still don't know how to choose the poles and zeros necessary to reproduce a given waveform, such as the glockenspiel and piano waveforms shown in Chapter 13. This chapter develops one general-purpose technique and applies it to the glockenspiel and piano waveforms. The technique developed here is variously called *maximum entropy* or *linear predictive spectral estimation*.

16.1 GENERAL LINEAR PREDICTIVE ESTIMATION

While the "maximum entropy" terminology has a certain appeal for theoretical reasons (at least if you are familiar with information theory), I prefer the "linear predictive" (LP) terminology, because it better describes the process. Linear predictive coding (LPC) is a technique used for signal compression. Linear predictive spectral estimation, explored in this chapter, is a nonlinear spectral estimation technique. In both cases the basic LP process is used to estimate a filter that could have produced the observed waveform given some assumed driving force. Thus, the more fundamental technique might be called linear predictive filter estimation.

You may be familiar with terms such as LPC-10, which is used for speech compression and means that a 10-coefficient version of linear predictive coding is used to compress speech waveforms. The idea is to estimate a filter that could have generated the observed waveform and then to transmit the filter coefficients instead of the speech waveform itself. At the receiving end, the waveform is reconstructed by stimulating the filter with an appropriate driving waveform. New filter coefficients are calculated and transmitted periodically, perhaps once every 10 ms or so, depending on the required quality and available bandwidth.

Speech compression is not the goal of this chapter, but the technique is the same. While LPC-10 uses an all-pole filter, this section shows how to compute a filter of any specified number of poles and zeros. This approach not only yields a technique with wider applicability; it also provides some useful insights on what exactly this technique is doing.

16.1.1   Preliminaries

The general idea is very straightforward. Let

$$\mathbf{X}_t = \begin{pmatrix} x_t \\ x_{t-1} \\ \vdots \\ x_{t-m} \end{pmatrix} \tag{16.1}$$

be the vector of $m + 1$ input values, and let

$$\mathbf{Y}_t = \begin{pmatrix} y_{t-1} \\ y_{t-2} \\ \vdots \\ y_{t-n} \end{pmatrix} \tag{16.2}$$

be the vector of n previous filter outputs. Then, according to Equations 14.18 and 14.21, a filter with m zeros and n poles can be represented by the vector equation

$$y_t = \mathbf{B}^\dagger \mathbf{X}_t + \mathbf{C}^\dagger \mathbf{Y}_t \tag{16.3}$$

where

$$\mathbf{B} = \begin{pmatrix} b_0 \\ b_1 \\ \vdots \\ b_m \end{pmatrix} \quad \text{and} \quad \mathbf{C} = \begin{pmatrix} -c_1 \\ -c_2 \\ \vdots \\ -c_n \end{pmatrix}$$

and for any matrix $\mathbf{M}$, $\mathbf{M}^\dagger$ is the transpose of $\mathbf{M}$. Notice that the $\mathbf{B}$ vector includes the constant b_0, which does not appear in Equation 14.18. This constant is the product of all the κ_ℓ's from Equation 14.21 as well as the α_k's of Equation 14.18. This also means that the b_j's in $\mathbf{B}$ have absorbed the α_k's of Equation 14.18, thus making the equations here easier to write.

16.1.2   The LP Equations

Now it is possible to concisely state the LP method. It is simply to find the vectors $\mathbf{B}$ and $\mathbf{C}$ in Equation 16.3 that minimize the difference between the calculated filter outputs and those actually observed. As usual, the least-squares technique is used, so the function to be minimized is

$$\Gamma(\mathbf{B}, \mathbf{C}) = \sum_{t=\tau}^{N-1} \left(y_t - \mathbf{B}^\dagger \mathbf{X}_t - \mathbf{C}^\dagger \mathbf{Y}_t \right)^2 \tag{16.4}$$

where we are assuming that x_t and y_t are both known for all times $0 \le t \le N-1$. In that case, the $\mathbf{X}_t$ vector is known for $m \le t \le N - 1$, and $\mathbf{Y}_t$ is known for $n \le t \le N$. The sum must therefore be from $\tau = \max(n, m)$ up to $N - 1$, the range of times over which $\mathbf{X}_t$ and $\mathbf{Y}_t$ are both known.

While Equation 16.4 is the natural way to write the poles and zeros, it is more convenient to combine $\mathbf{B}$ and $\mathbf{C}$ into one vector for the following development. For this purpose, write the vector

$$\mathbf{Q}_t = \begin{pmatrix} q_{t,0} \\ q_{t,1} \\ \vdots \\ q_{t,n+m} \end{pmatrix} = \begin{pmatrix} \mathbf{X}_t \\ \mathbf{Y}_t \end{pmatrix}$$

which means that

$$q_{t,j} = \begin{cases} x_{t-j} & \text{if } j \le m \\ y_{t+m-j} & \text{if } m < j \le n + m \end{cases}$$

The coefficient vectors are combined according to

$$\mathbf{A} = \begin{pmatrix} a_0 \\ a_1 \\ \vdots \\ a_{n+m} \end{pmatrix} = \begin{pmatrix} \mathbf{B} \\ \mathbf{C} \end{pmatrix}$$

so that

$$a_j = \begin{cases} b_j & \text{for } j \le m \\ -c_{j-m} & \text{for } m < j \le n + m \end{cases}$$

With this notation, Equation 16.4 becomes

$$\Gamma(\mathbf{A}) = \sum_{t=\tau}^{N-1} \left(y_t - \mathbf{A}^\dagger \mathbf{Q}_t \right)^2 \tag{16.5}$$

As always for least-squares problems, the vector $\mathbf{A}$ that minimizes this sum is found by differentiating with respect to $\mathbf{A}$ and solving for the vector that makes the derivative vanish. Taking the derivative one component at a time gives

$$D_{a_j}\Gamma(\mathbf{A}) = -2\sum_{t=\tau}^{N-1}\left(y_t - \mathbf{A}^\dagger\mathbf{Q}_t\right)q_{t,j}$$

$$= 2\mathbf{A}^\dagger\sum_{t=\tau}^{N-1}\mathbf{Q}_t q_{t,j} - 2\sum_{t=\tau}^{N-1}y_t q_{t,j}$$

Setting this equal to zero gives the equations

$$\mathbf{A}^\dagger\sum_{t=\tau}^{N-1}\mathbf{Q}_t q_{t,j} = \sum_{t=\tau}^{N-1}y_t q_{t,j}$$

This system of $n + m + 1$ equations can be expressed as a single matrix equation by writing them as follows:

$$\mathbf{A}^\dagger\mathbf{R}^{\mathbf{QQ}} = \sum_{t=\tau}^{N-1}y_t\mathbf{Q}_t^\dagger \tag{16.6}$$

where, of course, the matrix $\mathbf{R}^{\mathbf{QQ}}$ is defined by the sum above. However, it is convenient to define the cross-correlation matrix, $\mathbf{R}^{WV}$, more generally for any pair of vectors, because this will be needed momentarily. Thus, assume that the sequences of vectors $\mathbf{W}_t$ and $\mathbf{V}_t$ are both known for all $\tau \le t \le N - 1$. The vectors need not be the same dimensions. Then define the cross-correlation matrix,

$$\mathbf{R}^{\mathbf{WV}} = \sum_{t=\tau}^{N-1}\mathbf{W}_t\mathbf{V}_t^\dagger \tag{16.7}$$

which, by definition, has the components

$$R_{ij}^{\mathbf{WV}} = \sum_{t=\tau}^{N-1}w_{t,i}v_{t,j} \tag{16.8}$$

where the components of $\mathbf{W}_t$ and $\mathbf{V}_t$ are written as was done for $\mathbf{Q}_t$ above. From these definitions and calculations, it is clear that $\mathbf{R}^{\mathbf{QQ}}$ is a symmetric matrix, so we can transpose both sides of Equation 16.6 to obtain the more commonly written equation

$$\mathbf{R}^{\mathbf{QQ}}\mathbf{A} = \sum_{t=\tau}^{N-1}y_t\mathbf{Q}_t \tag{16.9}$$

This equation is solved by inverting the matrix $\mathbf{R^{QQ}}$. Because the vectors $\mathbf{A}$ and $\mathbf{Q}_t$ are composed as they are, it is convenient to break the matrix into similar parts. Careful inspection of the definition of $\mathbf{R^{QQ}}$ and the definition of $\mathbf{Q}_t$ shows that we can write

$$\mathbf{R^{QQ}} = \begin{pmatrix} \mathbf{R^{XX}} & \mathbf{R^{XY}} \\ \mathbf{R^{YX}} & \mathbf{R^{YY}} \end{pmatrix} \tag{16.10}$$

where each of these component matrices is a cross-correlation matrix, as defined in Equation 16.7. Notice that this means

$$\mathbf{R^{XY}} = \mathbf{R^{YX\dagger}}$$

which, in fact, is necessary, since $\mathbf{R^{QQ}}$ is symmetric. When we actually calculate these matrices, it is necessary to write out their components separately, which is done as follows:

$$R_{ij}^{\mathbf{XX}} = \sum_{t=\tau}^{N-1} x_{t-i} x_{t-j} \tag{16.11}$$

$$R_{ij}^{\mathbf{YY}} = \sum_{t=\tau}^{N-1} y_{t-1-i} y_{t-1-j} \tag{16.12}$$

$$R_{ij}^{\mathbf{XY}} = \sum_{t=\tau}^{N-1} x_{t-i} y_{t-1-j} \tag{16.13}$$

Some expositions claim that $\mathbf{R^{QQ}}$ is a *Toeplitz* matrix, which means that the matrix entries are constant on each diagonal. This is, in fact, not true and can lead to considerable confusion when the resulting programs do not produce expected results. To see that the matrix is not Toeplitz, look, for example, at the main diagonal of $\mathbf{R^{YY}}$. The first element is

$$R_{00}^{\mathbf{YY}} = \sum_{t=\tau}^{N-1} y_t^2$$

while the second diagonal element is

$$R_{11}^{\mathbf{YY}} = \sum_{t=\tau}^{N-1} y_{t-1}^2$$

The difference between these two elements is

$$R_{00}^{\mathbf{YY}} - R_{11}^{\mathbf{YY}} = \sum_{t=\tau}^{N-1} y_t^2 - \sum_{\ell=\tau}^{N-1} y_{\ell-1}^2$$

which, by substituting $t = \ell - 1$ in the second sum, becomes

$$= \sum_{t=\tau}^{N-1} y_t^2 - \sum_{t=\tau-1}^{N-2} y_t^2$$

$$= y_{N-1}^2 - y_{\tau-1}^2$$

Of course, if the number of points N is large, then these differences are probably small. In any case, it is important to get it right if you expect your algorithm to work well in all cases. There is an advantage to assuming the matrix is Toeplitz, because then there is an efficient way (called *Levinson recursion*) to solve Equation 16.9 without inverting the matrix. This is frequently a good approximation, especially if N is large, and is much more efficient. However, this approach is not explored here.

16.1.3   Example: Uncorrelated Driving Force

The linear predictive technique is not linear. The LP spectral estimate of the sum of two signals is not equal to the sum of the LP spectral estimates of the individual signals. The behavior of the linear predictive spectral estimates is therefore sometimes difficult to understand. I think it helps to examine the matrix values in certain special cases. This investigation helps explain some of the behavior of the LP technique in special cases.

Suppose, for example, that the driving waveform x_t is uncorrelated and has zero mean. Then $\mathbf{R^{XX}}$ is easily estimated for large values of N:

$$R_{ii}^{\mathbf{XX}} \approx (N - \tau)V^2$$

where V is the RMS value of the noise, and

$$R_{ij}^{\mathbf{XX}} \approx 0 \qquad \text{if } i \neq j$$

because we assumed the driving force is uncorrelated.

In this case, the matrix $\mathbf{R^{XY}}$ also reduces to a surprisingly simple form, involving only the impulse response of the filter and the power of the input noise. Even though we are considering a general filter with both poles and zeros, we know from Chapter 13 that every filter is completely described by its impulse response. Following Equation 13.2 on page 242, let $\mathcal{G}$ be the impulse response of the filter, so we can write the equation

$$y_t = \mathcal{G} * x(t) = \sum_{k=0}^{\infty} \mathcal{G}_k x_{t-k}$$

allowing for an infinite impulse response. Using this equation, we can calculate

$$\sum_{t=\tau}^{N-1} x_{t-i} y_{t-j} = \sum_{t=\tau}^{N-1} x_{t-i} \sum_{k=0}^{\infty} \mathcal{G}_k x_{t-j-k}$$

Interchanging the order of the sums gives

$$= \sum_{k=0}^{\infty} \mathcal{G}_k \sum_{t=\tau}^{N-1} x_{t-i} x_{t-j-k}$$

$$\approx \sum_{k=0}^{\infty} \mathcal{G}_k (N - \tau) V^2 \delta(i - j - k)$$

Because x is assumed uncorrelated,

$$\approx \begin{cases} \mathcal{G}_{i-j}(N - \tau)V^2 & \text{if } i \geq j \\ 0 & \text{otherwise.} \end{cases}$$

In particular, this means that

$$\mathbf{R}^{\mathbf{XY}} \approx (N - \tau)V^2 \begin{pmatrix} 0 & 0 & 0 & 0 & \cdots & 0 \\ \mathcal{G}_0 & 0 & & & & 0 \\ \mathcal{G}_1 & \mathcal{G}_0 & 0 & & & 0 \\ \mathcal{G}_2 & \mathcal{G}_1 & \mathcal{G}_0 & 0 & & 0 \\ \vdots & \vdots & \vdots & \ddots & \ddots & \vdots \\ \mathcal{G}_{m-1} & \mathcal{G}_{m-2} & \mathcal{G}_{m-3} & \cdots & \mathcal{G}_0 & 0 \end{pmatrix}$$

It also means that the right-hand side of Equation 16.9 can be approximated as

$$\sum_{t=\tau}^{N-1} y_t \mathbf{Q}_t \approx (N - \tau)V^2 \begin{pmatrix} \mathcal{G}_0 \\ \vdots \\ \mathcal{G}_m \\ r_{01} \\ \vdots \\ r_{0n} \end{pmatrix}$$

where

$$r_{ij} = \frac{1}{(N - \tau)V^2} \sum_{t=\tau}^{N-1} y_{t-i} y_{t-j}$$

Putting this all together, the matrix equation for this case is approximately

$$
\begin{pmatrix}
\begin{pmatrix} & & 1 & \end{pmatrix} & \begin{pmatrix} 0 & \cdots & \cdots & 0 \\ \mathcal{G}_0 & \ddots & & \vdots \\ \vdots & \ddots & \ddots & \vdots \\ \mathcal{G}_{m-1} & \cdots & \mathcal{G}_0 & 0 \end{pmatrix} \\
\begin{pmatrix} 0 & \mathcal{G}_0 & \cdots & \mathcal{G}_{m-1} \\ \vdots & \ddots & \ddots & \vdots \\ \vdots & & \ddots & \mathcal{G}_0 \\ 0 & \cdots & \cdots & 0 \end{pmatrix} & \mathbf{R}^{\mathbf{YY}}/(N-\tau)V^2
\end{pmatrix}
\begin{pmatrix} \mathbf{B} \\ \mathbf{C} \end{pmatrix}
\approx
\begin{pmatrix} \mathcal{G}_0 \\ \vdots \\ \mathcal{G}_m \\ r_{01} \\ \vdots \\ r_{0n} \end{pmatrix}
\tag{16.14}
$$

This equation is not used for any calculations. It does, however, provide some insights into what the linear predictive process is doing.

16.1.4   Example: No Driving Force

The other special case to consider is $x_t = 0$ for all t. In other words, the filter is not driven during the period of time covered. In that case, $\mathbf{R}^{\mathbf{XX}} = 0$ and $\mathbf{R}^{\mathbf{XY}} = 0$, so the equation reduces to

$$
\mathbf{R}^{\mathbf{YY}}\mathbf{C} = \sum_{t=\tau}^{N-1} y_t \mathbf{Y}_t
\tag{16.15}
$$

Nothing can be discovered about any zeros that might be present in the filter. In other words, an all-pole filter will be calculated.

16.1.5   Example: The All-Pole Case

If an all-pole filter is desired even if the filter is being driven, then $m = 0$ and Equation 16.14 reduces to

$$
\begin{pmatrix} (N-\tau)V^2 & 0 \\ 0 & \mathbf{R}^{\mathbf{YY}} \end{pmatrix}
\begin{pmatrix} b_0 \\ \mathbf{C} \end{pmatrix}
\approx
\sum_{t=\tau}^{N-1} y_t \begin{pmatrix} x_t \\ \mathbf{Y}_t \end{pmatrix}
\tag{16.16}
$$

Notice that the only difference between Equation 16.16 and Equation 16.15 is that b_0, which is simply a scale factor, can be calculated from Equation 16.16 and not from 16.15. In other words, this method is essentially identical for both of these cases. It delivers approximately the same filter coefficients, whether the filter is driven with uncorrelated noise or not driven at all.

16.2 AN LP PROGRAM

The first step towards testing this technique is to write a program that implements it. This is a fairly straightforward problem since the equations are relatively simple, but it does result in a fairly long routine.

The only special subroutine required is one to calculate the cross-correlation elements, as defined in Equations 16.11, 16.13, and 16.12. One difference between the actual program and the formalism used above is that the vectors $\mathbf{X}_t$ and $\mathbf{Y}_t$ are never actually formed. Instead, the program uses a vector of all inputs and another vector of all filter outputs, both of length N. In this program, the variable `order` is used in place of τ in the theoretical development.

This cross-correlation routine is used to calculate all the matrix entries as well as the vector components on the right-hand side of Equation 16.9.

```
#include <generic.inc>
#include <numeric.inc>
#include <matrix.inc>
#include <stdlib.h>

/* Must have order >= v_delay and order >= w_delay, but
 * this is not checked here.
 */
static double cross_correlation(int order,
VectorDouble *v, int v_delay,
VectorDouble *w, int w_delay)
{
    double sum = 0;
    if(v && w)
    {
        int vs = v->spacing, ws = w->spacing, n
                = v->length - order;
        double *vp = v->buffer + v->first
                + (order - v_delay)*vs,
               *wp = w->buffer + w->first
                + (order - w_delay)*ws;

        for(; n--; vp += vs, wp += ws) sum += *vp * *wp;
    }
    return sum;
}
```

The `lpfe` (for linear predictive filter estimate) routine itself takes, as arguments,

x	the vector of filter inputs
y	the vector of filter outputs
zeros	a vector that returns $\mathbf{B}$
poles	a vector that returns $-\mathbf{C}$ (actually the coefficients of the polynomial $P(y)$ defined in Equation 14.21, including $c_0 = 1$)

The number of zeros is one less than the length of the vector **zeros**, and likewise the number of poles is one less than the length of the vector **poles**. Either of these vectors may be a **NULL** pointer, but not both. If the number of zeros requested is 0, then the **x** vector may also be a **NULL** pointer. The routine returns 0 on error; otherwise, it returns 1.

```
int lpfe(const VectorDouble *x, const VectorDouble *y,
VectorDouble *zeros, VectorDouble *poles)
{
    /* Calculate the number of zeros and poles */
    int n_zeros = zeros ? zeros->length - 1 : 0,
        n_poles = poles ? poles->length - 1 : 0,
        /* The order is the larger of these values */
        order = (n_zeros > n_poles) ? n_zeros : n_poles,
        /* This is the dimension of the square matrix */
        length = n_zeros + n_poles + 1,
        status = 0;

    /* The auto-correlation matrix */
    MatrixDouble *r = new_MatrixDouble(length, length);
    /* The correlation vector and the vector of
     * coefficients */
    VectorDouble *v = new_VectorDouble(length),
                 *a = new_VectorDouble(length);

    if(!r || !v || !a)
        error_message("lpfe---Out of memory");
    else if(!x && n_zeros)
        error_message("lpfe---"
        "Cannot estimate the zeros without the forcing"
        " function");
    else if(!y)
        error_message("lpfe---"
        "Filtered vector must exist");
    else
    {
        /* Calculate the matrix and vector of
         * correlations */
```

```
{
    int i = length, vs = v->spacing;
    double *vp = v->buffer + v->first +
                 (length - 1)*vs;
    for(; i--; vp -= vs)
    {
        int j = length;
        if(i > n_zeros)
            *vp = cross_correlation(
                order, y, 0, y, i - n_zeros);
        else
            *vp = cross_correlation(
                order, y, 0, x, i);

        while(--j >= i)
        {
            double t = 0;
            if(i > n_zeros)  /* Autocorrelation */
                t = cross_correlation(order, y,
                    i - n_zeros, y, j - n_zeros);
            else if(j > n_zeros)
            /* Cross correlation */
                t = cross_correlation(
                    order, x, i, y, j - n_zeros);
            else  /* Autocorrelation of x */
                t = cross_correlation
                    (order, x, i, x, j);
            *MatrixElement(*r, i, j)
                = *MatrixElement(*r, j, i) = t;
        }
    }
}


/* If there are no inputs, then the RXX part
 * of the matrix should be set to the identity
 * matrix, otherwise r will not be invertible. */
if(!x)
{
    int i = 1 + n_zeros;
    while(i--) *MatrixElement(*r, i, i) = 1;
}


/* The solution is the inverted matrix times v.
 * invert_matrix is a routine that inverts the
```

```
        * matrix in its first argument, returning the
        * inverted matrix in its second argument.
        */
    if(!invert_matrix_d(r, r))
        error_message("lpfe---"
        "Could not invert the matrix");
    else
    {
        status = 1;
        /* a = rv, where r is the inverted matrix */
        matrix_x_vector_d(r, v, a);
        /* Now fill in the pole and zero vectors
         * from a */
        if(zeros)
        {
            int i = zeros->length, zs = zeros->spacing;
            double *z = zeros->buffer + zeros->first,
                    *c = a->buffer;

            for(; i--; c++, z += zs) *z = *c;
        }
        if(poles)
        {
            int i = poles->length - 1, ps =
                poles->spacing;
            double *p = poles->buffer + poles->first,
                    *c = a->buffer + n_zeros + 1;

            *p = 1;
            for(p += ps; i--; p += ps, c++) *p = - *c;
        }
    }
}
    if(v) old_VectorDouble(v);
    if(r) old_MatrixDouble(r);
    if(a) old_VectorDouble(a);
    return status;
}
```

16.3   THE GAIN OF A FILTER

The only remaining program required is one that can calculate the gain of
the filter, given the pole and zero coefficients derived from the **lpfe** routine.

The required program is easily obtained from Equation 14.24 on page 270, especially since the constants in that equation are already absorbed in the **B** coefficients. First, a short routine that evaluates a polynomial at any given location is required. The polynomial is real, but the location is complex—on the unit circle for our purposes. The required routine is

```
#include <numeric.inc>
#include <Complex.inc>
#include <stdlib.h>

Complex polynomial_value_dC(VectorDouble *p, Complex z)
{
    int cs = p->spacing, i = p->length;
    Complex sum = {0, 0};
    double *c = p->buffer + p->first + (i - 1)*cs;

    if(p && i > 0)
    {
        sum.x = *c;

        for(c -= cs; --i; c -= cs)
        {
            Cmul(z, sum, sum);
            sum.x += *c;
        }
    }
    return sum;
}
```

Using this routine, it is trivial to write a routine that returns the gain of a filter at any given radian frequency:

```
#include <numeric.inc>
#include <Complex.inc>
#include <math.h>
#include <filter.inc>

double filter_gain_d(FilterDouble *fd, double w)
{
    Complex z, gz = {1, 0}, gp = {1, 0};
    z.x = cos(w);
    z.y = sin(w);
    if(fd->poles) gp = polynomial_value_dC(fd->poles, z);
```

```
    if(fd->zeros) gz = polynomial_value_dC(fd->zeros, z);
    z = cquot(gz, gp);      /* Calculates gz/gp */
    return Cab2(z);   /* Return the magnitude squared */
}
```

16.4   TESTING THE LP METHOD

Before trying the `lpfe` routine on the glockenspiel and piano waveforms, we
should test it in a situation where the desired result is known. The glockenspiel
will be modeled using an all-pole filter because, except for the instant during the
hammer blow, the glockenspiel waveform is not driven by any energy input. The
LP technique will therefore be used without any driving force x, and this forces
us into the all-pole model. We should, therefore, test the routine on an all-pole
filter.

First, test it on a filter with four poles: a pair at $z = -0.01 \pm j0.13\pi$ and
another pair at $z = -0.01 \pm j0.17\pi$. The first 500 points of the impulse response
of this filter are plotted in Figure 16.1. Figure 16.2 is the actual frequency
response of the four-pole filter, shifted down by 62 dB; all plotted frequency
responses have been shifted down by this same amount for convenience of
plotting. The LP estimate for a four-pole filter is identical to the actual filter.

The dashed line in Figure 16.2 is the LP filter estimate for a two-pole filter.
There is no point in trying a three-pole LP estimate, since in that case the
remaining single pole must be at frequency 0 or π.

These two curves show a quite reasonable progression of the LP estimate.
The two-pole estimate places the pole pair in the center between the two actual
pole pairs.

In this test, we know that the four-pole LP estimate will probably be the
best, since the waveform was produced by a four-pole filter. However, in practice
we do not know the number of poles in advance, so it is important to consider
what happens as the number of poles used in the estimate increases. Ideally the
additional coefficients in this case will be zero or nearly so, in which case the LP
filter will remain nearly constant.

Figure 16.3 compares the actual filter response with the six-pole LP estimate. Surprisingly, the extra pole pair has been introduced near the frequency
0.83π. Worse, the discrimination between the two actual frequency peaks has
been eroded, and they are not as sharp as in the four-pole estimate.

Figure 16.4 compares the actual filter response with the eight-pole LP estimate. This time the separation of the two actual pole pairs has been completely lost, and the extra pair of poles has been introduced near the frequency
0.7π.

Evidently, unless you know the answer beforehand, the LP technique is not
very useful for spectral estimation. However, it does provide the filter coefficients

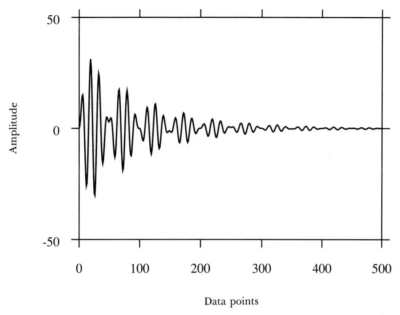

Figure 16.1   The impulse response of a four-pole filter with a pole pair at $-0.01 \pm j0.13\pi$ and another pair at $-0.01 \pm j0.17\pi$.

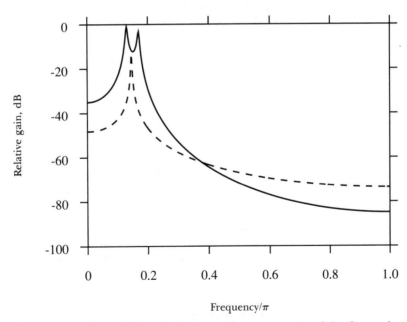

Figure 16.2   The solid line is the actual frequency gain of the four-pole filter. The dashed line is the two-pole LP approximation of this filter.

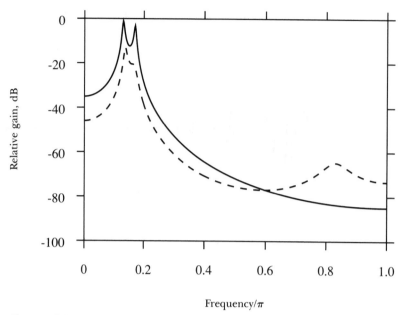

Figure 16.3   Six-pole LP approximation.

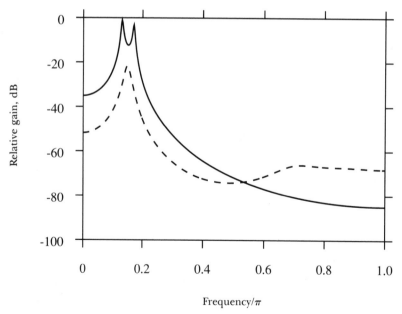

Figure 16.4   Eight-pole LP approximation.

as its final output, which is just what we are after. It may be—in fact, it will be—necessary to coerce the LP technique into giving us the spectral estimate we require, but in the end, we will have a filter that reproduces input waveform accurately.

16.5 LP AS A SPECTRAL ESTIMATOR

One claim that is frequently made for this technique as a spectral estimator is that only a few data points are required to obtain an accurate spectral estimate. However, careful testing shows this is not actually the case. The uncertainty principle, Theorem 8.11 on page 129, fundamentally limits the amount of frequency information that can be obtained from a short-time sample. For example, Figure 16.5 shows the LP estimates of the spectrum obtained from only 25 data points from Figure 16.1 (the points between 50 and 75). The solid line is the actual frequency response of the filter and also the four-pole estimate obtained from these 25 data points. The curve that peaks between the two peaks of the of the actual spectrum is the two-pole LP estimate, and the remaining curve is the six-pole LP estimate.

It is surprising that the four-pole LP estimate with only 25 points matches the actual filter response precisely. However, the fact that four is the correct number of poles represents ancillary information, not obtained from the waveform itself. You might think that this fact could be discerned by some qualitative difference between the spectral estimates obtained for the different number of poles assumed. In this test case, there is no noise in the waveform, and the filter that produced it is exactly represented by two pole pairs. In practice, neither of these conditions is ever realized. There will be no obvious choice to make between the various LP spectral estimates.

The time uncertainty in a 25-point rectangular window is $\Delta t = 7.21$, and since the uncertainty principle shows that $\Delta t \Delta \omega > \frac{1}{2}$, we can easily calculate

$$\Delta \omega \geq 0.022\pi$$

In other words, 25 points is enough to calculate the frequency to within ± 0.022 on the frequency scale of Figure 16.5. Obviously, the LP process is nowhere near this accuracy.

The Fourier transform can be used to achieve a much more accurate frequency estimate from these same 25 points. Figure 16.6 is the Fourier transform of these same points after applying a cosine-squared window. There are only 13 points in this spectrum, but the spectral peak is in the right place, and no ancillary information was required. The time uncertainty for the cosine-squared window of 25 points is $\Delta t = 3.68$, which implies a frequency uncertainty of at least

$$\Delta \omega \geq 0.043\pi$$

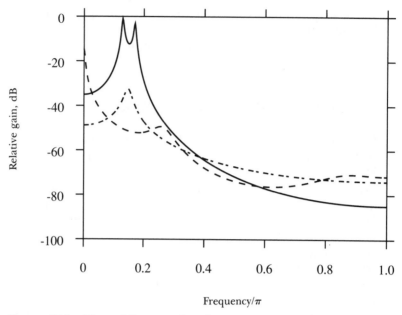

Figure 16.5 These LP spectral estimates were obtained from only 25 points of the waveform in Figure 16.1. The curve with only one peak is the two-pole estimate. The four-pole estimate (solid curve) matches the actual frequency response of the filter. The six-pole estimate (dashed curve) doesn't even come close to the right frequency.

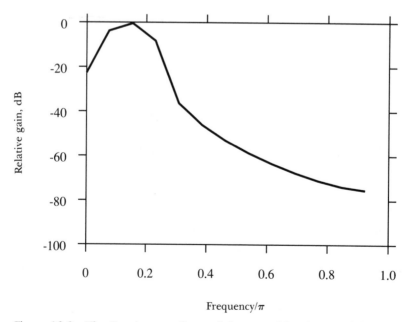

Figure 16.6 The Fourier transform of the same 25 points used for the LP spectral estimates of Figure 16.5 does not identify the spectral peaks independently but does correctly place the main spectral peak.

Since the two spectral peaks are at the frequencies 0.013π and 0.017π, it is not possible to resolve them independently.

16.6 LP APPLIED TO THE GLOCKENSPIEL

Now let's apply the LP technique to the glockenspiel waveform from Figure 13.11 on page 252, with spectra as plotted in Figure 13.12. The job is not as easy as it might at first seem. We will have to force the LP process to deliver a satisfactory spectral estimate and, therefore, a satisfactory filter.

16.6.1 The Tape Noise

The first thing to check is the background noise. How much of the spectral energy is due to tape noise and other sources that we are not interested in? Figure 16.7 is a spectral plot of a waveform obtained from the tape when no instrument was playing, in the same room and at the same time that I initially recorded the glockenspiel and piano waveforms. The dotted curve is the spectrum of the glockenspiel waveform for comparison. The strong component of tape noise below 200 Hz might be a significant problem for the LP method.

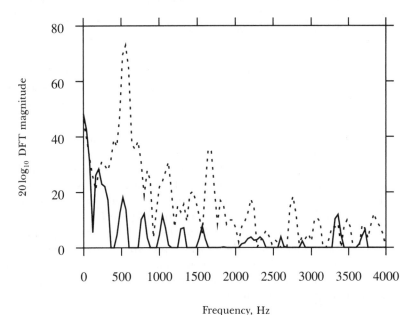

Figure 16.7 The tape noise and other background sources has a spectrum that is particularly strong in the low frequencies. In fact, below about 200 Hz the spectrum of the music is lost in the tape noise. The dotted curve is the spectrum of the glockenspiel waveform.

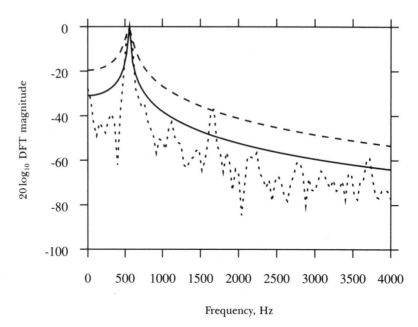

Figure 16.8 This plot shows the 2-, 4-, and 8-pole LP spectral estimates of the glockenspiel waveform. The solid line is both the 4- and 8-pole estimate. The dashed line is the 2-pole estimate. All curves have been normalized to have unit length.

Figure 16.8 shows the normalized spectrum of the glockenspiel along with the two-, four-, and eight-pole LP spectral estimates, also normalized. The solid curve is for the four- and eight-pole estimates, which essentially coincide in this frequency range. The dashed curve is the two-pole LP estimate. None of these curves picks up the third harmonic at all, although all of them accurately locate the fundamental.

Figure 16.9 shows the glockenspiel spectrum once again, along with the 16- and 32-pole LP spectral estimates. The solid curve is the 32-pole estimate. The 16-pole estimate shows a slight bump near the third harmonic, but at too high a frequency and not well defined. The 32-pole LP estimate successfully locates this harmonic but also responds to the low-frequency tape noise.

Visual inspection of the glockenspiel spectrum suggests that two pole pairs (four poles) would be sufficient at least to represent the two principal features (the fundamental and the third harmonic), yet the LP method requires approximately 32 poles (16 pole pairs).

16.6.2 After Filtering Out Low-Frequency Noise

Perhaps we can do better by filtering out the low-frequency tape noise before applying the LP technique. After all, this low-frequency noise is actually somewhat stronger than the third harmonic. Figure 16.10 shows the frequency response

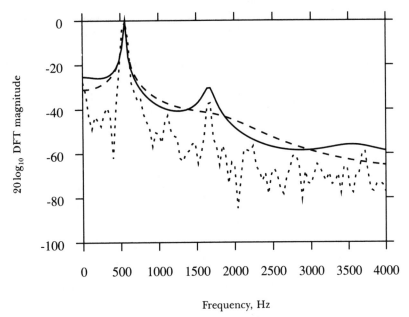

Figure 16.9 This plot shows the 16- and 32-pole LP spectral estimates of the glockenspiel waveform. The solid line is the 32-pole estimate.

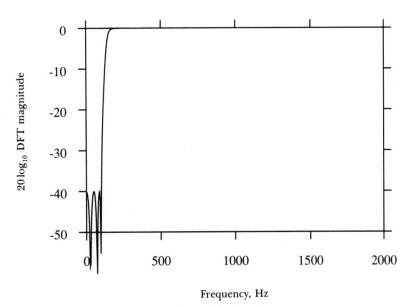

Figure 16.10 This high-pass inverse Chebyshev filter was used to attenuate the low-frequency tape noise in the glockenspiel waveform.

of a high-pass, inverse Chebyshev filter (for a discussion of Chebyshev filters see [8]) that has a flat response above 200 Hz and is 40 dB down below 100 Hz.

Figure 16.11 shows the LP spectral estimates obtained after filtering the waveform through the high-pass filter shown in Figure 16.10. The dashed line is for 16 poles, the solid line for 32 poles. Indeed, filtering out the low-frequency noise eliminated the low-frequency response of the LP spectral estimate, but it did not significantly improve the LP estimates of the third harmonic.

16.6.3   Where Are All the Poles?

So where are all these extra pole pairs being used? Figure 16.12 provides the answer. This figure is the same as Figure 16.11, but the spectral curves are plotted all the way out to 20 kHz, the Nyquist frequency. Each wiggle in the LP spectral estimates represent at least one pole pair. In fact, a careful count of the bumps in the 16-pole estimate reveals 8 upward wiggles, accounting for all 16 poles. A similar count of the wiggles in the 32-pole estimate accounts for 26 poles. Evidently the other 6 poles (3 pairs) are either nearly coincidental with others or so weak that they do not make their own discernible contribution.

It is surprising that the LP estimates respond to the much weaker noise spikes while not adequately modeling that third harmonic. The 16-pole LP estimate barely notices the harmonic yet responds to the spikes near the Nyquist frequency, the strongest of which is 22 dB weaker than the third harmonic. It even responds to the lower noise levels between 5 and 15 kHz.

16.6.4   Filter Out the High-Frequency Noise

I can't really explain why the LP method does this, but we can change its behavior with another filtering of the glockenspiel waveform. This time, we knock down the high-frequency noise, hoping to eliminate the LP response at these higher frequencies. Figure 16.13 shows the frequency response of the Chebyshev filter used for this purpose.

Figure 16.14 shows the four- and 16-pole LP spectral estimates of the glockenspiel waveform after filtering it with both the high-pass filter of Figure 16.10 and the low-pass filter of Figure 16.13. The dotted line is the DFT spectrum, the dashed line is the four-pole LP estimate, and the solid line is the 16-pole estimate. It is gratifying that the four-pole estimate already responds to that third harmonic. However, neither the four-pole nor the 16-pole estimate locates this harmonic accurately. In fact, the peak identified by the LP estimates wanders back and forth around the actual frequency, not in any discernible pattern, as the number of poles is increased.

16.6.5   Increasing the Number of Data Points

Increasing the number of points used to calculate the LP estimate does not improve this wandering of the location of the third harmonic, but it does change the

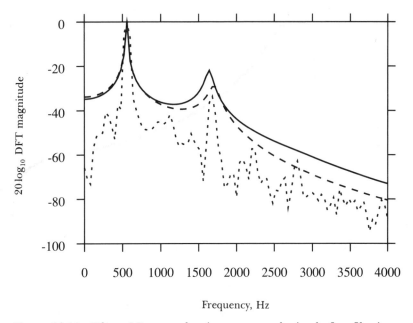

Figure 16.11   These LP spectral estimates were obtained after filtering the glockenspiel waveform to eliminate the low-frequency tape noise. The dashed line is a 16-pole LP estimate, the solid line is for 32 poles.

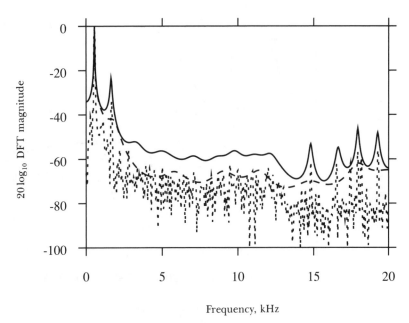

Figure 16.12   This figure shows the same LP spectral estimates as does Figure 16.11, but plots them all the way out to 20 kHz, the Nyquist frequency. Each wiggle of the LP estimates is caused by a pair of poles.

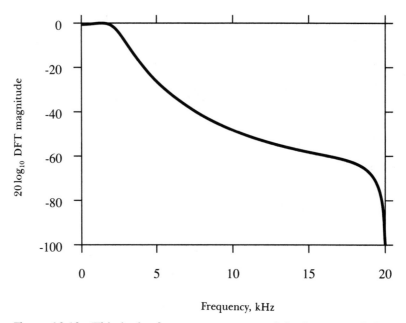

Figure 16.13 This is the frequency response of the low-pass Chebyshev filter used to attenuate the high-frequency noise in the glockenspiel waveform.

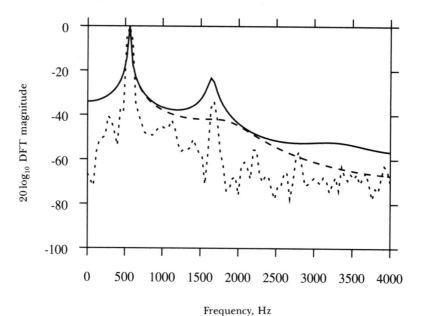

Figure 16.14 This figure shows the LP spectral estimates of the glockenspiel waveform after filtering out the high frequency noise. The dashed line is the four-pole LP estimate, the solid line is the 16-pole estimate.

spectral estimate. Figure 16.15 compares the LP spectral estimates obtained from 3000 points and 1000 points, both for 16 poles. The upper curve is the 3000-point estimate. Increasing the number of points used has not altered the location of the poles, but it did raise the estimated magnitude of the third harmonic.

16.6.6   The Impulse Response of the LP Filter

The solid line in Figure 16.15 is the Fourier transform magnitude of a waveform generated from the 16-pole LP filter estimate (using 3000 points). Specifically, the first 1000 points of the impulse response of this filter were windowed with the cosine-squared window and then transformed. The fundamental frequency is nearly a perfect match to the original spectrum, and the third harmonic is a reasonably good match.

Why is the spectrum of this portion of the waveform so different from the theoretical LP filter response? Simply because it is only a short segment of the waveform, which does not take into account the initial transient or the gradual decay of the impulse response. If the full impulse response were used, the Fourier transform magnitude would match the theoretical response exactly.

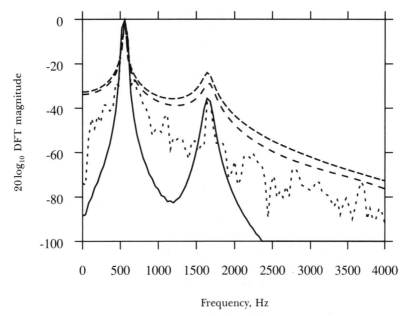

Figure 16.15   This figure shows the 16-pole LP spectral estimate obtained from 1000 points, as in Figure 16.14, and from 3000 points. The upper dashed curve is the 3000-point estimate; the more open dashed curve just below it is the 1000-point estimate. The solid line is the Fourier transform magnitude of an actual waveform obtained from the 3000-point, 16-pole LP filter.

Figure 16.15 looks like a great success for the LP filter estimation method. However, there is a disappointment in store for us when the spectrum of a later portion of the waveform is considered. The fundamental frequency does not change, but that third harmonic quickly disappears! There is a good reason for this. The LP technique produced a filter with the right overall response, but the pole pair that generates the third harmonic has much more damping than the pole pair for the fundamental. That is the only way a cascade of filters can produce this kind of spectrum. Evidently that is the wrong model for a glockenspiel. The glockenspiel should probably be modeled using the sum of two (or more) parallel filters rather than the cascade of pole pairs used here. The relative magnitudes could then be controlled by the strength of the force driving each of the parallel filters instead of by varying the damping.

Evidently the LP filter, while not the right model for a glockenspiel, does give approximately the right overall frequency response. However, the evolution of the tone will be wrong. The initial sound will be too strong in the third harmonic relative to the fundamental, but it dies out much too quickly.

16.7   LP APPLIED TO THE PIANO

Having obtained rather mixed results on the glockenspiel waveform, dare we try the LP method on the more complicated piano waveform? The LP spectral estimate required 32 poles to approximate the fundamental and third harmonic of the glockenspiel. How could we ever obtain an LP filter estimate that represents the rich harmonic structure of the piano, as displayed in Figure 13.7 on page 248?

The answer is that there is no hope of obtaining a filter whose impulse response will recreate the piano waveform. There is a fundamental reason for this, as we saw in the case of the glockenspiel. No matter what technique is used to obtain the filter estimate, all harmonics present at amplitudes lower than the amplitude of the fundamental will be represented by pole pairs with greater damping than the pole pair that produces the fundamental. These other harmonics will therefore die out quickly, whereas in the actual piano waveform they remain at nearly the same strength throughout the sustain.

One approach is to use parallel filters, one for each harmonic, instead of a cascade of poles and zeros. However, that approach will not be tried here. There is an easier method that works for a wide range of instruments.

The method used here is to drive the filter with periodic impulses instead of a single impulse. For example, the piano waveform has a fundamental frequency of approximately 235 Hz. The spectrum of a train of impulses delivered with equal spacing 235 times per second will be a line spectrum, all lines with equal magnitude, spaced 235 Hz apart. For example, Figure 16.16 is the first 2 kHz of the spectrum of 1000 points of such a pulse train, using a cosine-squared window. If a longer pulse train were used, the spectral lines would be correspondingly narrower and the nulls deeper.

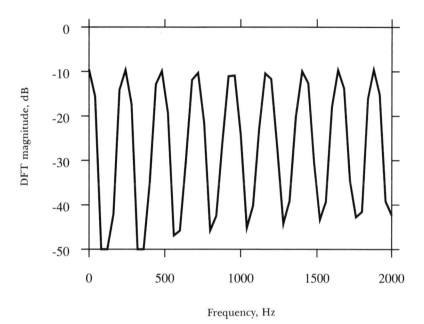

Frequency, Hz

Figure 16.16 The spectrum of a regular train of pulses is a line spectrum, each line having equal magnitude. In this case the pulse spacing was $\frac{1}{235}$ of a second, and the spectrum was obtained by applying the cosine-squared window to a 1000-point segment of the waveform.

The goal now is to find a filter that will shape these spectral lines to look more like those in Figure 13.7. As it turns out, this is easily done using the LP filter estimation method. Figure 16.17 shows the spectrum of the piano waveform (dotted line), the 16-pole LP filter estimate (dashed line), and the 32-pole estimate (solid line). Of these, the 32-pole estimate seems to be the best choice.

The simulated piano waveform obtained by driving this 32-pole LP filter estimate with a train of impulses (235 per second) has the spectrum shown in Figure 16.18 (solid line) which compares favorably with the actual spectrum (dotted line). Notice that the peaks of the simulated spectrum follows the LP filter estimate exactly (dashed line).

Figure 16.19 is the simulated piano waveform. The spectrum of Figure 16.18 was obtained from the steady-state part of this waveform after the initial transient. Compare this waveform with Figure 13.4 on page 244. The sustained part of the waveform is a reasonable representation of the actual waveform. The differences can be attributed to phase changes and to the errors in the relative magnitudes of the harmonics.

However, the attack of the actual piano waveform, Figure 13.1 on page 239, is far more complicated than the initial transient of the simulated piano. This makes a big difference in the perceived sound, particularly if the piano is played staccato, or very rapidly. We have successfully represented the sustain but not the initial attack.

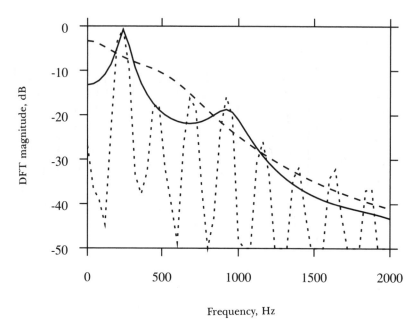

Figure 16.17   This figure compares the 16- and 32-pole LP filter estimates for the piano with the spectrum of the piano waveform. The dotted line is the spectrum of the piano waveform, the dashed line is the 16-pole estimate, and the solid line is the 32-pole estimate.

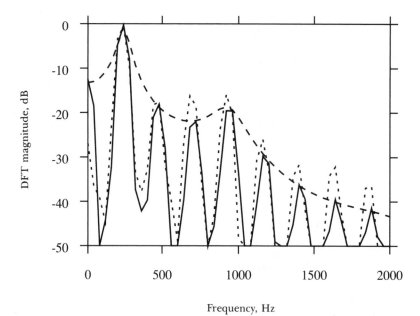

Figure 16.18   The spectrum of the original piano waveform (dotted line) is compared with the spectrum of the simulated piano waveform (solid line). The dashed line is the 32-pole LP filter used.

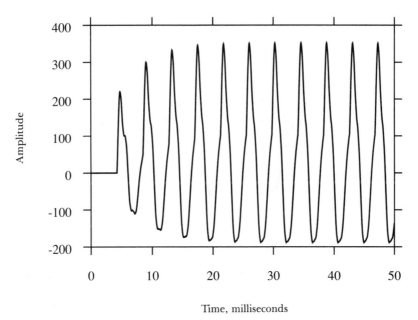

Figure 16.19   This is the simulated piano waveform. Compare it with the actual waveform plotted in Figures 13.1 and 13.4.

16.8   OTHER INSTRUMENTS AND ADDITIONAL CHALLENGES

Waveforms for the glockenspiel, piano, trumpet, and French horn are included on the program disk, which you can order separately. The piano waveform and spectrum is already plotted in Figures 13.3 and 13.7. Figures 16.20 and 16.21 show a sample of the trumpet waveform and its spectrum. Figures 16.22 and 16.23 show a sample of the French horn waveform and its spectrum. All three of these instruments show the same pattern: a narrow fundamental frequency and many strong harmonics.

Notice that the third harmonic of the French horn note is actually about 3 dB stronger than the fundamental frequency. Despite this fact, the human listener perceives the fundamental frequency as the note being played. Human perception of music is much more complicated than you might at first suppose.

The line spectrum observed for the trumpet, French horn, and piano suggests using a periodic driving force, as we did for the piano. This certainly makes sense for the French horn and trumpet. The driving force in any brass instrument is the periodic rush of air out of the player's lips as they part and close repeatedly in response to the instrument's impedance characteristics and the air pressure applied behind the lips.

But what about the piano? Should such a periodic driving force be used? At first sight, the piano is simply a percussive instrument. However, it is much more complicated. The string, once struck, serves as a source of energy that drives

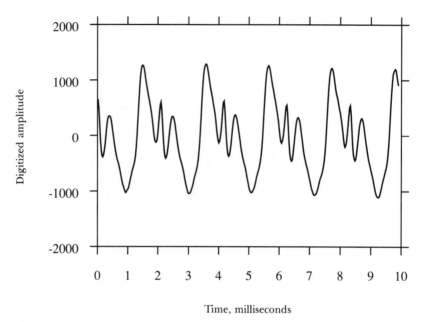

Figure 16.20   The sustained trumpet waveform is far from sinusoidal but highly regular.

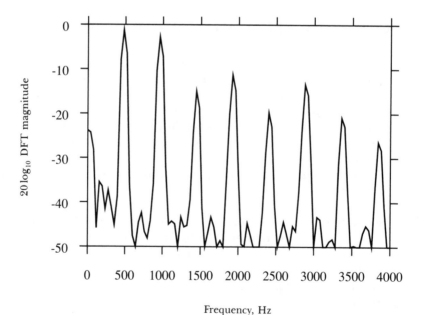

Figure 16.21   The Fourier transform of a trumpet waveform shows a basic line structure. It is the strong harmonics that supply the rich tone.

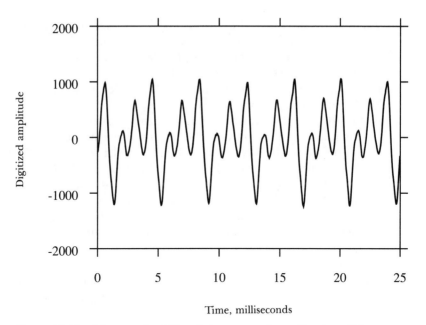

Figure 16.22 The sustained French horn waveform, like that of the trumpet, is highly regular.

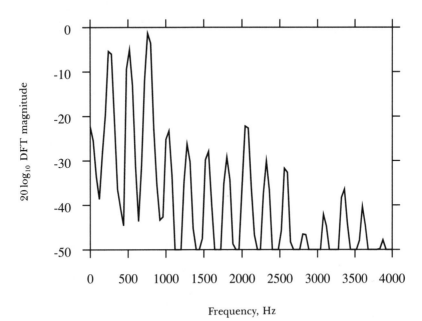

Figure 16.23 The Fourier transform of a French horn waveform also shows a strong line structure. Notice that the third harmonic is actually stronger than the fundamental.

the filter composed of the sound board, instrument case, and the enclosed air space. If you think of the piano as a filter driven by the vibrations of its strings, then the proposed model makes physical sense.

In any case, we leave it to you, the reader, to undertake modeling the trumpet and French horn and to improve the models of the piano and glockenspiel. Much remains to be done to incorporate any of these instruments into the music synthesizer of Part I. Even if we ignore the problem of the initial attack of these instruments and focus only on the sustain, how can different notes be modeled? Will a different LP filter estimate be required for each note? Or can one filter be driven with waveforms of different fundamental frequencies? The fact that most brass instruments have three valves suggests that eight different filters will be needed for each brass instrument, which can then be driven with different input waveforms to obtain all possible notes. What about the piano? Is it more complicated? These questions are left for you to investigate.

If you have purchased the optional program disk, the menu-driven DSP environment supplied is sufficient to try any model you might envision. Once you are satisfied with your model, you can then use the Companion Library routines to build your own unique music synthesizer. Good luck. It's lots of fun.

References

[1] Bachman, George. *Elements of Abstract Harmonic Analysis.* New York: Academic Press, 1965.

[2] Benade, Arthur H. "The Physics of Brasses." *Scientific American*, 229(1):24–35, July 1973.

[3] Bracewell, R. N. "Numerical Transforms." *Science*, 248:697–704, May 1990.

[4] Gabor, D. "Theory of Communications." *J. Inst. Elec. Eng. (London)*, 93:429–457, February 1946.

[5] Gauss, C. F. *Werke*, Volume 3. Göttingen: Royal Society of Sciences, 1876.

[6] Kottick, Edward L., Kenneth D. Marshall, and Thomas J. Hendrickson. "The Acoustics of the Harpsichord." *Scientific American*, 264(2):110–115, Februrary 1991.

[7] Oppenheim, Alan V., and Ronald W. Schafer. *Discrete-Time Signal Processing.* Englewood Cliffs, NJ: Prentice Hall, 1989. An updated and significantly modified version of their earlier book on the same subject.

[8] Parks, T. W., and C. S. Burrus. *Digital Filter Design.* New York: John Wiley & Sons, 1987.

Index

A

Abelian groups, 147, 148, 180, 183–184, 197–199, 204–215
Abelian harmonic analysis, 177
Adaptive signal processing, 11
Additivity, 193
Aliasing, 7
All-pole equations, 257–258
    negative half-plane, 258–259
    zeros from differential equations, 259–260
ANSI standard for C, 71, 72, 101
    function prototypes, 62, 72–73, 80, 95–96
    rules for, 97–98
    type checking, 62, 72–73
    variable lengths, 74
Anti-aliasing filter, 245
Anti-Hermitian operator, 133

B

Bachman, George, 107, 178, 317
Bandpass sampling, 7
Bell(s), 43, 46–48, 50–51
Bell choir:
    audio outputs, obtaining, 68
    C structures, 56
    dynamics markings, 68
    efficiency, 64–65
    function prototypes, 62
    graphing, 66
    header file, 58–60
    musical notation, 66–68
    parsing, 65
    planning the project, 55
    playing, 65–66
    routines, 58, 60–61, 62–64
    structure for the bell, 57–58
    type definitions, 56–57
Benade, Arthur, 317
Bias, 49
Borland® Graphics Interface (BGI), 66
Bra, 49
Bra-and-ket notation, 69, 110–111, 113, 121–122
Bracewell, R. N., 317
Bracket notation, *see* Bra-and-ket notation
Brute force method, 213–214
Buffers, 65–66, 273, 274–276
Burrus, C. S., 317

C

Cauchy-Schwarz inequality, 117, 131–132, 134, 138, 140, 202
C++ compiler, 75, 86, 100, 105
Characteristic function, 115
Characters, 114, 143, 146, 197–199
Chebyshev filter, 306, 308
Circular buffers, 274–276
Commutative groups, 177, 180
Companion Library, 69, 70, 71, 95. *See also* ANSI standard for C
    complex numbers, 100
    C++ version of, 75
    error messages, 61, 97, 99–100
    examples from, 96–99
    fast Fourier transform routine, 177

319

Companion Software Available

Companion DSP Environment: the graphical, menu-driven DSP environment allows testing of all techniques in this book (and many others) on any digitized waveform without any programming. Includes some digitized music waveforms. *NOTE:* Requires IBM-PC compatible with a mouse and an EGA, VGA, or Hercules graphics display.

Companion Library: the source code library of DSP and supporting routines. Includes numerous routines not discussed in the text but needed for general DSP applications.

Additional planned products you may be interested in:

C++ version of the library   Pascal version of the library

Apple MacIntosh version of the Companion DSP Environment   '386 version of the Companion DSP Environment

Reid Associates Companion Software
P.O. Box 495
Chelmsford, MA 01824

1-800-374-7343 (Visa and Mastercard only)

Quantity	Item Description	Each	Price
	Companion DSP Environment	$34.50	
	Companion Library	$44.50	
	Environment and Library	$64.50	
Express delivery		$ 6.00	
Shipping outside USA		$ 4.00	
Total			

	5.25", 1.2 Megabyte		3.50", 1.44 Megabyte
	5.25", 360 Kilobyte		3.50", 720 Kilobyte

Visa No. _____ Exp. Date: _____

M/C No. _____ Exp. Date: _____

Name on card (print): _____

Signature: _____

Billing Address: _____

Telephone (in case of problems): _____